I0121691

Consequential Museum Spaces

Consequential Museum Spaces

Representing African American History and Culture

Bettina Messias Carbonell

LEXINGTON BOOKS
Lanham • Boulder • New York • London

Rowman & Littlefield
Bloomsbury Publishing Inc, 1359 Broadway, New York, NY 10018, USA
Bloomsbury Publishing Plc, 50 Bedford Square, London, WC1B 3DP, UK
Bloomsbury Publishing Ireland, 29 Earlsfort Terrace, Dublin 2, D02 AY28, Ireland
www.bloomsbury.com

Published by Lexington Books
An imprint of The Rowman & Littlefield Publishing Group, Inc.
4501 Forbes Boulevard, Suite 200, Lanham, Maryland 20706
www.rowman.com
86-90 Paul Street, London EC2A 4NE

Copyright © 2023 by The Rowman & Littlefield Publishing Group, Inc.

All rights reserved. No part of this publication may be: i) reproduced or transmitted in
any form, electronic or mechanical, including photocopying, recording or by means of
any information storage or retrieval system without prior permission in writing from
the publishers; or ii) used or reproduced in any way for the training, development or
operation of artificial intelligence (AI) technologies, including generative AI technologies.
The rights holders expressly reserve this publication from the text and data mining
exception as per Article 4(3) of the Digital Single Market Directive (EU) 2019/790.

British Library Cataloguing in Publication Information available

Library of Congress Cataloging-in-Publication Data

Names: Carbonell, Bettina Messias, author.
Title: Consequential museum spaces : representing African American history and culture
    / Bettina Messias Carbonell.
Other titles: Representing African American history and culture
Description: Lanham : Lexington Books, [2023] | Includes bibliographical references
    and index.
Identifiers: LCCN 2022049996 (print) | LCCN 2022049997 (ebook) |
    ISBN 9781666919547 (cloth) | ISBN 9781666919554 (epub)
Subjects: LCSH: African Americans—Museums. | African Americans—Exhibitions. |
    Museums and minorities—United States. | Slavery in museum exhibits—United
    States. | Collective memory—United States.
Classification: LCC E185.53.A1 C38 2023 (print) | LCC E185.53.A1 (ebook) |
    DDC 973/.04960730075—dc23/eng/20221021
LC record available at https://lccn.loc.gov/2022049996
LC ebook record available at https://lccn.loc.gov/2022049997

Contents

List of Illustrations   vii

Acknowledgments   ix

Introduction: Figure/Ground Relationships   1

Chapter One: Frames   25

Chapter Two: Themes, Part I: Contributions to the Region and the Nation   57

Chapter Three: Themes, Part II: Cultural Achievements—The Art Exhibition as a Rhetorical Space   83

Chapter Four: Themes, Part III: Representing Difficult History in an Activist Present   111

Chapter Five: Publics   145

Bibliography   175

Index   195

About the Author   211

List of Illustrations

Figure 0.1. Seated Figure—The National Mall at 14th Street
(2009)—Future Site of the National Museum of African
American History and Culture.   7

Figure 0.2. Smithsonian Orientation Plaque (2009) showing future
site of the National Museum of African American History and
Culture at lower right.   8

Figure 0.3. National Museum of African American History and
Culture—Under Construction (2012).   9

Figure 1.1. Charles H. Wright Museum of African American
History, Detroit/Sims-Varner & Associates, Inc., Architects.   29

Figure 1.2. Charles H. Wright Museum of African American
History, Detroit/Sims-Varner & Associates, Inc., Architects.
Driveway.   29

Figure 1.3. Birmingham Civil Rights Institute, Birmingham,
Alabama/Davis Brody Bond, Architects.   30

Figure 1.4. National Underground Railroad Freedom Center,
Cincinnati, Ohio/Blackburn Architects with BOORA Architects.   31

Figure 1.5. National Underground Railroad Freedom Center/
Interior Lobby.   32

Figure 1.6. Charles H. Wright Museum of African American
History/Ford Freedom Rotunda—Dome.   34

Figure 1.7. Charles H. Wright Museum of African American
History/Ford Freedom Rotunda—*Ring of Genealogy* (Detail).   34

Figure 1.8. Harvey B. Gantt Center for African-American Arts + Culture/Lobby and Stairway. 37

Figure 1.9. Reginald F. Lewis Museum of Maryland African American History and Culture/Stairway. 38

Figure 1.10. Birmingham Civil Rights Institute/Exterior—Stairway. 39

Figure 1.11. National Underground Railroad Freedom Center/ Stairway. 41

Figure 2.1. Museum of African American History, Boston/African Meeting House. 60

Figure 2.2. African American Museum in Philadelphia/*Audacious Freedom: African Americans in Philadelphia, 1776–1876.* 62

Figure 2.3. African American Museum in Philadelphia/*Philadelphia Conversations* (Detail), James Forten. 63

Figure 2.4. DuSable Black History Museum and Education Center/ Founders Hall. 66

Figure 4.1. National Underground Railroad Freedom Center/Slave Pen Exterior. 116

Figure 4.2. National Underground Railroad Freedom Center/Slave Pen Interior. 117

Figure 4.3. National Underground Railroad Freedom Center/Slave Pen Interior and Surrounding Ancillary Materials. 118

Acknowledgments

The subjects of this book have been in (not merely on) my mind for more than ten years, and in that time I have discussed ideas, concerns, and goals with good friends and patient colleagues—many of whom are probably not only excited but relieved that the author has finally crossed the finish line. You know who you are!

However strong and insistent ideas may be, writing doesn't happen at all, and certainly doesn't succeed, without careful and candid readers. I am deeply grateful to the members of my writing group: Paul Lauter, Erica Burleigh, Susan Harris, and the late Jon Christian Suggs.

However determined and committed an author/researcher may be, she can't get anywhere (literally) without time and funding. I am grateful for the help of John Jay College's Office of the Advancement of Research and the staff members who have guided me as I sought internal and external funding as well as a less quantifiable resource—time to do the work. The Research Foundation of the City University of New York has also been extremely generous in terms of travel grants to support essential field work as well as the release time in which to accomplish it.

My efforts to identify relevant contexts—scholarship, exhibition catalogues, and other printed matter—would have been impossible without the libraries I have relied on so heavily. I am grateful to the New York Public Library: the Stephen A. Schwarzman Building (which the lions protect), their Center for Research in the Humanities (which has provided a second home for reading and writing in their research study rooms), and the Schomburg Center for Research in Black Culture. The Lloyd Sealy Library at John Jay College of Criminal Justice, the librarians, and the entire City University of New York library system have also been essential resources.

Finally and collectively, I am grateful to the many museums and staff members at every level who have welcomed me and responded to my questions. I am thinking about both the museums I have written about here and so many others I have visited and been inspired and deeply affected by. In general, some of my most potent memories are spatial, and this must be one reason museums are so clearly consequential spaces for me. I have tried to do justice to them by interrogating what they do and how—by trying to describe the power they hold that sets them apart from other communicative and argumentative forms.

Introduction

Figure/Ground Relationships

On October 1, 2016, one week after the official opening of the National Museum of African American History and Culture (NMAAHC), I made my way from New York to Washington, DC, for my first visit, hoping that the lingering haze over Amtrak's Northeast Corridor would soon disappear. I realized that I had pictured ideal atmospheric conditions for my first direct experience of the museum. I had been keeping up with media coverage, including interviews with the architects,[1] and I had been monitoring the museum's interactive website to track the structure as it rose from its foundation on the National Mall. The long-awaited opening had become a prominent point on my horizon. I had also been following mainstream media coverage of the museum's development and had begun to learn about the century-long history of the idea. While my personal expectations—and impatience—were running high, I was keenly aware that many others had been waiting much longer for this essential dimension of our national history and culture to be recognized and appropriately represented in the nation's capital. The moment was, to say the very least, a long time coming.[2]

The research project that resulted in this book was triggered by my growing interest in the gradual emergence of the national museum, but it did not stop there. As an academic specializing in American literature and the representation of American history, and as an "Americanist" focusing on museum studies, my interests inevitably expanded to include the entire American landscape. Seeking to expand my limited knowledge of regional African American museums, I narrowed my focus and embarked on several years of field work/museum visits. I also began to read more deeply and critically, focusing on how African American history and culture is—and historically has been—represented in and beyond the museum.[3] As I finally made my way to the NMAAHC, the generative source of this project, I contemplated the ongoing challenges of additional field work, secondary research, and writing.[4] The result is a book that is descriptive in its documentation of what I have seen, critical and analytical in its consideration of relevant primary and secondary literature, and argumentative in its insistence on the need for greater interest in the subject matter. My goal is to contribute to an ongoing intersectional dialogue about the work of culturally specific museums.[5] That consequential work warrants consideration from multiple perspectives, while keeping several intimately related subjects and goals in mind: memory and history, corrective history, intergenerational trauma, human rights, and historical consciousness.

These subjects have certainly received extensive attention from multiple disciplinary perspectives, but the work of culturally specific—and in this case African American—museums has not yet received the degree of attention it deserves. Looking back thirty years to an essay by John E. Fleming (who at the time was director of the National Afro-American Museum and Cultural Center in Wilberforce, Ohio) we find an interrogation of the "American ideal" and an indictment of the exclusion of African American history from the identification and preservation of cultural values. Fleming explains that museums have a key role to play as a corrective to systemic exclusion: "Rather than being marginal institutions, African-American museums grow directly from the culture and history of African Americans. They grow out of a desire to preserve what is of value to the people"; moreover, they "inherit the responsibility of the griot tradition—they are modern-day keepers of the culture."[6] Recently, in a contribution to a special theme issue of *The Public Historian* (2018) which was devoted to African American museums, Fleming reiterated and reinforced this claim: "The Black community has come to learn and appreciate that museums are rewarding spaces for understanding who we are as a people, repositories for what we wish to remember about our past, and the values we hope to pass on to our descendants." *Consequential Museum Spaces* offers a comparative and selective examination of how this "rewarding" work is being carried out. It also attempts to illustrate how serious consideration of that work can inform—and be informed by—broader museum studies discussions. It is still possible to say of "the nation's museums" (as James Horton and Spencer Crew had done in 1989) that "the burgeoning scholarship in black history has not found its way into the public presentations that have shaped the historical consciousness of millions of Americans."[7] It is also possible, however, to find that museum studies scholarship now lags behind in acknowledging and incorporating the significance and specific accomplishments of African American museums.

THE POWER OF PLACE

The presence of certain buildings, the memorials to certain events, and the absence of others speak eloquently, though with great ambiguity, about the vast structure of national recollection that is mythos (Fath Davis Ruffins, "Culture Wars Won and Lost, Part II").[8]

Even if most observers understand that the Mall's memorial landscape can never remain fixed, neither in reality nor in the subjective imagination of its visitors, efforts continue to take control of the commemorative system and seal off at least some of it from further change. (Kirk Savage, *Monument Wars*).[9]

My comparative study of regional African American museums took shape at a time when our national depth of field—the amount of material we could maintain in sharp focus—was finally expanding to accommodate a new museum in the Smithsonian Institution complex. Yet the nation was not quite ready to award it pride of place on the National Mall,[10] a well-ordered yet often densely populated space spanning a two-mile area from the Capitol Building to the Lincoln Memorial and from Constitution Avenue to the Jefferson Memorial. On an unusual day—Marian Anderson's Easter Sunday concert (April 9, 1939), the March on Washington for Jobs and Freedom (August 28, 1963), the Black Panther Revolutionary Convention (June 19, 1970), or the March for Racial Justice (August 29, 2020), for example—it becomes a scene of instruction on matters of national importance as well as a space of "insurgent citizenship."[11] At all times the National Mall is both a symbolic and literal/physical space, but in times of heightened sensitivity it can function as a "dialectical" space in which we may come to recognize an embedded but hidden aspect of our national lives.

Thinking more abstractly about "aspects," it is worth considering a serial question raised by Ludwig Wittgenstein in *Philosophical Investigations* during his analysis of the process of perception. In the classic duck-rabbit example of what we sometimes refer to as a "dialectical image," a single image contains the possibility of seeing either a duck or a rabbit; however, as Wittgenstein explains: "You only 'see the duck-rabbit aspects' if you are already conversant with the shapes of these two animals." After a lengthy examination of the phenomenon, he asks: "Could there be human beings lacking in the capacity to see something *as something*—and what would that be like? What sort of consequences would it have?—Would this defect be comparable to colour-blindness or to not having absolute pitch?—We will call it 'aspect blindness.'"[12] This is exactly the question raised when we are exposed to previously unrecognized aspects of our national history and culture.

Historian Lucy G. Barber notes that "Capital spaces" like the National Mall are "filled with a potent mixture of actual policy making and national symbolism" and "are a rich source for understanding how people actually imagine themselves as members of the nation."[13] What we see in the case of diverse reactions to the location of a new national museum is that the Mall can function as a pragmatic space in which structures, people, and events become future-oriented, transnational, and consequential.[14] It is not surprising, then, that the emergence of new construction on that multi-dimensional plane of reality and representation might require a slight, moderate, or even radical readjustment of focus, depending on a visitor's original subject position and physical location.

The opening of the NMAAHC in 2016 marked more than 100 years in the long history and slow realization of an idea that had been preceded by more than fifty years of foundational work at the regional level.[15] While the national, often highly politicized commitment to the status of African American history and culture continued to meet with resistance, important gains were being made in regional museums. The examples I examine in *Consequential Museum Spaces* are comprehensive and wide-ranging in their focus on history and culture and present a wealth of material for close study. They include: the Reginald F. Lewis Museum of Maryland African American History and Culture (Baltimore); the Museum of African American History (Boston); the Harvey B. Gantt Center for African-American Arts + Culture (Charlotte, NC); the DuSable Black History Museum and Education Center (Chicago); the Charles H. Wright Museum of African American History (Detroit); the California African American Museum (Los Angeles); the African American Museum in Philadelphia; the August Wilson African American Cultural Center (Pittsburgh); and the Museum of the African Diaspora (San Francisco). The two exceptions that adopt a specific focus are the National Underground Railroad Freedom Center (Cincinnati) and the Birmingham (Alabama) Civil Rights Institute. In practice, however, that focus is not limited to a single subject or limited time period.[16]

Charting the detailed history of each museum is not my purpose. That challenging and necessary work is being undertaken by others. For example, in *From Storefront to Monument: Tracing the Public History of the Black Museum Movement* (2013), Andrea Burns has traced the "origin stories" of several regional museums (in Chicago, Detroit, Washington, DC, and Philadelphia) and placed them in their broader socioeconomic and activist historical contexts.[17] Mabel Wilson has expanded that focus to demonstrate that the formation of "the first grassroots museums" (in Chicago, Boston, and Detroit) occurred within a global sphere. In *Negro Building: Black Americans in the World of Fairs and Museums* (2012), Wilson contextualizes that local struggle for representation in the late nineteenth and early twentieth centuries within an international climate of colonialism, stereotyping, and institutionalized marginalization.[18]

Consequential Museum Spaces focuses on the physical, symbolic, dialectical, and pragmatic properties of regional institutions and their historiographic work. It examines a cross-section of major regional institutions that have staked their claim on the American landscape. Based on an analysis of site-based fieldwork, I investigate the concrete physical terrain; equally important, I contextualize these primary sites within current multidisciplinary global conversations about the intersections of memory and history, and the ethics and efficacy of collections, exhibitions, and narratives, particularly those devoted to the subject of difficult history. The book engages in the dialogue about ends and means by offering a comparative analysis of culturally specific regional institutions (that are inevitably national and global in historical scope) and examining both their individual character and their common ground. By considering how these museums perceive their missions and how they carry them out, my goal is to bring some discrete points into the critical foreground and add them to a map that now includes a national institution.[19]

Several questions recur in this analysis: What primary themes, narratives, and subtexts are represented at each site? How does *regional* history bear upon the representation of *national* history? How are recent developments in museology reflected in museum narratives and strategies of display? I address the last of these questions most directly at the end of each chapter in a subsection devoted to contexts and theory. Broader underlying issues are also revealed here, including the aesthetic and ideological dimensions of representing history and culture in museums, the political dimensions of representing national history in a period "post"–nation-building, the personal, collective, and national character of historical consciousness, and the consequential relationship between museums and civic life.

ON THE HORIZON: THE NATIONAL MUSEUM OF AFRICAN AMERICAN HISTORY AND CULTURE

The conviction that the nation needed a site dedicated to the collection, preservation, and exhibition of African American history and culture can be traced back to 1915 when a group of black Civil War veterans sought to create interest in and support for "a memorial honoring black contributions to the country."[20] Robert L. Wilkins, a Washington attorney who conducted extensive research on the early years of that movement and was eventually appointed to the presidential commission formed in 2002 to develop a plan for the national museum, explains that the black veterans of the Union Army had come to Washington to participate in a celebration of the fiftieth anniversary of another gathering from which they had been excluded: a "triumphant parade down Pennsylvania Avenue" at the end of the Civil War. The veterans who had survived to experience a gradual change were finally accommodated on the parade route half a century later, but the substantial "discrimination and segregation" they suffered in the process moved them to create a "'colored citizens' committee" and engage in the process of building a memorial to their military achievements.[21]

Participants in that movement later included Mary McLeod Bethune, head of the National Council of Negro Women, and Mary Church Terrell, charter member of the NAACP. Although Congress eventually created a National Memorial Commission in 1929, necessary funding was not allocated. The initiative lost momentum and then stagnated during the Depression. In the late 1960s, civil rights leaders and prominent artists became involved.[22] Formal proposals repeatedly failed and were not taken up again for another twenty years. By then, two of the regional museums I include in this study had opened their doors: the DuSable Museum of African American History in Chicago (founded in 1961) and the Charles H. Wright Museum of African American History in Detroit (founded in 1965).

Efforts to establish a national museum continued, led by Representative John Lewis (D-Georgia). Beginning in 1988 and yearly thereafter he tried without success to achieve passage of necessary legislation.[23] By this time the vision and mission had expanded well beyond the celebration of achievements imagined by the Civil War veterans. In an op-ed piece published on June 4, 2001, in *The Washington Times*, for example, Representative Lewis, Senator Sam Brownback (R-Kansas), Senator Max Cleland (D-Georgia), and Representative J. C. Watts (R-Oklahoma) argued that: "One of the most important chapters in our national story of human freedom and dignity is the history and legacy of the American march toward freedom, legal equality and full participation in American society."[24] A twenty-three-member commission was soon charged with creation of a "Plan for the National Museum of African American History and Culture" (Public Law 107–106, December 28, 2001). Two years later, President George H. W. Bush signed the legislation that established the NMAAHC (Public Law 108–184, December 16, 2003). This was followed by years of extensive planning and continued debate about whether there was room for another museum on the National Mall and, if so, where?[25] However, as Lonnie Bunch, the founding director of the NMAAHC, would insist: "For African Americans, there's no greater symbol than being in view of the Capitol, the Lincoln Memorial and the White House. It reminds people of America's promise. Not only am I protesting, but I am using your symbols of power as a way to mirror and remind us of what America doesn't do."[26]

Figure 0.1. Seated Figure—The National Mall at 14th Street (2009)—Future Site of the National Museum of African American History and Culture.
Source: Author's Photo

In 2006 a site was eventually selected at Constitution Ave NW between the National Museum of American History and 15th Street (see *Figure 0.1*), next to the Washington Monument.[27] A competition was held to select the design team, and in April 2009 the Freelon Adjaye Bond/SmithGroup was chosen.[28] The ground-breaking ceremony was held on February 23, 2012. (*Figure 0.2.*) These important developments were accompanied by a protracted, contentious, and at times regressive public and political journey and the need to overcome one remaining obstacle: the assertion that there might not be sufficient space for this institution—in proximity to other national art, science, technology, and history museums—on the National Mall in Washington, DC. (*Figure 0.3.*)

The problem was arguably less about real estate acreage and/or maintaining the integrity of a master building plan and vision for the National Mall than it was about making room "at the geographic center of American civic identity"[29] for centuries of political, social, and cultural history that had been ignored, under-represented and/or marginalized.[30]

Figure 0.2. Smithsonian Orientation Plaque (2009) showing future site of the National Museum of African American History and Culture at lower right.
Source: Author's Photo

THE BACKGROUND: SYMBOLIC SPACES, SINGLE-POINT PERSPECTIVE, NATION-BUILDING, AND THE COURSE OF EMPIRE

The composition of a thematic *and* believable arrangement of space in a work of visual art may be achieved by the assertion of an ideal viewing point, a stable subject position. In the realm of statecraft, the circumscription of space through nation-building, and often through empire-building, is achieved in similar ways.[31] The construction of that realm of symbolic/physical space also entails identification of a center—an ideal vantage point from which to see and experience vistas, thoroughfares, pathways, buildings, or objects, including statues and other monuments. However, despite deliberate planning, a vital/living public space will inevitably experience interventions and distractions.

Erwin Panofsky explains in *Perspective as Symbolic Form* that "it is not only the effect of perspectival construction, but indeed its intended purpose, to realize in the representation of space precisely that homogeneity and boundlessness foreign to the direct experience of that space." He then goes

Figure 0.3. National Museum of African American History and Culture—Under Construction (2012).
Source: Author's Photo

on to note that "the history of perspective may be understood . . . as a triumph of the distancing and objectifying sense of the real, and as a triumph of the distance-denying human struggle for control.[32] That willfully encompassing project may also be applied to individual buildings, a point I will address in chapter 1 (*Frames*) with respect to regional African American museums.

Within the boundaries of the National Mall numerous sites—monuments, memorials, federal buildings, and museums—seek to create, control, perpetuate, and reinforce a coherent (and for some this means homogeneous) center of national identity. The addition in 2004 of the National Museum of the American Indian, however, proved the point made by Kylie Message in *New Museums and the Making of Culture* that museums may also "bring a certain heterogeneity to key national spaces like the Mall."[33] Yet the "problem" of finding adequate space on the Mall for a National Museum of African American History and Culture revealed that questions about inclusion persisted, and that making room for this building would require fundamental perspectival adjustments.

In the case of the United States and the National Mall in particular, a more expansive and accurate representation of identities insists that we reject the limitations of the univocal and accommodate the multiple and the dialogical. This calls for what Roger Kennedy, former director of the National Museum of American History, described as "a capacious concept of culture and an inclusive definition of nationhood."[34] It involves an acknowledgment of the dynamic effect of what lies outside a simplistically nation-oriented frame. Writing from the perspective of a specialist in the psychology of art, Rudolf Arnheim has explained in *The Power of the Center* that if "the given parts of an object point compellingly toward a center outside the frame, that center, although not seen, will participate with its weight and location in the play of the compositional forces." In a chapter titled "Centers as Hubs," he observed that: "Throughout the ages and in most cultures, the central position has been used to give perceivable expression to the divine or some other exalted power. The god, the saint, the monarch, dwells above the pushes and pulls of the milling throng."[35] Thus we might want to ask: What higher powers were at work when the National Mall was initially configured? What powers are disturbed by the intrusion of new buildings—and points of view?

Arnheim's observations about what we might call the centripetal force of the center reveal what is at stake in a field of vision and representation like the National Mall, where the relationship between a unified sense of identity and the secular divinity of the political/social/cultural center is made visible. The quasi-religious dimensions of the Mall have been analyzed by Jeffrey Meyer from the vantage point of religious studies and he has identified many instances of "civil religion" and pilgrimage in the nation's capital. Along similar lines, anthropologists Edith L. B. Turner and Frederick Turner have used the metaphor of pilgrimage to describe the "mystical participation" and spirituality in our secular attachment to the space.[36] However, our twenty-first-century wisdom insists that all centers—especially those that house seats of power and enable the exhibition of iconic objects—are vulnerable. This is reflected at a macro level when we recognize changes on the National Mall like the emergence of the NMAAHC. Such changes suggest a productive decentering of our traditional understanding of American history and culture. Although less often recognized, similar changes in perspective have existed at the regional/micro level for at least fifty years.

THE MIDDLE GROUND: CULTURAL AWAKENINGS

The compositional shift from a national history based on single-point perspective to a more inclusive history based on multiple subjects and vantage points entailed (and continues to require) a morally urgent and politically insurgent—but slow—awakening to African American history, material culture, individual and collective achievement, and their importance to the fabric of the nation. That awakening arguably constitutes the dawning of a new "museum age" in the representation of our national history.[37]

When presenting an expansive overview of *The Museum Age* in 1967, curator Germain Bazin drew a distinction between Europe and the United States regarding the relative influence that a central political/ideological power might exert on the formation of a museum. He identified, yet arguably idealized and miscalculated, the forces that propel the founding of an American museum: "American museums," he observed, "are not created by laws and decrees but are the spontaneous product of American life."[38] Bazin was writing at a time when regional African American museums were emerging on the American scene but when formidable elements of "American life" continued to insist on distinctions between center and margins. Significant political, artistic, and academic movements, in addition to concerted efforts by African American museum founders, helped to create disturbances at that center. The New Social History of the 1960s, the culture wars of the 1990s, increasing pressure on cultural institutions to attend to diversity, and earlier "democratizing forces" helped to create a hospitable climate for change.[39] These developments became visible in essay collections like *Presenting the Past: Essays on History and the Public* (1986), where editors signaled a "new kind of history" that "explores long-neglected subjects."[40] But this announcement was simultaneously tempered by a warning that economic support for (revisionist) research projects might diminish with shifts in the political power base.

Conferences, symposia, museum exhibitions, and resulting anthologies made their contribution to the movement. A series of three essay collections, developed in connection with conferences supported by the Rockefeller Foundation and the Smithsonian Institution, are a case in point. In the Introduction to the first collection, *Exhibiting Cultures: The Poetics and Politics of Museum Display* (1991), Ivan Karp and Steven D. Lavine warned that "judgments of power and authority " are visible in the presentation of cultures in museums, that "exhibition designers still are struggling to invent ways to accommodate alternate perspectives," and that "we need experiments in exhibition design that try to present multiple perspectives or admit the highly contingent nature of the interpretations offered."[41] While these points may stand as foundational assumptions for ongoing research, analysis, and professional museum practice, they were not immediately reflected in mainstream museum exhibitions or in museum studies analyses.[42]

The essays collected in the third volume of the Smithsonian series, *Museum Frictions: Public Cultures/Global Transformations* (2006), included critical analyses of the representation of slavery in the United States and the representation of marginalized and elided peoples and their histories in Ghana, South Africa, Australia, and Cambodia.[43] Yet many mainstream museum efforts—and scholarly analyses of those efforts—continue to suffer from "aspect blindness," from the propensity to discriminate between narratives and "counternarratives," and from a reflex action that designates some stories as primary and others as "ancillary."[44] In the Preface to *Museum Frictions* Ivan Karp and Corinne Kratz reflected on the earlier Smithsonian conferences. Alert to the demands of "the new millennium," they emphasized a decision to adopt "a critical concept of globalization," to move "beyond the United States," and to include "a greater range and weighting of international cases." In the foreword, Lynn Szwaja and Tómas Ybarra-Frausto noted the issue-oriented global focus on "race, gender, and ethnicity," developing countries, and "transnational or diasporic issues and identities." They pointed out that in recent years the Rockefeller Foundation had sought to "address, . . . interrogate and theorize notions of cultural heritage (both tangible and intangible)" and to encourage "community cultural development projects that use oral history and dialogic exhibitions to probe histories of repression and conflict and to safeguard memory."[45] While "long neglected subjects" and "alternate perspectives" were slowly finding a place in museum representations, however, it would be an overstatement to describe those developments as evidence of a "new age" or a paradigm shift to an emphasis on diversity and inclusion.

THE FOREGROUND: CONSEQUENTIAL/ PRAGMATIC SPACES, REGIONAL MUSEUMS, MISSIONS, AND MANDATES

In an introductory statement on its website, the National Museum of African American History and Culture asserts the importance of history to the nation and its people as it notes the nation's tendency toward forgetfulness. In doing so it announces the "four pillars" on which its mission stands:

> It provides an opportunity for those who are interested in African American culture to explore and revel in this history through interactive exhibitions. It helps all Americans see how their stories, their histories, and their cultures are shaped and informed by global influences. It explores what it means to be an American and share how American values like resiliency, optimism, and spirituality are reflected in African American history and culture. It serves as a place of collaboration that reaches beyond Washington, D.C. to engage new audiences and to work with the myriad of museums and educational institutions that have explored and preserved this important history well before this museum was created.

The very existence of the National Museum stresses the act and potential consequences of remembering and it creates an implicit mandate for a course of action, at least at the level of personal memory.[46]

Similar keywords are used by the sites examined in *Consequential Museum Spaces* to describe their missions, values, and goals. Some are neutral (history, remembering, stories, dialogue, lens), but others are more politically and ethically inflected terms (race, reconciliation, freedom struggles, healing). Some include verbs that encourage a response (help, stimulate, foster) and terms that evoke more kinetic and active experiences (create, explore, revel). In these statements we also find evidence of the new "future-oriented commemorative paradigm" that Louis Bickford and Amy Sodaro identify with institutions that seek "to use knowledge of the past—and especially its traumas and violence—to create a better present and future."[47] As Lonnie Bunch has observed, "history—especially African American history—provides useful tools and lessons that can help us navigate contemporary life."[48] Overall, the statements are aspirational.

Perhaps all museums are, or are quickly becoming, focused on a reassessment of primary goals. This is particularly true of museums that view their mandate in terms of civic and/or global responsibility, a common goal for many of the museums I discuss here—although other aspects of their missions and methods may differ. Their mission statements express broad major goals, as we might expect, but they are often accompanied by separate "vision" statements that articulate what the outcomes of a successful mission may yield. The mission statement of the African American Museum in Philadelphia emphasizes "greater appreciation of the Black experience" but the vision statement takes this a step further, as it seeks to "make a meaningful impact on visitors' lives"—thus to be *consequential*.[49] The mission statement of the Charles H. Wright Museum in Detroit maintains that its work "opens minds and changes lives through the exploration and celebration of African American history and culture." Its vision statement brings that goal into sharper relief by imagining "a world in which the adversity and achievement of African American history inspire everyone toward greater understanding, acceptance, and unity!"[50] The National Underground Railroad Freedom Center in Cincinnati seeks to "pursue inclusive freedom by promoting social justice for all, building on the principles of the Underground Railroad." The vision statement repeats that core value by seeing itself as "the preeminent cultural learning center for inclusive freedom—locally, nationally and globally."[51]

A comparative analysis suggests that while their mission statements vary in degree and emphasis depending on foundational principles and collections, each of the museums I examine here extends the conventional attention to collection, preservation, and exhibition. Keywords indicate values—inclusiveness, understanding, appreciation of diversity, shared heritage, equality—and high expectations for affect and visitor/civic response—inspiration, involvement, enrichment, and empowerment. The museum's role as a custodian for the future—dedicated to the preservation and communication of history and heritage—is often addressed, as is the museum's role as a forum for discussion of contemporary struggles for freedom and human rights and, increasingly, the museum as an active agent in those struggles. In some cases we find specific attention to the region: on Marylanders (Reginald F. Lewis Museum); on Boston and New England (Museum of African American History); on California and the Western United States (California African American Museum); on Western Pennsylvania (the August Wilson Center). While not every museum highlights the diaspora in their mission statement, the focus is often present—even prominent—in the museum's permanent or special exhibitions.[52]

FOCUS AND METHOD

Chapter 1 (Frames) considers geographical locations, immediate surroundings, and the routes visitors may take in their approach to a museum. In turning to buildings themselves, I consider how they may exert an affective and directive power beyond their most obvious practical functions. In the case of African American and other culturally specific/"first voice" institutions, the design and communicative power of a building may carry greater meaning and bear more responsibility. These buildings hope to speak to visitors who self-identify with the institution's culturally specific subject position as well as those who do not. They aim to create greater understanding, greater respect, and more just and ethical relationships between individuals, groups, societies, and even nations. Thus, the visitor's engagement with the building may involve a significant learning experience. I describe and analyze entrances, orientation/introductory devices (which may involve greeters, an orientation video, an exhibit), the allocation of space, and iconographic programs—the ways in which visitors are encouraged, explicitly or subtly, to move through and between spaces. Architecture in general is a subject that has generated a multidisciplinary canon of critical discussion about how, and how much, a building matters, and in the "Contexts and Theory" section—a recurring feature in each chapter—I review the ongoing debate about architecture and cultural identity. This includes newer not yet canonical voices (architects and cultural critics) who address what has been termed "Afrocentric architecture"—its origins, its traditions, its features, and its status in the creation of new African American museums.

Chapter 2 (Themes, Part I: Contributions to the Region and the Nation) is one of three chapters in which I investigate common thematic goals and the ways that individual museums communicate key themes as they establish the unique history and culture of their specific geographical location. I focus on two major themes in this chapter: 1) settlement narratives and the instrumental role of African Americans in the founding and development of cities and regions, including the establishment and flourishing of all-black communities, and 2) historical eras and events, including key movements and/or individuals in political, social, and military history. I address how the museum works with scale, presentation of textual and visual narratives, and use of objects. In order to avoid totalizing or essentialist claims, I consider the relative importance of these major themes to an individual museum's overall program and I emphasize the unique qualities of the museum's strategies of representation. In the "Contexts and Theory" section, I turn to how once buried histories are made visible in formative exhibitions, supplementary catalogues, and revisionist—or what I frame as "rhetorical"—history texts, and I place them in the broader context of object-based epistemology and the gradual emergence of relevant objects in museum collections. In recognizing the political, ethical, as well as museological problems of inclusion, collection, preservation, and exhibition, I contextualize prominent themes in African American museums within broader interdisciplinary discussions that address collective and regional memory, approaches to difficult history, cultural continuity, correctives to and/or gaps in national master narratives, and the missions and demands of local constituencies and communities.

Chapter 3 (Themes, Part II: Cultural Achievements—The Art Exhibition as a Rhetorical Space) considers the role of the visual arts in making the larger case for the vision, talent, and achievements of African Americans in the arts. I emphasize the corrective nature of art exhibitions that establish links to unrecognized, buried, and/or marginalized cultural traditions. In examining major exhibitions devoted to the work of African American artists, I offer a selective survey of foundational exhibitions that have been mounted by both African American and mainstream museums over the last half-century. In the "Contexts and Theory" section, I consider the influence/rhetorical power of art exhibitions and art history texts—those that elide as well as those that document the work of African American artists—and the longstanding tradition of debate surrounding what has been termed "the black aesthetic."

Chapter 4 (Themes, Part III: Representing Difficult History in an Activist Present) continues the comparative analysis of themes but shifts the focus to: 1) the treatment of slavery—the African, transatlantic, and American slave trade, and the long history of slavery as an institution in the United States; 2) the status of Africa—the continent and individual countries and regions—as a source of origins and traditions and a destination for reconnection with the past; and 3) activism and human rights. I examine the fact that some but not all the museums included in this study foreground slavery and ties to Africa. In several cases, although slavery-related themes and objects are foregrounded, they are often juxtaposed with or surrounded by contrasting material that introduces physical, political, and cultural forms of resistance. While a reconstructed slave pen marks the physical center of the National Underground Railroad Freedom Center, for example, invisible slavery today is also a dominant theme. In the "Contexts and Theory" section, I consider the importance of trauma studies, memory studies, and the relationship between empathy and efficacy in working through traumatic events; in particular I address the treatment of difficult history and the representation of human suffering.

Chapter 5 (Publics) examines the relationship between the institution and its actual and potential visitors. I look at how African American museums fulfill the mission-related dimensions of public programming and how those programs extend a museum's borders as they further its mission. I explore mounting evidence that public programming is not necessarily collection or exhibition related, that it may also include debates and community conversations, and that activism has begun to occupy the foreground of public programs as a defining rather than ancillary element. I focus on recent events that have placed systemic racism, social injustice, inequality, and the fight for human rights in the foreground, and I describe how these harsh realities have led to explicitly action-oriented rather than more conventional educational or curatorial museum activities. I also consider how the COVID-19 pandemic has exerted a similar pressure to bring communities together to identify problems and offer solutions. In the "Contexts and Theory" section, I review the ongoing debate among museum professionals and scholars regarding the role of the museum as an agent of change. Finally, I return to the question of efficacy and unsettle the assertion in the book's title: How can museums be consequential spaces?

In a brief coda, I approach the keyword *consequential* in the context of shared states of emergency—locally, nationally, and globally—and I recall some generative notes I took early in this project. My notes were based on a reading of an essay by Thomas Laqueur in which he argues for the efficacy of "the humanitarian narrative." Laqueur deals with the genre in its appearance as a verbal text—one that "describes particular suffering and offers a model for precise social action."[53] My argument in *Consequential Museum Spaces* is that, like (strictly) verbal humanitarian narratives, African American museums can have this pragmatic effect. As a model, however, they transcend the category of suffering. They attest to achievement—under the most difficult circumstances—and they call for equal opportunity as well as equal recognition.

NOTES

1. See for example: Calvin Tomkins, "A Sense of Place," *New Yorker*, September 23, 2013; an interview with Philip Freelon on *All Things Considered*, NPR, Feb. 22, 2010; and Jacqueline Trescott's ongoing, in-depth coverage over many years in *The Washington Post.*

2. James F. Brooks, editor of *The Public Historian's* special theme issue on "The State of Black Museums" (compiled in honor of the fortieth anniversary of the Association of African American Museums), titled his introductory essay "A Long Journey to the Washington Mall." The contributors to the volume, including Fath Davis Ruffins, John E. Fleming, Jeff Hayward, and Christine Larouche, delineate the work that led up to this historical moment. See "State of Black Museums: Historiography Commemorating the Founding and Existence of Black Museums over Four Decades," ed. James F. Brooks, *The Public Historian* 40, no. 3 (August 2018).

3. Two excellent studies document the founding of African American museums, but they do not analyze their contemporary practices. See Andrea A. Burns, *From Storefront to Monument: Tracing the Public History of the Black Museum Movement* (Amherst: University of Massachusetts Press, 2013) and Mabel O. Wilson, *Negro Building: Black Americans in the World of Fairs and Museums* (Berkeley: University of California Press, 2012).

4. This project began with and continued to be driven by on-site visits to each of the museums I discuss. However, it was not possible to keep up with the evolution of individual museums, rotations in the use of collections, changes in permanent exhibitions, the remodeling of physical spaces, and changes in leadership and focus. The need to rely on remote access also increased with the onset of the COVID-19 pandemic but, fortunately, so did the development of websites and listservs that afforded more and more imaginative and extensive access to exhibitions and collections. I have drawn on all these sources in an effort to address the subjects, approaches, methods and issues that form the focus of the book—and which are inevitably contingent upon evolving events and new perspectives.

5. I am mindful of the reservations quoted—but not endorsed—by Fath Davis Ruffins in her outline of the achievements and underlying beliefs of artist and museum founder Margaret Burroughs. Ruffins notes the "tensions" and "resentment" Burroughs expressed regarding "academic scholars who 'want to tell us about us.'" Like Ruffins, I am "acutely sensitive" to these concerns. I appreciate not only her own extensive body of work (often cited in this book) but her efforts to "incorporate a diversity of voices, while regarding each one with respect." See Fath Davis Ruffins, "Building Homes for Black History: Museum Founders, Founding Directors, and Pioneers, 1915–1995," *The Public Historian* 40, no. 3 (August 2018), n. 64 page 40.

6. See John E. Fleming, "African-American Museums, History, and the American Ideal," *The Journal of American History* 81, no. 3 (December 1994): 1021; and John E. Fleming, "The Impact of Social Movements on the Development of African American Museums," *The Public Historian* 40, no. 3 (August 2018): 72.

7. James Oliver Horton and Spencer Crew, "Afro-Americans and Museums: Towards a Policy of Inclusion," in *History Museums in the United States: A Critical*

Assessment, ed. Warren Leon and Roy Rosenzweig (Urbana: University of Illinois Press, 1989), 216.

8. Fath Davis Ruffins, "Culture Wars Won and Lost, Part II: The National African-American Museum Project," *Radical History Review* 70 (Winter 1998): 99. Copyright 1998, MARHO: The Radical Historians' Organization, Inc. All rights reserved. Republished by permission of the copyright holder, and the Publisher. www. dukeupress.edu.

9. Kirk Savage notes that some view the Mall as a "'work of civic art'—a complete and finite system" which is both an "important legacy (and fiction)" of the original 1901 plan. He suggested (in 2009) that we "abandon the idea that the National Mall is a 'completed work of civic art,'" yet he also made "a modest proposal" that we have a ten-year moratorium during which "ephemeral monuments" will be created. Savage recommended that at the end of that period an "independent body" could enter into discussion/consultation regarding "the memorial landscape of the future." Kirk Savage, *Monument Wars: Washington, D.C., The National Mall, and the Transformation of the Memorial Landscape* (Berkeley: University of California Press, 2009), 310–12. © 2009, University of California Press.

10. Two new Smithsonian museums are now in the planning stages: the National Museum of the American Latino (approved by Congress in 2020) and the American Women's History Museum (currently in the development/initiative stage). The proposed sites for the former include The Arts and Industries Building on the National Mall—the site initially proposed for the NMAAHC and firmly rejected by that planning committee in favor of new construction.

11. Savage finds that the Anderson concert "established the Mall as more than a national stage set designed by art professionals. It was now a space of moral principle, defined by the citizens who occupied it." Savage documents some of the injustices, hypocrisies, and daily realities that existed side-by-side with the development of the Mall as a place of national pride. His focus, however, is on monuments rather than museums. Savage, *Monument Wars*, 257. Also see Lawrence J. Vale on James Holston's analysis of "'insurgent citizenship'" and "the ways that subsequent citizen action alters the meanings of officially sanctioned and designed places." Lawrence J. Vale, *Architecture, Power, and National Identity*, 2nd ed. (London: Routledge, 2008), viii.

12. Ludwig Wittgenstein, *Philosophical Investigations*, trans. G. E. M. Anscombe (Oxford: Blackwells, 1997), volume II, xi: 207e and 213e.

13. Lucy G. Barber, *Marching on Washington: The Forging of an American Political Tradition* (Berkeley: University of California Press, 2002), 8.

14. Kylie Message explains that the NMAAHC has "attempted to balance the tensions arising from the needs of its local content with the often competing demands of the transcultural discourse with which it also seeks engagement." Kylie Message, *New Museums and the Making of Culture* (Oxford: Berg, 2006), 8.

15. This book is not an attempt to chart the course of our national journey toward retrieval, recognition, and representation. Such a project requires a thorough analysis of often-stalemated debates about need, funding, and location, as well as vital decisions involving architecture, collections, exhibition design, and major themes.

Founding director Lonnie G. Bunch III provides a thorough history of the creation of the NMAAHC in *A Fool's Errand: Creating the National Museum of American History and Culture in the Age of Bush, Obama, and Trump* (Washington, DC: Smithsonian Books, 2019). Also see Mabel O. Wilson, *Begin with the Past: Building the National Museum of African History and Culture* (Washington, DC: Smithsonian Institution Press, 2016).

16. I want to acknowledge the suggestion made by Lonnie Bunch—when I sought his advice in the early stages of the project—that I consider including the National Underground Railroad Freedom Center and the Birmingham Civil Rights Institute in my field work; unlike my other cases in point, these were subject-specific institutions but they proved to be an important basis of comparison.

17. See Andrea Burns, *From Storefront to Monument*, for extensive details about the public history of The African American Museum of Philadelphia, The Du Sable Museum in Chicago, and the Charles H. Wright Museum in Detroit. Also see Amina Jill Dickerson, *The History and Institutional Development of African American Museums* (MA thesis, The American University, Washington, DC, 1988).

18. Mabel Wilson asks, for example, what it means "for black Americans to claim a physical space in the nation's symbolic cultural landscape and a symbolic space in the nation's historical consciousness?" See *Negro Building*, 3.

19. In 2009, Juanita Moore, then president/CEO of the Charles H. Wright Museum, noted that "'The national museum has to broaden the impact of the stories that we tell already. It has to show African-American history is American history.'" Quoted in Deborah K. Dietsch, "Storyteller of Black America; Director Shapes Mission of Smithsonian's Newest Museum," *Washington Times*, September 27, 2009, M08. NMAAHC Director Lonnie Bunch was reported to have been acutely aware of the need to avoid stepping on "the territory of the regional museums that house African American history." See DeNeen L. Brown, "Looking Forward and Back at Once," *Washington Post*, February 19, 2012, E07.

20. See Lynette Clemetson, "Long Quest, Unlikely Allies: Black Museum Nears a Reality," *New York Times*, June 29, 2003, 1.1.

21. Robert L. Wilkins. "A Museum Much Delayed," *Washington Post*, March 23, 2003, B08. Wilkins subsequently published a book-length overview: *Long Road to a Hard Truth: The 100 Year Mission to Create the National Museum of African American History and Culture* (Washington, DC: Proud Legacy Publishing, 2016). For details about the research undertaken by Wilkins, see Clemetson ("Long Quest") and Peter Slevin, "Black History Museum Has Artifacts but No Building; Organizer Envisions Center on Anacostia Waterfront," *Washington Post*, January 9, 2000, C09.

22. For an overview of debates within 1) multiple African American constituencies, 2) the Smithsonian Institution, and 3) the US Congress, see Ruffins, "Culture Wars Won and Lost."

23. Representative John Robert Lewis (1940–2020) was present at the opening of the NMAAHC in 2016.

24. John Lewis, Sam Brownback, Max Cleland, and J. C. Watts, "400 Years of Turbulent History: An African American Space at the Smithsonian." *Washington Times*, June 4, 2001, A17.

25. See, for example, Zack Hale, "Monuments Face a New Landscape," *Roll Call,* March 22, 2010, n.p., for a summary of the position articulated by Kirk Savage.

26. Lonnie Bunch is quoted in Jacqueline Trescott, "Grounds for Serious Reflection; As African American Museum Site Is Weighed, The Mall Looms Large," *Washington Post,* January 30, 2006, C01. Trescott provides a good overview here of the historical background of Washington, DC, in general, and what is now the geographical space of the National Mall.

27. For details on the four sites that made the final round see: Petula Dvorak, "African American Museum Poses a Siting Dilemma," *Washington Post,* November 17, 2005, B01); Jacqueline Trescott, "Study Weighs Four Sites for Museum; African American History Location to Be Chosen in January," *Washington Post,* December 6, 2005, C01; and Lynette Clemetson, "Smithsonian Picks Notable Spot for Museum of Black History," *New York Times,* January 31, 2006, A16.

28. For details on the finalists see: Jacqueline Trescott, "Black History's Future; Grand Plans Unveiled for African American Museum on the Mall," *Washington Post,* March 28, 2009, C01; Deborah K. Dietsch, "Building New History; Black Museum Plan Picked," *Washington Times,* April 15, 2009, B05; Jacqueline Trescott. "Designer Chosen for Black History Museum; Team Wins Bid with Crown-Shaped Plan," *Washington Post,* April 15, 2009, C01); and Randy Kennedy, "Architects Chosen for Black History Museum," *New York Times,* April 15, 2009, C01.

29. In terms of physical space within the Mall landscape, Nathan Glazer noted that the NMAAHC would "have to be shoehorned in" to fit its designated place. See Glazer's introduction to *The National Mall: Rethinking Washington's Monumental Core,* ed. Nathan Glazer and Cynthia R. Field, (Baltimore: Johns Hopkins University Press, 2008), 6. The contributors to that edited volume offer important historical background regarding the original United States Senate Park Commission, "the McMillan Plan," and the ways in which that plan was modified, and for some disregarded. See in particular Judy Scott Feldman (chair of the National Coalition to Save our Mall), "Turning Point: The Problematics of Building on the Mall Today" in *The National Mall,* 135–58. The political history, the evolving design, and the manifold uses of the Mall over more than a century are highly complex and I do not seek to oversimplify that complexity. Also see Kate Taylor, "The Thorny Path to a National Black Museum," *New York Times,* January 23, 2011, A01.

30. See Mabel O. Wilson on the exclusion of blacks from the "mainstream public sphere." *Negro Building,* 7.

31. Links between empire-building, nation-building, and the role of museums in the exposition/presentation of a synthesized national narrative have been well established. In *The Museum Age* (see note 38 below) Germain Bazin identified their function in the "rationalization" of empire and their use in marking the culmination of a civilization. The importance of museums in promotion of the "concept of a homogeneous national identity" has also been established, as Annie Coombes points out, with specific reference to the British Empire; museums can accomplish this goal as they function as "useful tools in the service of the colonial administration." See Annie Coombes, "Museums and the Formation of National and Cultural Identities," *Oxford Art Journal* 11.2 (1988). However, Barbara Kirshenblatt-Gimblett notes that the

"dissolution of colonial empires and (rise of) new postcolonial nations" may also be reflected in new exhibitions—and in newly created museums. See "From Ethnology to Heritage: The Role of the Museum," SIEF Keynote, Marseilles, April 28.4 (2004). On the persistence of empire as "a systematic condition" and a "new paradigm governing the global order" see Saloni Mathur, "Social Thought and Commentary: Museums and Globalization, *Anthropological Quarterly* 78.3 (Summer 2005).

32. Erwin Panofsky, *Perspective as Symbolic Form*, trans. Christopher S. Wood (New York: Zone Books, 1997), 30–31, 67. In the introduction to his translation of Panofsky, Christopher Wood explains that perspective "encourages a strange kind of identification of the art-object and the world-object. It is perspective, after all, that makes possible the metaphor of a Weltanschauung, a worldview, in the first place" (13). For an analysis of Panofsky on the illusory nature of perspective in relation to museum exhibitions, see Bettina Carbonell, "The Afterlife of Lynching: Exhibitions and the Re-Composition of Human Suffering," *Mississippi Quarterly* 61.1–2 (Winter–Spring 2008): 197–215. Also see art historian Stephen Bann's "'Views of the Past'—Reflections on the Treatment of Historical Objects and Museums of History," in *Picturing Power: Visual Depiction and Social Relations*, ed. Gordon Fyfe and John Law. *Sociological Review Monographs* 35 (London: Routledge, 1988), 40. As Bann explains: the "implication that perspective established a regime of strictly determined visibility, and so facilitated the creation of discourses of power over bodies and classes of objects, has been advanced and tested in many different contexts."

33. Kylie Message, *New Museums and the Making of Culture*.

34. See Roger Kennedy, "Some Thoughts about National Museums at the End of the Century," in *The Formation of National Collections of Art and Archaeology*, ed. Gwendolyn Wright (National Gallery of Art, 1996). Also see Stephen Weil on the "grand stories of history [which] may serve to legitimize the present for nations and for empires," and the (prescriptive) "burden of accommodating" other "realities." "Speaking about Museums: A Meditation on Language," *Alberta Museums Review* 18 (Spring–Summer 1992).

35. Rudolf Arnheim, *The Power of the Center: A Study of Composition in the Visual Arts* (Berkeley: University of California Press, 1988); see "Limits and Frames," 62 and "Centers as Hubs," 109.

36. Meyer notes that Pierre Charles L'Enfant, first architect of the "Capital City," often used "imperial terms like 'vast empire'" to describe the nation. See Jeffrey F. Meyer, *Myths in Stone: Religious Dimensions of Washington, D.C.* (Berkeley, U of California, 2001). Also see Edith L. B. Turner, "The People's Home Ground," 69–78, and Frederick Turner, "Washington as a Pilgrimage Site," 79–92, in *The National Mall*, ed. Nathan Glazer and Cynthia R. Field.

37. See Jeanne Theoharis for a comprehensive analysis of the "perilous silences," "dilutions," and distortions" that characterize the "popular" representation of the civil rights movement. She argues that a "national fable" has minimized its "unpopular, disruptive, and deeply persevering" nature. Theoharis critiques the statue of Martin Luther King Jr. on the Mall, which "bears little resemblance to the civil rights leader himself, or to the collective spirit of dissenting witness he embodied." *A More*

Beautiful and Terrible History: The Uses and Misuses of Civil Rights History (Boston: Beacon Press, 2018), xxiii, 5, 9.

38.Germain Bazin observed that: "Only when men sense the waning of a civilization do they suddenly become interested in its history and, probing, become aware of the force and uniqueness of the ideas it has fostered." However, he made what seems to be a contradictory point about American museums: "In order to understand the museological phenomenon in America, one must realize that in the political life of the country the State does not have that authority—shaped by Roman jurisprudence, monarchical absolutism, revolutionary nationalism, Hegelian metaphysics, Prussian militarism, Machiavellian cynicism, and Marxist dialectic—which is unquestioned in old European countries." Germain Bazin, *The Museum Age*, trans. Jane van Nuis Cahill (New York: Universe Books, 1967), 260, 278.

39. See Bill Adair, Benjamin Filene, Laura Koloski, "Introduction: Letting Go?: Sharing Historical Authority in a User-Generated World," In *Letting Go?: Sharing Historical Authority in a User-Generated World*, ed. Bill Adair, Benjamin Filene, and Laura Koloski (Philadelphia: Pew Center for Arts and Heritage, 2011). In "Where Are the Best Stories? Where Is My Story?—Participation and Curation in a New Media Age," Steve Zeitlin puts the emergence of Web 2.0 within a larger historical frame. He credits the early twentieth-century "invention and dissemination of recording devices and phonographs," developments in radio and television, and the establishment of initiatives like the American Folklife Center, that "celebrated the stories of ordinary people," as steps that preceded Web 2.0 as a "democratizing force in American culture" (*Letting Go?* Zeitlin, 37).

40. *Presenting the Past: Essays on History and the Public*, ed. Susan Porter Benson, Stephen Brier, and Roy Rosenzweig (Philadelphia: Temple University Press, 1986).

41. See Steven D. Lavine and Ivan Karp, "Introduction: Museums and Multiculturalism" in *Exhibiting Cultures: The Poetics and Politics of Museum Display*, ed. Ivan Karp and Steven D. Lavine (Washington, DC: Smithsonian Institution Press, 1991), 2, 4, 7.

42. For a focused examination of this problem see Alan Wallach, "Revisionism Has Transformed Art History but Not Museums," in *Exhibiting Contradiction: Essays on the Art Museum in the United States* (Amherst: University of Massachusetts Press, 1998), although Wallach arguably assigns too much credit to the "transformation" of the field of art history.

43. *Museum Frictions: Public Cultures/Global Transformations*, ed. Ivan Karp, Corinne A. Kratz, Lynn Szwaja, and Tomás Ybarra-Frausto (Durham: Duke University Press, 2006). See Ivan Karp and Corinne A. Kratz, Preface: "Museum Frictions: A Project History," xv–xxii.

44. On the preferential treatment given to certain master narratives see Edward Said, *After the Last Sky: Palestinian Lives* (New York: Pantheon, 1986), 140. On the lack of regard for the experiences of the African American community and the tendency to see these events as "exotic ancillary" stories, see Lonnie G. Bunch III, "Embracing Ambiguity: The Challenge of Interpreting African American History in Museums," *Museums and Social Issues* 2.1 (Spring 2007).

45. Lynn Szwaja and Tomás Ybarra-Frausto, foreword, *Museum Frictions*, xi–xiv.

46. "The Vision for the Future of the National Museum of African American History and Culture," nmaahc.si.edu/about/about-museum accessed 6/14/2022.

47. Louis Bickford and Amy Sodaro, "Remembering Yesterday to Protect Tomorrow: The Internationalization of a New Commemorative Paradigm," in *Memory and the Future: Transnational Politics, Ethics and Society*, ed. Yifat Gutman, Adam D. Brown, and Amy Sodaro (London: Palgrave Macmillan, 2010), 67.

48. Lonnie G. Bunch, III, "Embracing Ambiguity."

49. See www.aampmuseum.org/about-us.html

50. See www.thewright.org/about

51. See freedomcenter.org/about/history/

52. The importance of the diaspora to African American identity was explored in *Making African America*, a three-week symposium (3/5/2021–3/21/2021) organized by The National Museum of African American History and Culture and the Center for Global Migration Studies at the University of Maryland College Park. Sessions were recorded and made available, along with descriptions of the panels and presenters, at: nmaahc.si.edu/making-african-america.

53. Thomas W. Laqueur, "Bodies, Details, and the Humanitarian Narrative," in *The New Cultural History*, ed. Lynn Hunt (Berkeley: University of California Press, 1989), 178.

Chapter One

Frames

If we are to have any real discussion about the impediments to full representative African-American architectural participation, we must acknowledge and understand that at the heart of the common understanding of space—key to the creation and production of architecture—is a fundamental spatial privileging of *whiteness* that is a primary part of the foundation of the architectural discipline . . . —Craig L. Wilkins. *The Aesthetics of Equity: Notes on Race, Space, Architecture, and Music*[1]

When we acquire knowledge or learn to appreciate new perspectives during a museum visit, we routinely give credit to exhibition content and interpretive labels, but how often do we acknowledge the building itself *as* content—and, therefore a source of enlightenment? The exterior and interior design are in fact essential parts of the *content* as well as the *context* of the museum experience. Architecture can be generative and capacious, but it can also function as an extension of repressive regimes that are indebted to fixed technical, aesthetic, and ideological forms. In the case of African American and other culturally specific/"first voice" institutions, the design and communicative power of a building may carry even greater meaning. The building itself may have to bear more weight than we can calculate with the laws of physics or realize through the arts of geometry and engineering. These buildings hope to speak to many visitors—those who self-identify with the institution's culturally specific subject position and those who do not. They seek to confront and counter existing notions of fact and value and aim to create greater understanding, greater respect, and more just and ethical relationships between individuals, groups, societies, and even nations. Thus, the visitor's engagement with the building may involve a significant learning experience. Art historian Vincent Scully notes that "the making and the experience of architecture, as of every art, are always critical-historical acts, involving what the architect and the viewer have learned to distinguish and to image through their own relationship with life and things."[2] The emphasis on what the user brings to the experience is also noted by architect and architectural historian Jonathan Hill: "There are two occupations of architecture: the activities of the architect and the actions of the user. The architect and user both produce architecture, the former by design, the latter by use. As architecture is experienced, it is made by the user as much as the architect. Neither are the two terms mutually exclusive. They exist within each other."[3] These perspectives underscore the reciprocal nature of the architectural experience but there is another key context that merits explicit attention—the power structures that decide how, why and by whom spaces are to be developed and used.[4]

THE POWER OF FORMS

In more than one sense of the word *regime*—the regulation of aspects of life, a method of government or control, an organization, a way of doing things, a "set of physical conditions and influences"[5]—African American museums present arguments in favor of regime change. This is a difficult undertaking given that well established regimes are embedded in assumptions regarding intellectual, social, and moral character.[6] Regimes of perception are commonly discussed in the context of strategies of display, the deployment of objects, and label documentation, but they can be extended to museum exteriors, including buildings and the subject positions of those who design them.

Some visitors react to a museum building with a mixture of awe, surprise, and approval, noting bold architectural forms, arresting façades, and decorative motifs. Once inside, some visitors recognize a narrative element in the physical floor plan or identify a teleology in the discrete pathways and divisions of interior space. They may be attuned to an arrangement of space that guides their movements and at the same time establishes hierarchies of value—an "iconographic program" that seeks to direct their progress *and* their reception of more explicit museum frames.[7] A well-constructed, functional space can communicate thematic messages, materialize structures of power, including aesthetic norms, and/or create new domains of thought.[8] Yet not all visitors respond (at least not consciously) to the aesthetic, affective, and directive power of buildings. Given wide variations in sensitivity and affect: How much can—or does—a building matter?

One answer—which I will go on to explore with reference to the Charles H. Wright Museum, the Reginald F. Lewis Museum, the Harvey B. Gantt Museum, the Birmingham Civil Rights Institute, and the National Underground Railroad Freedom Center—is that the dynamic aspects of the museum event may be inspired and facilitated by architecture and interior design as well as by objects and exhibitions. If a visitor's encounter with the museum is active and "constructive"—if the museum's communication strategies transcend the "transmission" model of learning—then what the visitor brings to the encounter may affect their experience and reception of the museum's overall program.[9] This give and take, in which the building arguably plays a role, is essential to the success of the reciprocal relationship between visitor and content, particularly when the museum mission is action oriented. For example, as Nelson Goodman observes in *Reconceptions in Philosophy and Other Arts and Sciences*, a building "may inform and reorganize our entire experience" and "give new insight, advance understanding, participate in our continual re-making of a world."[10] Although we may be accustomed to granting such power to museum objects—especially when they are glossed by exhibition themes, narratives, and label copy—we may be less likely to grant similar agency to museum buildings. However, architect Bernard Tschumi insists that we raise "the question of the events that take place within" buildings and thereby fully acknowledge their "dynamic aspects."[11]

This mandate seems particularly relevant to the study of African American museums. In most but not all cases the museums I focus on here were sited, designed and constructed specifically *as* museums. To borrow Tschumi's terms, these buildings merit recognition as "events" (not only as the site of events).[12] They can be analyzed from at least three perspectives: the immediate affective power of architectural forms—a topic that has received much art historical/theoretical attention; the language of forms—a topic that has also been considered in depth, both in theory and through practical examples; and the consequences of our engagement with forms. The third perspective has received less critical attention, perhaps because it involves the most elusive dimension of the event: what we make of and what we may retain of the museum experience, and how we might think and act in the future as a result of that experience.[13]

The museum building is not only a concrete *manifestation* of the institution and its program. It also affords space—museologically speaking, it can become a forum—for extra-institutional engagement. Public programs such as lectures, gallery tours, and other organized activities immediately come to mind, and I will explore them in the last chapter of this book, but engagement can also include events that are solitary, silent, or shared in small social groups and private conversations. With a focus on the agency of buildings, political scientist Murray Edelman asserts that "striking and original conceptions in the design of buildings encourage the onlooker to think in unconventional terms, even about matters that have no obvious connection with architecture." He maintains that buildings may "objectify some aspect of the polity or the social order," including "divine will" or "the public interest" or "communism" or "democracy" or "justice." In this context we might recall the resistance and finally the proud placement of the National Museum of African American History and Culture on the Mall in Washington, DC. The project and its monumental building seem to prove that previous efforts to describe "the nation" can be countered and that, in the process, a site can take on new meanings.[14]

More to the point, we can also consider the museums I focus on here; they merit the analysis of their traditional formal elements and, equally important, the analysis of the new regimes of perception they establish and the extra-museological goals they seek to attain. These striking, creative, and bold museum buildings suggest that if the "program" of a museum is essentially a body of thoughts about its functions then architectural and interior design not only make those functions known they make them possible. We may agree with art historian Henri Focillon that a building is able to discover and demarcate a world of its own: "the profound originality of architecture," he insists, "resides perhaps in the internal mass. In lending definite form to that absolutely empty space, architecture truly creates its own universe." However, we may disagree with his inclination to minimize the inspiration, the pressure, and the influence of external contexts.[15] Inspired by and in response to external pressures, the African American museum building—in concert with other elements—can become a *consequential* space that has the potential to alter a visitor's lifeworld. Of course, however intentionally designed that space may be, it must also allow for personal paths and (de) tours, making it possible for the visitor to freely observe, appreciate, and be inspired by the museum's themes, exhibitions, and collections.

APPROACHES AND FIRST ENCOUNTERS

At the Charles H. Wright Museum of African American History (Sims-Varner and Associates, Inc., Architects) a curving path leads to and echoes the circular structure of the 125,000 square foot museum building and the large glass dome (100 feet in diameter and 65 feet high) that forms its apex (*Figure 1.1* and *Figure 1.2*). Great bronze doors signal the structure's significance; aluminum and gold-plated masks mounted on the façade mark a zone of contact with deeply rooted cultural values and traditions.[16] As a form of articulation, the decorative façade is part of the building, yet it has an independent identity.[17]

The 72,000-square-foot home of the Reginald F. Lewis Museum of Maryland African American History and Culture (Freelon Group with RTKL, Architects) is sited on a rectilinear lot at the edge of Baltimore's Inner Harbor tourist district and can be seen from a substantial distance. The saturated colors of the façade (red, black, and yellow) announce its presence, suggest

Figure 1.1. Charles H. Wright Museum of African American History, Detroit/Sims-Varner & Associates, Inc., Architects.
Source: Author's Photo

Figure 1.2. Charles H. Wright Museum of African American History, Detroit/Sims-Varner & Associates, Inc., Architects. Driveway.
Source: Author's Photo

a distinct cultural identity, and set the building apart from nearby commercial structures. A striking "Red Wall of Freedom"—a monumental interior structural element—is also visible from the street. The detailing on this wall of steel comes into focus gradually on approach. Large windows allow for the communication of the interior to those outside. The reciprocal effect—the windows also let the outside in—creates an opportunity to acknowledge and make connections to the historic Jonestown neighborhood surrounding the museum.[18]

As visitors approach the Birmingham Civil Rights Institute (David Brody Bond, Architects), perhaps by crossing directly from historic Kelly Ingram Park, they occupy a primary site of the civil rights movement, once a scene of peaceful protests and violent "Public Safety" retaliation (*Figure 1.3*). This historical ground also includes the 16th Street Baptist Church where, on September 15, 1963, a bombing resulted in the deaths of four young girls, Denise McNair, Carole Robertson, Addie Mae Collins, and Cynthia Wesley.[19] The imposing 58,000 square foot brick and stone structure is a formal and material instantiation of enduring strength, dignity, and fortitude.

The National Underground Railroad Freedom Center (Blackburn Architects with BOORA Architects) is a formidable three-story, 158,000-square-foot building that may be reached from the city's side streets or from the riverfront (*Figure 1.4*). The visitor's ability to experience the full effect of the museum's siting on the Ohio River—formerly a visible north/south boundary line between slavery and relative freedom—depends on their route to the building but it can also be appreciated once they are inside (*Figure 1.5*). The museum

Figure 1.3. Birmingham Civil Rights Institute, Birmingham, Alabama/Davis Brody Bond, Architects.
Source: Author's Photo

Figure 1.4. National Underground Railroad Freedom Center, Cincinnati, Ohio/ Blackburn Architects with BOORA Architects.
Source: Author's Photo

looms large, particularly when viewed from the south. Curving walls on the east and west elevations, made of rough travertine stone blocks, are congruent with the rough journey to freedom. Copper cladding covers the north and south facing walls. The glazed walls of the first-floor interior are also visible from the street and command attention from vantage points on the riverfront.

Each of these buildings draws the visitor into an experience that begins at a distance, leads to an arresting façade, and continues in the encounter with an often dramatic entrance, an orientation gallery, and explicit framing devices. Each building exploits the potential of a dramatic siting on an urban and in some cases historically inflected landscape, thus increasing the museum's visibility and emphasizing the act of approach. Architect Philip Johnson has made provocative claims for the importance of approach, explaining that memory "plays a much larger part in architectural experience than is acknowledged." He refers, for example, to our memory of the "spaces traversed" on the way to a theater seat. This sensitivity to the guided yet still highly subjective experience of approach foregrounds the importance of how we are directed to and through a destination—and the formative power of what we encounter along the way. The siting may also

Figure 1.5. National Underground Railroad Freedom Center/Interior Lobby.
Source: Author's Photo

establish a reciprocal relationship with the museum's themes and collections. The Charles H. Wright Museum, the Birmingham Civil Rights Institute, the National Underground Railroad Freedom Center, and the Reginald F. Lewis Museum are bold examples. The buildings themselves function as meaningful surrounding and introductory frames for collections and exhibitions, and as experiential frames for the visitor's experience.

In terms of a visitor's reception of these forms, the actual visitor is not a stock character and the architect's intentions do not guarantee the outcome of the individual visit. As architecture critic Paul Goldberger notes: "Every building exists within a social and cultural context, and receives much of its meaning from it, and that backdrop is not static. . . . Indeed, the culture within which you see a building is likely to change more often, and more completely, than your own eye . . . " Goldberger emphasizes "the notion of common ground" to describe the relationship between a building and those who, once within it, may become a community, be it familial or public.[20] Establishing that bond is arguably one of the main objectives at African American museums.

Size, principal shape(s), and materials may communicate monumentality, spirituality, individual and collective accomplishments, and cultural affinities. The façade—cladding, moldings, decorative motifs—may introduce additional cultural connections and point toward specific origins, traditions, and aesthetic norms. While these architectural elements are often culturally specific, they have the potential to envelop and embrace every visitor, including those who do not enter the building with conscious cultural connections to the museum or its focus. An "architecture of substance," as architectural historian Leland Roth notes, has multiple functions beyond the utilitarian: It "springs from impulses that might be described . . . as ethical and cosmological." This requires the manipulation of physical space but also the manipulation of "perceptual . . . conceptual . . . and behavioral space."[21] The buildings examined here exhibit those impulses: they seem to have clear designs on the visitor—who is or who might become a perceptive and active occupant.

Most museums have a mandate to collect, conserve, and exhibit. Yet the building may not announce the cultural identity of the content, particularly in the universal survey museum where collections are wide ranging.[22] With few exceptions, however, African American museums proudly announce their cultural identity. The use of traditional African-based architectural forms, motifs, patterns, and spatial values speaks concretely to issues of restoration and continuity. These formal references re-establish an attachment to Africa that had been ruptured but not destroyed by the slave trade and the diaspora. However, these buildings may also show evidence of the longstanding art-historical argument that certain forms appear across cultures and have universal meaning. This element of universality may be crucial to the goal of communicating to a wide audience.

In *The Dynamics of Architectural Form* Rudolf Arnheim observed that "the architect is concerned first of all with the broad metaphoric quality of perceptual expression" rather than "conventional limited symbols." He insisted that the "most powerful symbols derive from the most elementary perceptual sensations because they refer to the basic human experiences on which all others depend." The cupola of a dome, he noted, "may no longer specifically signify a religious image of heaven; but as an overarching and surrounding hollow it forever preserves a spontaneous affinity with the natural sky and shares some of its principal expressive connotations." In even more general terms, Arnheim claimed that "viewing a work of architecture lets the observer sense within himself perceptual forces of load and resistance, of pull and push."[23]

The transparent dome of the Charles H. Wright Museum (*Figure 1.6*) and the large entrance hall it encloses (*Figure 1.7*) exemplify what Goldberger has described as the affective potential of a museum building and the way that "space unfolds in stages as we move within it." In *Architecture as Art: An Aesthetic Analysis*, Stanley Abercrombie probed the "structural

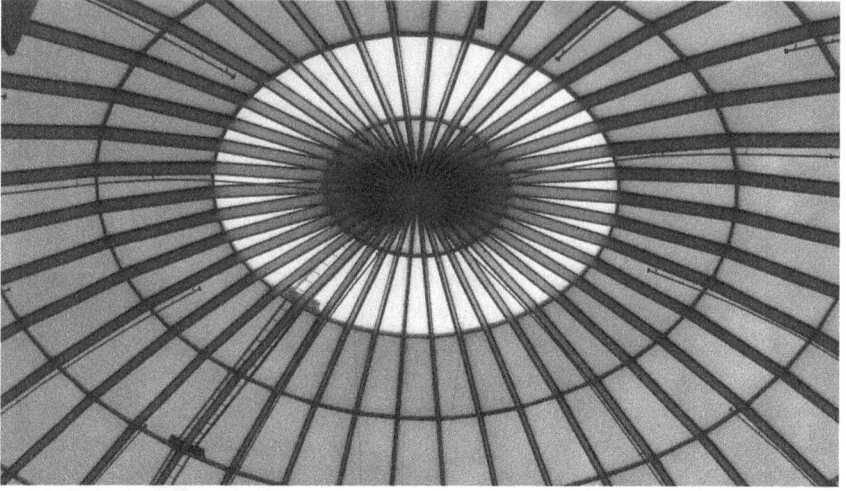

Figure 1.6. Charles H. Wright Museum of African American History/Ford Freedom Rotunda—Dome.
Source: Author's Photo

Figure 1.7. Charles H. Wright Museum of African American History/Ford Freedom Rotunda—*Ring of Genealogy* (Detail).
Source: Author's Photo

accomplishment" of the dome, as well as the pyramid and obelisk, observing that "these forms not only have an 'external surface' but suggest their 'internal space and organization.'" In doing so he reaches beyond the western tradition for examples—including a small stupa on the site of Sirkap, Taxila,

West Pakistan—in order to demonstrate that: "Inside or outside, it is often the most simple masses or volumes that appeal most strongly."[24] In the case of the dome at the C. H. Wright, the imposing exterior literally foreshadows the formative experience that lies ahead. On entering, depending on the weather and time of day, the visitor may find the interior bathed in natural light. If the rotunda calls to mind a sacred space, it also invites active engagement rather than quiet contemplation.

In a review of the museum upon its (re)opening in a new building and location in 1997, Jane Lusaka noted that the dome was "the architect's rendition of an African design concept that represents the union of heaven and earth." Drawing upon statements made by one of the architects, Harold Varner, Lusaka reported that "the dome also reflects the African hut form and the strong sense of community and family in African and African-American cultures," and that the building's sculptural columns are "based on a traditional African rope motif."[25] Architect Melvin Mitchell also notes that this "large domed" museum was designed "with the stated intent of homage to the West African roots of African American culture."[26] On the occasion of the architect's death, his daughter Kimberly Varner Tandy recalled that, for her father, this rotunda was "'an example of things he had experienced as we traveled to Africa. He wanted it to be more of a gathering place than a museum. That's really what he was trying to impart into that building—a place to come and experience the culture as well as celebrate our heritage.'"[27]

While Varner's inspiration comes from particular cultural experiences, the dome can also be related to—but not overdetermined by—Goldberger's remarks on the Pantheon in Rome, which he sees as an example of a "great circular temple" with an "enveloping dome" and, in this case, light emanating from the oculus above. As a result of such structural achievements—and Goldberger is also thinking about other "great" spaces including Borromini's Sant'Ivo church—we're "jolted into a higher level of perception."[28] David Adjaye's intentions for the National Museum of African American History and Culture in Washington are particularly relevant in this context: "'I wanted to create this feeling of weight bearing down on you at the entrance, a powerful impression of timber, like a great forest. In the way that cathedrals used vaults and arches to make people feel the immensity of the space, I'm trying for something with a different effect—I want the architecture to make you feel the weight of an enormous body of history, which you will then go in and explore.'"[29]

Affording space for enlightenment is clearly a goal at the C. H. Wright: the floor of the Ford Freedom Rotunda contains a circular thirty-six-foot terrazzo *Ring of Genealogy* mural created by Detroit artist Hubert Massey and the flags of ninety-two African nations hang beneath the dome above. The mural includes figures of an African woman, who "kneels beside a body representing young slaves who died during the Middle Passage," and an African American woman, who "embraces a body" that stands for uncounted lives lost after arrival and across generations in the United States. The mural also includes outline maps of Africa and the United States, representative of their "connected spirit and culture." The three concentric circles that surround the mural contain brass nameplates that commemorate the achievements of "historically prominent Africans and African Americans" (Charles H. Wright Museum *Fact Sheet*).[30] A new focus is selected each year and exemplary names are added to the evolving archive. Visitors who stop, look up, look down, and engage with these materials—and perhaps with the greeter who hovers close by—will likely find this area strong, arresting, and impressive. There is much to absorb, see, and read, yet for some visitors this very large entry area may seem too empty to serve as a framing experience.[31]

LITERAL MOVEMENT/SYMBOLIC ACTION

Like the dome, stairways are a significant architectural element that may afford both the practical and symbolic experience of ascension. Although Philip Johnson regretted that "the great increase in population has made the great staircases obsolete,"[32] African American museums provide substantial evidence to the contrary. For example, stairways are key structural and experiential features at the Harvey B. Gantt Center, the Reginald F. Lewis Museum, the Birmingham Civil Rights Institute, and the National Underground Railroad Freedom Center. One way to explain their importance may be found in the universalist claim, as expressed by Arnheim, that "the gratification in climbing consists in the conquering of one's own inert heaviness for the purpose of attaining a high goal—an experience inevitably endowed with symbolic connotations. Climbing is a heroic liberating act; and height spontaneously symbolizes things of high value, be it the value of worldly power or of spirituality." Arnheim admits that "a set of stairs or a staircase" can be "a mere geometrical configuration," but he notes that we may also perceive "the gradual rising of the steps from the ground as a dramatic crescendo" and recognize "an expressive quality, which carries a self-evident symbolism."[33] Several of the African American museum buildings examined here demonstrate that stairways may convey fundamental messages about strength, vision, endurance, and a literal/physical rise to heights once denied.[34]

At the Harvey B. Gantt Center (*Figure 1.8*) the large interior stairway is a dominant functional feature; the stairway motif on the façade also makes reference to "a thriving African American community that was slowly displaced during the 1960s by the post-segregation expansion of the central business district." The Freelon Group notes on their website that the Gantt Center

Figure 1.8. Harvey B. Gantt Center for African-American Arts + Culture/Lobby and Stairway.
Source: Author's Photo

"takes design inspiration from the Myers School that was located nearby. The school's prominent exterior staircases inspired its byname—'Jacob's Ladder School.'" They also note that this "historic reference became one of

Figure 1.9. Reginald F. Lewis Museum of Maryland African American History and Culture/Stairway.
Source: Author's Photo

the guiding ideas for the Gantt Center's design," now visible in the stairs, escalators, and central atrium.[35]

At the Reginald F. Lewis Museum an interior stairway is also a main structural element (*Figure 1.9*). According to Jeremy Kargon, it is "as muscular

Figure 1.10. Birmingham Civil Rights Institute/Exterior—Stairway.
Source: Author's Photo

a piece of contemporary sculpture as one will find at any art gallery." The "curved metal-framed walls . . . through which the staircase rises" are "the figurative heart of the museum."[36]

At the Birmingham Civil Rights Institute (*Figure 1.10*) a graduated exterior stairway achieves the effect of a stepped altar platform, calling attention to the entrance and the visitor's approach. The experience of entering is gradual: the space-defining courtyard and flight of stairs recall the slow and deliberate movement toward equal rights. The use of large exterior spaces in African architecture may also be seen as a cultural reference point. As architect and historian Nnamdi Elleh notes, "courtyards had high religious and fellowship functions as places of gathering and socialization."[37] Similarly, architect David Hughes includes the "great courtyard (precedent to the universal African adaptation of space as an outside/inside dominant relationship)" as one of the characteristic elements of African and Afrocentric architecture.[38]

In the dark interior, a circular design encourages but docs not insist that we move through the exhibition galleries in a specific order. Architect Bradford C. Grant emphasizes the specific local and historical dimensions, explaining that the BCRI "embodies the idea of the 'march' as community activism through the design of the long upward walk from the main gate to the building's main entry. One starts at street level and 'marches' up through a rising exterior entry court to the main rotunda." He notes that "The rotunda's roof form and geometry topped with copper relates to African or African American culture" and that the "primary use of brick, the scale, and the roof forms . . . clearly relate to the materials, scale, and roofs of the adjacent churches and residential buildings." In relation to the community of which it is a part, Grant focuses on the siting of the BCRI in a prominent part of the Birmingham Civil Rights District: "The representation of memory, of the collective cultural memory of the Birmingham African Americans and of the Civil Rights experience, is perhaps the greatest contribution of the district and its buildings."[39]

Laura Anderson, former archivist and director of special projects at the BCRI, describes how the architecture and design of the exterior and interior spaces—along with gallery content and narratives—collaborate in the Institute's overall intentions:

> Empathy, . . . within the context of the Birmingham Civil Rights Institute would be defined as intentional and grounded in storytelling. It was the aim of [Odessa] Woolfolk and other creators of the BCRI permanent exhibition to craft an experience immersive enough in voices from Birmingham's recent past to provoke emotional responses in visitors. Founding task force members fully embraced the concept of using symbolic, physically expressed architecture designed to lead visitors in a literal climb—only gradually and not too steeply—through the unfolding story of the movement for civil and human rights in Birmingham, Alabama, in the twentieth century.

Anderson notes that the narrative of struggle is embodied not only in the representation of persons and events but in the floor coverings and topography—"wood turns to concrete and pavement slants upward"—and in a deliberate constriction of gallery space.[40] As I will discuss in the last chapter (Publics), empathy is viewed by some theorists as a key element in the cultivation of human rights activism on the part of museum visitors. The common ground of struggle can be denotative and explicit, or it can be connotative and implied. Both "meanings" can be conveyed through a museum's architecture as well as its objects, images, and texts.[41]

In the 8,000-square-foot Welcome Hall on the second floor of The National Underground Railroad Freedom Center a large spiral staircase (*Figure 1.11*) enables visitors to ascend and move between the building's three pavilions which are connected by sky bridges. Late in the design phase the position of the stairway was moved from the center to the periphery of the building, making room for a two-story exhibition space that contains the museum's central artifact—a restored slave pen—the stairway and rotunda, however, retain an imposing, functional presence.

Figure 1.11. National Underground Railroad Freedom Center/Stairway.
Source: Author's Photo

The concrete physical aspects of the buildings described here support an underlying narrative of continuity and attest to the ongoing evolution of forms. These buildings create space for the presentation of complicated historical and contemporary narratives and warrant a prominent place in the analysis of aesthetic/communicative strategies that include objects, labels, and explicit framing devices. To more fully comprehend their power, we also need to look behind/beyond their explicit physical and sensory presentations and consider the principles, questions, preconceptions, and misconceptions that influence what can be imagined, designed, built, experienced—and appreciated—by museum visitors.

CONTEXTS AND THEORY: CULTURAL IDENTITY, CONTINUITY, INCLUSION, INDIVIDUALITY

The production of the architecture of the museum must also be recognized as taking place at the level of the individual, and here we are concerned with the plays of power between architects, designers, project managers, directors,

curators, users and all those involved at an individual level in the production of a specific site. Importantly, this production does not stop when a new building is complete and before the doors of the museum open; rather, production is continual and ongoing through occupation and use.
    —Suzanne MacLeod. "Rethinking Museum Architecture: Towards a Site-Specific History of Production and Use"[42]

Art historians, philosophers, and political scientists continue to acknowledge the universal language of forms and find that some forms function similarly across cultures, thus attesting to the universality of human experience. Yet Western examples are generally the basis for their illustrations and cases in point. When an African or other non-Western architectural tradition or example is invoked, it is often used to support an assertion of universals rather than to identify culturally specific forms and meanings. This results in a tendency to elide central questions, such as those raised by editor Lesley Naa Norle Lokko and other contributors to *White Papers, Black Marks: Architecture, Race, Class, Culture*. Lokko asks, for example, "what importance does 'race' have as any kind of category in the study of architecture and the shaping of the built environment? In making, using and studying architecture, does 'race' matter? Should it?"[43]

In a contribution to this collection entitled "The Unsound Space," Ethiopian-born architect Araya Asgedom underscores the shortcomings of this almost exclusively Western-European knowledge base and insists—with his own training as a crucial example—that "we are educated in the ocular language of Western architecture." As a counterpoint, Asgedom explicitly identifies with and "cares for" a "contaminated space" made up of "my African experiences, my major disciplinary training whose historical and theoretical loci are of European origin, and the affecting presence of African and African-American sonorous cultures." He uses the terms *improvisation*, *repetition*, *polyphony*, and *polyrhythmy* to suggest how, in some traditions, the "consistency of things known is joined together with the dynamism of things hoped for."[44] An analysis of African American museum buildings can benefit from the use of this expansive description insofar as these museums aspire to share knowledge of the actual (which includes the historical) and to create the foundations, materials, and skills to build a better future.

Yet the analytical discourse on the meaning and affect/effects of architectural elements continues to be dominated by art historians and cultural critics whose training, areas of study, and focus tend to privilege Western traditions. In contrast, a consideration of the presence (or absence) of "Afrocentric" characteristics is often central to the analysis of African American museum buildings, although the criteria are widely debated. Discussions of Afrocentricity and its presence within African American culture inevitably foreground three intimately related factors: tradition, continuity, and identity. Jocelyn Robinson-Hubbuch, former director of the African American Museums Association, noted that African American museums have a "dual identity" and "dual responsibility" to "tell the African-American story while at the same time telling a broader American story"; yet she admitted that this is complicated by "our need first to know our 'pre-American' identity." When the ancestral traditions "have been stripped or stolen" that knowledge will have to be acquired before it can be passed on.[45] The broken or interrupted circuits—the content and the forms of that continuity—must be re-established, and as Sterling Stuckey has argued, doing so can be a "formidable task" for those would "attempt to establish the Negro's humanity by reclaiming his heritage."[46] Clearly the aesthetic, ethical, and political stakes could not be higher when we seek to identify and then establish the relationships between tradition, continuity, and identity. Those stakes are underscored by Jane M. Jacobs, Kim Dovey, and Mathilde Lochert in "Authorizing Aboriginality in Architecture" when they point out that the putative absence of "a 'formal' architectural tradition" has been used as evidence of the "primitive" state of indigenous peoples.[47]

In her introduction to *White Papers/Black Marks* Lokko asks: "Does architecture serve to evoke or enforce hidden signs of racial (spatial) superiority and cultural hegemony?"[48] The contributors to this volume address that question in various ways. Edward Ihejirika observes that architecture is not only "a product" but a "cultural process." Both an architect and educator, Ihejirika insists on the urgency of asserting "black identities in architectural discourse." He explains that his "black perspective" is informed by his birth in the United Kingdom, his Nigerian parents, his early education in Benin, and his postsecondary education in the United States. He employs the term "intensive continuity" to address the "fragmentation," the breaks, and the losses suffered during slavery and the diaspora, and the need for repair. Cultural continuity, he argues, must be recovered and restored in architectural history and practice, and this project will involve a correction: "A paradox exists in that architectural discourse remains exclusive of alternative notions of identity, despite a prevailing sense of the cultural pluralism and relativism of Western society."[49]

Further complicating the discussion is the fact that responses to the architecture and interior design of African American museum buildings often address a key normative question: *should* these culturally specific museum buildings exemplify, refer to, reflect, and reflect upon African and/or African American architectural traditions and legacies? Several issues that emerge in the ongoing commentary and critical commonplaces bear directly upon the museums I focus on here. One issue is the assertion of universal meaning; while this may underscore commonality and point toward the fact of a common humanity (and perhaps universal human rights) it may also demote, dilute, or erase the integrity of particular cultural differences. Another issue is the primacy of origins and traditions as determinants of present practice; this bears directly on a diasporic present, the right to originality, and the goals of an aspirational future. Finally, there is the interplay between the formal properties of a building, the cultural groundings of the receiver (visitor/scholar/ critic), the vagaries of aesthetic judgment, and human subjectivity. When the primary subject is a museum that hopes to "speak" to many visitors—those who self-identify *a priori* with the institution's culturally specific subject position and those who do not—these issues take on even greater importance.

A foundational moment in the discussion of the relationship between personal identity, cultural identity and creativity is available in the record of "The Black Artist in America: A Symposium" held at the Metropolitan Museum of Art in 1969 and transcribed in *The Metropolitan Museum of Art Bulletin*. This event was structured as a conversation among seven artists, including Romare Bearden as moderator, occasioned by a heated debate surrounding the conception and eventual mounting of the exhibition *Harlem on My Mind: Cultural Capital of Black America, 1900–1968*. Bearden, Sam Gilliam, Richard Hunt, Jacob Lawrence, Tom Lloyd, William Williams, and Hale Woodruff revealed a variety of perspectives and points of disagreement regarding the "problems of the Black artist in America." They included the lack of recognition by critics and collectors, the scarcity of Black historians and Black aestheticians, the shortage of opportunities for exhibition and opportunities for training, the lack of exposure at an early age to art and museums, and the failure of museums to extend their audiences and provide a higher "quality of aesthetic experiences." The critical questions they raised included: Is it possible to identify forms as "uniquely black?" Is there an identifiably "'Black art'"? Who should "control Black programs"?[50]

A case in point of the enduring presence of these questions appears in the coverage of the designs proposed for the National Museum of African American History and Culture. After a site was secured in 2006, and a three-year selection process for the architectural design team began, concerns about the status of cultural identity in the submissions inevitably emerged. They were summarized by David Sokol in "Marrying Content to Container" and are representative of the ongoing debate. While his primary focus was the announcement of the Freelon Adjaye Bond and Smith Group as the museum design team, Sokol's coverage of the process and the finalists' designs illuminated a much larger practical, theoretical, and ethical landscape. He observed that the winning design "does not represent a literal architectural expression of black identity, and the five other finalists' proposals similarly avoid such symbolism." He posited that a modernist vocabulary was apparent among the entries and that its presence "intimates that Modernism is the architectural vocabulary of African-Americans." Evidence of his claim can be found in frequent references to Modernism in the broader critical discourse about Afrocentric architecture.

Explicit as well as indirect references to African architectural elements and African/American history were evident in many of the finalists' designs for the NMAAHC.[51] Reporting on the results of the competition, Clay Risen noted that it called attention to "an ongoing debate over the appropriateness of African architectural elements in contemporary design." After a brief review of positions Risen concluded that cultural institutions must "speak simultaneously to the particular and the universal, the diverse and the collective whole. The NMAAHC will be the first, and hopefully not the last, to do just that."[52] While the NMAAHC may be the first national institution to speak from this culturally specific platform, regional African American museums have already declared this mission and sought this diverse audience.

In "Discovering African Identity in African-American Architecture," a two-part article published in 2007, Stephen A. Kliment tackled the question of "architectural identity in work by a particular racial or ethnic group" and outlined the positions on the role of cultural identity in/and architecture He focused in part on a summary of position statements by practicing architects, including Bradford C. Grant and Max Bond, and in part on practical considerations, including the "use of materials, siting, detailing, ornament, forms and space flow." In interviewing practitioners, Kliment raised a two-part question: "What are the characteristics of African architecture and how are they used in African American architecture?" Responses were diverse but several main elements appeared: continuity with African traditions, recognition of spiritual beliefs, and adaptation to new environments, uses, and communities.[53]

In the scholarship produced by practicing architects and teachers, some of whom were included in Kliment's coverage, we hear that using the term "Afrocentric" may serve to collapse a continent that comprises many individual nations and cultures into a monolith and threatens to homogenize diverse histories that encompass millennia. In *Architecture in Black*, for example, Darell Wayne Fields argues that the "term 'African' homogenizes Africa: it neutralizes and makes indistinguishable cultural and political determinants that make Libyans different from Egyptians different from Nigerians different from South Africans." He goes on to observe that the "construction of the term 'African-American,' relative to its assumptions of meaning is nothing more than a rhetorical colonizing strategy that in actuality denies and suppresses socio-political realities and culture rather than providing, say, a more precise race term that clarifies present political identities and circumstances." The tension between finding common ground and protecting individual originality is clear: "If one speaks of black culture in this country," Fields explains, "one of its major determinants is an ongoing struggle against stereotypical, formal, and historical definitions that attempt to limit or conceal it." In order to facilitate deeper analysis, he makes a distinction between "heritage" (which "implies" continuity, longevity, a formal identity) and "culture" or "functional identity" (which is "infinitely more complex"). Fields notes that culture is "more sporadic and unpredictable because it defines itself around particular circumstances or events." Summing up, but of course not solving the puzzle, Fields argues that "If the term 'African-American' is anything, it is an artifact of the struggle between the formal and functional identities that 'we' have constructed for ourselves."[54]

Concerns about the suppression of originality are longstanding. Nigerian architect Olufemi Majekodunmi, for example, took an emphatically critical and controversial position on the question of "Afro-centricity" in an address to members of the National Organization of Minority Architects (NOMA) in 1993. For Majekodunmi, the use of the term was "disturbing" and restrictive, insofar as it "denoted a self-conscious attempt to put an 'African' stamp on every building designed by the African-American architect, simply as a means of identifying the origins of the designer." He insisted instead that one must "study" and "document" but not be overly burdened, and he looked ahead to a time when an organization such as NOMA "will no longer be of relevance."[55] Yet NOMA celebrated its fiftieth anniversary in 2021 and, in the midst of the heightened attention to issues of inclusion, the organization has never been more relevant.[56]

A number of studies have also analyzed the shortage of African American architects in the profession and the dense landscape of underlying causes. For example, Bradford C. Grant describes "environmental design's relationship to race, especially to African Americans, as part of their continuous struggle with a strategy of accommodation and resistance in our society." In doing so he traces "three historical periods." The first is slavery, when "African craftsmen-slaves were the primary builders of the South, usually under the strict control of a 'master,' yet often in a role of 'supervisor-designer-builder.'" The second is the Jim Crow Era during which "the Jim Crow economy discriminated against and marginalized newly free Black builders-designers." Grant explains that, in general, architecture "was practiced within the isolation of the Black community with Black clients and Black users." During the civil rights movement, "legal barriers to the active involvement of the African American architect in all segments of the profession" were "lifted as a result of civil rights law" but "discriminatory practices existed, and hidden discriminatory practices are still part of the profession today." Thus the "client base" and "main building type" has shifted "to the government and quasi-government institutions." Adding to the lack of opportunities is the invisibility of some important buildings by African American architects,

John Moutusseme's North Pier Towers (Chicago), for example, which tend to receive critical attention.[57]

In contrast to those who insist that the classification "African American architecture" could present a restrictive frame for the practicing architect, and act as a constraint on those who evaluate the results, David Hughes insists that everything has cultural origins. He presents a theory of Afrocentric architecture designed to provide "a methodological format for identification, analysis, critique and design in the modern built environment which manifests distinct elements in space, form and aesthetic derived from the historical, cultural or environmental origins of the continent of Africa." In very practical terms, Hughes seeks to create opportunities for "academicians, scholars and practitioners, to define and develop distinct architectural styles" and looks forward to a future in which "African American architects will be the vanguard in defining and designing a new architecture that is appropriately representative of the diverse cultural groups that inhabit our inner cities." His major claim is that "African archetypes in architecture, from antiquity to this day, have had a significant and substantive impact on all global architecture and now forms [sic] a solid foundation for Afrocentric architecture." Hughes is clearly writing a critical historical corrective, given that the topic has (until now) been "ignored or marginalized in architectural scholarship." He describes and locates the "formal heritage," identifies traditional Afrocentric elements—including the great courtyard, the use of polychromatic patterning and cut stonework on the façade, and recurring symbolic forms—and he shows how they have influenced buildings in Africa and throughout the Diaspora. Once again, the stakes of the debate are high: "Afrocentrists should not seek or accept values of other cultures as measures of the worth of their creativity, but must establish vehicles and forums to judge and evaluate work using self-determined criteria."[58]In a syncretic analysis that admits the presence of multiple influences and allows for a broader assessment, Nnamdi Elleh uses a "Triple Heritage Concept" to note the indigenous, Western, and Islamic dimensions of African architecture.[59]

Critical attention to African American traditions and their bearing on contemporary practice has clearly not been as robust as the subject warrants but significant contributions have been made. Among the earliest was Robert Farris Thompson's foundational study "African Influence on the Art of the United States" published in 1969. Part of the collection *Black Studies in the University: A Symposium,* this exemplary survey of the subject matter engages in a probing critique of existing scholarship on the continuity of African traditions in African American creative forms. "The assumption," Thompson wrote, "has been that slavery in the United States destroyed the creative memories of newly arrived Africans, so that today no African influence can be discerned in this country, apart from fragments in the verbal arts, music, and the dance." He goes on to indict endemic race prejudice (and a need to protect the status quo) as a major cause of aesthetic blindness: "Artistic autonomy implies social autonomy." Despite the suppression of evidence, Thompson was eloquent and comprehensive in locating a creative "sensibility which could not be policed out of existence." He imagined a future when "the contours of an entire tradition will emerge, sufficient to discredit the apriorists" who fail to acknowledge direct antecedents. He then made a significant contribution to that understanding in *The Flash of the Spirit: African and Afro-American Art and Philosophy* (1984), a wide-ranging study of architectural, sculptural, decorative, and performance traditions.[60]

The subject of cultural continuity has also been studied in terms of vernacular architecture. An early example of this would include the work of John Vlach, who traced "residential domains" and the still "ubiquitous southern shotgun house" to its African roots.[61] At the outset of his analysis, however, Vlach warned that the "links to Africa are not simple and direct." The project of recovering these origins and influences remains incomplete; links are waiting to be discovered and traced but important work continues to be done.[62] Several of the museum buildings I examine here contribute to that work as they look back to African origins and traditions, encompass the realities of American history and create an identifiably Afro-American and potentially "defiant" architecture. Visitors who approach, enter, and inhabit these buildings can reap the benefits: new knowledge, greater understanding, and a deeper appreciation of cultural traditions and adaptations.

NOTES

1. Craig L. Wilkins, *The Aesthetics of Equity: Notes on Race, Space, Architecture, and Music* (Minneapolis: University of Minnesota Press), 2007, 26. Copyright 2007 by the Regents of the University of Minnesota.

2. Vincent Scully, "Introduction—Note to the Second Edition," in Robert Venturi, *Complexity and Contradiction in Architecture*, 2nd ed (New York: Museum of Modern Art, 1977), 12.

3. Jonathan Hill, Introduction, in *Occupying Architecture: Between the Architect and the User*, ed. Jonathan Hill (London: Routledge, 1998), 5.

4. As Vincent Pecora explains: "Whatever its pretensions otherwise, architecture will always serve some function, for someone, and will do so in the context of already existing social struggles among classes, races, genders, and other social groupings over the control of social space and the right to make use of it." See Vincent P. Pecora. "Towers of Babel" in *Out of Site: A Social Criticism of Architecture*, ed. Diane Ghirardo (Seattle: Bay Press, 1991), 75.

5. "regime, n." OED Online. June 2022. Oxford University Press (accessed June 16, 2022).

6. Tony Bennett reminds us that such "sensory regimes" can find their way *into* the museum and the "didactics" of display. "Pedagogic Objects, Clean Eyes, and Popular Instruction: On Sensory Regimes and Museum Didactics," *Configurations* 6.3 (1998).

7. Carol Duncan and Alan Wallach, "The Universal Survey Museum," *Art History* 3.4 (December 1980).

8. Writing about architecture in the "New South," specifically in Raleigh and Wilmington, North Carolina, Catherine W. Bishir notes that "in the decades just before and after 1900, political and cultural elites drew on the imagery of past golden ages to shape public memory in ways that supported their authority." This included "reviving architectural themes from Colonial American, classical Roman, and Renaissance sources." See "Landmarks of Power: Building a Southern Past in Raleigh and Wilmington, North Carolina, 1885–1915," in *Where These Memories Grow: History, Memory, and Southern Identity*, ed. W. Fitzhugh Brundage (Chapel Hill: University of North Carolina Press, 2000), 141.

9. See Eilean Hooper-Greenhill, "Changing Values in the Art Museum: Rethinking Communication and Learning," *International Journal of Heritage Studies* 6.1 (March 2000).

10. Nelson Goodman, "How Buildings Mean," in *Reconceptions in Philosophy and Other Arts and Sciences*, ed. Nelson Goodman and Catherine Z. Elgin (London: Routledge, 1988).

11. Bernard Tschumi, *Architecture and Disjunction* (Cambridge: MIT Press, 1994), 16, 23.

12. Tschumi insists that "space and action are inseparable" and that architecture "is only an organism engaged in constant intercourse with users, whose bodies rush against the carefully established rules of architectural thought" (122–23). That encounter is active and it can become combative: "Architecture and events constantly transgress each other's rules, whether explicitly or implicitly." *Architecture and Disjunction*, 122–23; 132.

13. Richard Sandell observes that museums are increasingly viewed as "agencies that are capable of reforming ways of viewing difference" and that audiences "are now widely viewed as active agents who do not simply absorb messages but are capable of constructing their own meanings that may radically differ from those intended at the point of production." However he admits that "little is known" about the processes that underlie these activities. Sandell suggests that "we need to look more closely at the audience-exhibition encounter." See *Museums, Prejudice and the Reframing of Difference* (London, Routledge, 2007).

14. Murray Edelman, *From Art to Politics: How Artistic Creations Shape Political Conceptions* (Chicago: University of Chicago Press, 1995), 89, 74, 75, 90. Regarding urban design, the relationship between architecture and existing power structures is also emphasized by Lawrence J. Vale, who notes that the "designs of particular parts" of capital cities "help to clarify the structure of power in that society." Power can be questioned, and symbols can be variously interpreted, of course, and Vale cautions that: "The relation between the social and the spatial is never a direct one. There are strong limits to it, occasioned in part by the value of abstraction in architectural design that permits the same place to have multiple meanings and prevents any single

interpretation of a building from becoming definitive." See *Architecture, Power, and National Identity* (London: Routledge, 2008), viii–ix.

15. Focillon grants architecture a unique power among the arts. It is "not that of surrounding and, as it were, guaranteeing a convenient void, but of constructing an interior world." He goes on to say that the builder "does not set apart and inclose (sic) a void, but instead a certain dwelling-place of forms, and, in working upon space, he models it, within and without, like a sculptor." Although Focillon hesitates to posit direct connections between art-making and prevailing political, social, and cultural influences, he does not wholly reject external contexts; for example, he acknowledges the creative influences of new materials and technological developments. See *The Life of Forms in Art*, trans. Charles B. Hogan and George Kubler (New Haven: Yale University Press, 1942), 24–25. For a compelling connection between musical form (specifically the blues) and Focillon's understanding of form as reciprocal—both stable and adaptive—see Brent Hayes Edwards, *Epistrophies: Jazz and the Literary Imagination* (Cambridge: Harvard University Press, 2017), 81.

16. Susan Denyer notes that "If architectural form can broadly be seen as a product of environment and social circumstance, decoration appears to be much more bound up with a society's value systems." *African Traditional Architecture: An Historical and Geographical Perspective* (London: Heinemann, 1978), 116.

17. For a discussion of ornamentation on building façades see David Hughes, *Afrocentric Architecture: A Design Primer* (Columbus, Ohio: Greyden Press, 1994), 53, 171. The Charles H. Wright façade also exemplifies several of the points made by Christian Norberg-Schulz. who points out that articulation is evidence of the "desire for individual characterization" beyond the marks of spatial organization and main building materials. He provides a broad analysis of spiritual beliefs, physical landscapes, and the ways in which buildings have reflected and served cultural ends, and he foregrounds "articulation" as a subheading in each chapter. In a section on Egyptian architecture, he includes plant motifs, relief sculptures, moldings, cornices, and columns as illustrations of articulation. This (in many ways exhaustive) study includes examples from non-Western traditions, yet it has been criticized for an emphasis on Egypt and lack of attention to other African countries and cultures. Christian Norberg-Schulz, *Meaning in Western Architecture* (New York: Praeger, 1975), 400.

18. Architect Jeremy Kargon notes that the museum's large window openings and billboards "create a large-scale symbolic gateway for the re-emerging Jonestown historic neighborhood behind the museum." See "Architecture: The Reginald F. Lewis Museum of Maryland African American History and Culture," *Curator* 49.1 (January 2006): 90–91.

19. See Leigh Raiford and Renee C. Romano, "Introduction: "The Struggle over Memory" in *The Civil Rights Movement in American Memory*, ed. Renee C. Romano and Leigh Raiford (Athens, Georgia: University of Georgia Press, 2006), xi–xxiv. In this collection also see Owen J. Dwyer, "Interpreting the Civil Rights Movement: Contradiction, Confirmation, and the Cultural Landscape" (5–27) on the redesigning of the park in 1992 "as 'A Place of Revolution and Reconciliation' to commemorate the protests that led to the desegregation of the city" (7). Dwyer describes the Park,

with its sculptures of "iconic figures from the protests," as "offering a spatial primer in the tactics of provocation and confrontation used by protestors to secure their rights" (8). Also see Renee C. Romano, "Narratives of Redemption: The Birmingham Church Bombing Trials and the Construction of Civil Rights Memory" (96–133) on the main themes that have emerged from the trials—and the coverage by the media. Romano argues that these themes "effectively remove civil rights crimes from their historical context" (99). In "The Birmingham Civil Rights Institute and the New Ideology of Tolerance" Glenn Eskew describes the original architectural plans by Bond, Ryder, James, and Associates, the exhibition design contributions of Richard Rabinowitz, and subsequent disagreements which led to completion of the museum by David Jones and Diversified Project Management.

20. Paul Goldberger, *Why Architecture Matters* (New Haven: Yale University Press, 2009), 174, x.

21. Leland M. Roth, *Understanding Architecture: Its Elements, History, and Meaning* (New York: Icon Editions, 1993).

22. Duncan and Wallach, "The Universal Survey Museum."

23. Rudolf Arnheim, *The Dynamics of Architectural Form* (Berkeley: University of California Press, 1977), 208–209.

24. Stanley Abercrombie, *Architecture as Art: An Aesthetic Analysis* (New York: Van Nostrand Reinhold, 1984), 37–42. Goldberger acknowledges Abercrombie's observations on shapes in architecture, agreeing that "basic geometric shapes have a wholeness and a completeness that is inherently compelling" yet difficult to explain. Goldberger, *Why Architecture Matters*, 82–83.

25. Jane Lusaka, "Finding A Voice," *Museum News* (July/August 1997).

26. Melvin L. Mitchell, *The Crisis of the African-American Architect: Conflicting Cultures of Architecture and (Black) Power,* rev. 2nd edition (New York: Writers Advantage, 2003), 342 n.3. In an acute analysis of how the museum "attempts to teach people—white and black—to see differently," Alison Landsberg notes the "new state of the art building" but does not focus on architectural elements; her primary interest is the central exhibition: "At the heart of the museum, and the core of the permanent exhibition, is a slave ship." See *Prosthetic Memory: The Transformation of American Remembrance in the Age of Mass Culture* (New York: Columbia University Press, 2004), 109, 81.

27. "Detroit Architect Harold Varner Dies at Age 78," *Associated Press*, December 18, 2013. The February 1998 issue of *Ebony* magazine had already included a highly favorable article on the opening of the Charles H. Wright Museum in its new building. Yet several months later Harold Varner's partner Howard F. Sims would have to insist in a letter to the editor that "there is one group of artisans . . . who garnered no reference" in their coverage. Sims then identified the architectural partnership: "Established in 1964 by Howard Sims, Sims-Varner & Associates is a Black-owned, comprehensive and diversified architectural/engineering/planning organization" (*Ebony* 53.8, June 1998):13.

28. Goldberger. *Why Architecture Matters*, 127, 112.

29. David Adjaye is quoted by Calvin Tomkins, "A Sense of Place." *New Yorker*, September 23, 2013. Adjaye explained that: "'I'm inventing an image of a classical

idea for African America, a kind of root for the future.'" He notes that the exterior design was "'adapted, through many prototypes, from the ornamental metal castings that were done by slaves and former slaves in Charleston and New Orleans before and after the Civil War—using techniques that had been developed much earlier in Benin and other African cultures.'" See 76,78.

30. The fact sheet I received from a greeter on my first visit to the Charles H. Wright Museum (10/01/2011) included the following details: A central figure "represents the Supreme Being, and the importance of spirituality in strengthening African Americans." Other elements include: (on right) an African woman kneeling beside a body "representing young slaves who died during the Middle Passage"; (on left) an African American woman "embraces a body, which symbolizes the loss of lives to violence in the United States"; (right of center) an outline map of Africa; (left of center) outline of the United States. "These depict the connected spirit and culture of Africans and African Americans." Also: a figure clutching a book (without words) "symbolizing a hunger for knowledge"; a figure with outstretched arm "seeking upward mobility"; gold chains with a "double meaning. . . . The chains that bound Africans in slavery" and the chains "that bind African Americans in unity today."

31. Supporters' names are also acknowledged on the interior walls of the rotunda; although the exterior walls are bare, the stone creates a compelling design.

32. Philip Johnson, "Whence and Whither: The Processional Element in Architecture," in Philip Johnson, *Writings* (New York: Oxford University Press, 1979).

33. Arnheim, *Dynamics of Architectural Form*, 33, 210.

34. In "The Universal Survey Museum" Duncan and Wallach explain how the use of stairways can establish a hierarchy of value by leading the visitor to the apex of Western European art. This point is also relevant—and yields different results—when we regard the African American museum and its "iconographic programme."

35. http://www.freelon.com/portfolio/273/Cultural#.Vpa_dk3Sly1per (accessed 1/13/2016).

36. Jeremy Kargon, "Architecture: The Reginald F. Lewis Museum of Maryland African American History and Culture," *Curator* 49.1 (January 2006).

37. Nnamdi Elleh, *African Architecture: Evolution and Transformation* (New York: McGraw-Hill, 1997), 48.

38. David Hughes, *Afrocentric Architecture: A Design Primer*, 17.

39. Grant observes that: "The power of the district is that it is an extended urban area and not just one building or museum" and that the "cultural symbols and messages leak out of the Civil Rights Institute into the [Kelly Ingram] park and streets, allowing the public to learn about the cultural and racial memory of a whole area and not just from the exhibit design of the institute." Bradford C. Grant, "Accommodation and Resistance: The Built Environment and the African American Experience," in *Reconstructing Architecture: Critical Discourses and Social Practices*, ed. Thomas A. Dutton and Lian Hurst Mann. *Pedagogy and Cultural Practice* vol. 5 (Minneapolis: University of Minnesota, Press 1996), 224, 226. Also see Priscilla Hancock Cooper's analysis of the design in "A City Embraces Its Past, Looks to the Future: A Perspective on the Evolution of the Birmingham Civil Rights Institute," *The Public Historian* 40, no. 3 (August 2018).

40. Laura Caldwell Anderson, "Walk With Me: The Birmingham Civil Rights Institute," in *Fostering Empathy through Museums*, ed. Elif M. Gokcigdem (Lanham, Maryland: Rowman & Littlefield, 2016), 268–69.

41. Umberto Eco discusses these "primary" and "secondary" functions in "Function and Sign: The Semiotics of Architecture," in *Rethinking Architecture: A Reader in Cultural Theory*, ed. Neil Leach (London: Routledge, 1997).

42. Suzanne MacLeod, "Rethinking Museum Architecture: Towards a Site-Specific History of Production and Use," in *Reshaping Museum Space: Architecture, Design, Exhibitions*, ed. Suzanne MacLeod (London: Routledge, 2005), 21. Used with permission of Taylor & Francis Informa UK Ltd – Books, © 2005, permission conveyed through Copyright Clearance Center, Inc.

43. Lesley Naa Norle Lokko, Introduction. In *White Papers, Black Marks: Architecture, Race, Culture*. Edited by Lesley Naa Norle Lokko (London: Athlone Press, 2000), 14.

44. Araya Asgedom, "The Unsound Space," in Lokko, *White Papers, Black Marks*, 242–243.

45. Jocelyn Robinson-Hubbuch, "African-American Museums and the National Conversation on American Pluralism and Identity," *The Public Historian* 19.1 (Winter 1997).

46. Sterling Stuckey, *Going Through the Storm: The Influence of African American Art in History* (New York: Oxford University Press, 1994), 124. Also see Sterling Stuckey, *Slave Culture: Nationalist Theory and the Foundations of Black America* (New York: Oxford University Press, 1987). The concept of lost or interrupted continuity is an ongoing theme in the study of African American cultural history and its roots in African sources, including the sources of African American rhetorical traditions. See, for example: Orlando Patterson, *Slavery and Social Death: A Comparative Study* (Cambridge: Harvard University Press, 1982), and *Understanding African American Rhetoric: Classical Origins to Contemporary Innovations*, ed. Ronald L. Jackson II and Elaine B. Richardson (New York: Routledge, 2003).

47. Jane M. Jacobs, Kim Dovey, Mathilde Lochert, "Authorizing Aboriginality in Architecture," in Lokko, 220.

48. Lesley Naa Norle Lokko, Introduction, *White Papers, Black Marks*, 29.

49. Edward Ihejirika. "Intensive Continuity," in Lokko, 186. In another essay in that volume, Felecia Davis explains that at the memorial and museum at the African Burial Ground in NYC the "sand-blasted glass covering [is] akin to a burial shroud." However, she is "not interested in the nostalgic inscription of an African-American architecture, but in critical invention which reconfigures 'African' and its traditions and allows for many identities to co-exist simultaneously." See Felecia Davis, "(Un)Covering/(Re)Covering" in Lokko, 353, 355.

50. "The Black Artist in America: A Symposium," Romare Bearden et al. *The Metropolitan Museum of Art Bulletin*, New Series, 27.5 (January 1969).

51. David Sokol, "Marrying Content to Container," *Architectural Record* 197.5 (May 2009). Sokol identifies a "direct reference" to a "Door of No Return" and other uses of directive "nomenclature" in the design by Moshe Safdie and Associates, 82.

52. Clay Risen, "Plinth and Crown," *Architect* 98.7 (July 2009).

53. Stephen A. Kliment, "Discovering African Identity in African-American Archi-tecture." Parts 1 and 2. *AIArchitect* (August 3, 2007 and September 7, 2007. In Part 1, Kliment presents an overview of arguments and positions, focusing on Darell Wayne Fields, David Hughes, Bradford C. Grant, David Lee, and Max Bond, all of whom have published books and/or opinion pieces. In part 2 he includes brief interviews with practitioners. He also summarizes the work of interior designer Sharne Algots-son, who identifies "five hallmarks": continuity—including the appearance of masks and figurines; technique—including gold casting /cire perdue; simplicity—using "'design and decoration as a kind of visual communication'"; spirituality—including the "'Reverence for ancestors and the forces of nature [which] permeated all forms of African art'"; and flexibility—characterized by blending and adapting. See part 2, 5–6.

54. Fields insists that "Black people and architecture don't mix. This is not to say that blacks can't do architecture or serve in every facet of the regime, but when they do, they are practicing the Whiteness of architecture as condoned by White his-tory, White theory, and White practice." Darrel Wayne Fields, *Architecture in Black* (London: The Athlone Press, 2000), 26–31, 49. In his Foreword to the book, Cornel West credits it as "the first theoretical treatment of race in architectural discourse." Foreword to *Architecture in Black*, xvii.

55. Majekodunmi emphasized the "freedom" and "responsibility" entailed in the architectural project and urged his audience to consider that: "Your origins are African, but you have transcended those origins"; "the most important part of your present-day identity now is the way you think and the way you feel within the context of present-day America"; "you are in a unique stage in the evolution of the black race" and bear a "position of greater responsibility, not only to the black race but to the rest of humanity . . . ; and, finally, "you are not designing for Africans, but for Americans." Olufemi Majekodunmi, "Afrocentric Architecture: Myth and Reality," *Architectural Record* (January 1994), 16.

56. See National Organization of Minority Architects: www.noma.net.

57. Grant, "Accommodation and Resistance," 202, 203, 207, 209, 211–13.

58. David Hughes, *Afrocentric Architecture: A Design Primer*, 6, 159, 52, 81. The characteristic elements Hughes identifies include: the great courtyard; building the "monumental from the minute unit"; creation of a "rhythmic pattern" through the "solid/void relationship" (179); and an emphasis on polychromatic patterns, mosa-ics in particular, on the façade. Specific forms include: the pyramid; the ellipsis; chevron detail; prominent use of the crown; the egg, which is a symbol of power in African cosmologies (88); the "cylindrical shape reminiscent of the drum as a form determinant" (95); the obelisk (as an archetype of 'modern skyscraper'); the conical tower and the rondavel. Hughes also notes specific structures: the Great Pyramids of Giza, an example of "monumental architecture as pure geometric form" (19); the Temple of Tamses II at Thebes, for its façade/masonry construction (27); the Obelisk of Luxor, as an archetype of modern skyscraper (31); and the Great Conical Tower of the elliptical temple of Great Zimbabwe (42, 45). He points out that Zimbabwe gives us the forerunner to unit masonry from cut stone which "allows for a broader expression in patterns, bonds and details wrought by the unit rather than the chisel"

(43). We see this clearly in the façade of the National Underground Railroad Freedom Center in Cincinnati.

59. Elleh identifies several "ancient Egyptian house forms" that include the tent, hoop-roofed house, round hut, and rectangular house, the sub-Saharan obelisk, vaulted roofs, and enclosed courtyards and forecourts. *African Architecture: Evolution and Transformation* (New York: McGraw-Hill, 1997), 22–28.

60. Thompson provides an overview of "seven traits" of Afro American sculpture that "suggest African influence": 1) Monochromy or bichromy, exemplified by "black or red monochrome" in "the West African economy of palette" [see the Reginald F. Lewis Museum]; 2) smooth, luminous surfaces, exemplified by "the relative glitter of carefully smoothed surfaces"; 3) equilibrated gestures, exemplified in statuary by standing or seated figures "in frontal position, with arms symmetrically disposed"; 4) frozen faces in "West African figural sculpture" that "present to the world a 'mask' uncompromised by signs of specific emotion"; 5) beaded, shell, or metal eyes that reflect a "larger pattern in West African cultures of mixed-media compositions"; 6) synoptic vision, characterized by "the simultaneous use of two or more vantage points within the same frame of visual reference" (in contrast to Western single-point perspective); and 7) the repertory of reptilian motifs that include "frogs, lizards, tortoises, alligators and serpents." Robert Farris Thompson, "African Influence on the Art of the United States," in *Black Studies in the University: A Symposium*, ed. Armstead L. Robinson et al. (New Haven: Yale University Press, 1969), 122, 124, 163–64. Also see Thompson's *The Flash of the Spirit: African and Afro-American Art and Philosophy* (New York: Vintage Books, 1984). Thompson establishes connections here between discrete African regions and traditions and their reappearance in the Black Atlantic, Mexico, and Central and South America. He offers a detailed look, for example, at "suspended patterning" in art, dance, and music, including the "rhythmized textiles" and "off-beat phrasing of melodic accents in African and Afro-American music" (xvii, 207).

61.Vlach explores the evolution of the "central building type" of Afro-American folk architecture during and after the slaveholding era and describes the shotgun as an "Afro-American artifact." In its basic form, this dwelling is "one-room wide and several deep, with its gable facing the street" and stands as an example of the influence and contribution of Africans and then of African Americans to dominant traditions and forms. In this case of "cultural borrowing," Vlach finds evidence of "proxemic continuities" between West Africa (particularly the Yoruba of Benin and their neighbors, the Edo), the slave trade, and the West Indies (particularly southern Haiti) in the "prototype" of the shotgun. As he explains: "The shotgun had been an element of the slave experience and became an architectural expression with a distinct mulatto identity. The house was a signal of difference and perhaps independence. It has been referred to an 'an architecture of defiance.'" Vlach also offers empirical evidence that free blacks were "active in the building trades" by 1850 and that there were "free black house builders from the start of the nineteenth century." John Michael Vlach, "The Shotgun House: An African Architectural Legacy," in *Common Places: Readings in American Vernacular Architecture*, ed. Dell Upton and John Michael Vlach (Athens: University of Georgia Press, 1986), 58–78.

62. For a comprehensive, fully illustrated analysis of vernacular architecture in West Africa see Jean-Paul Bourdier and Trinh T. Minh-ha, *Vernacular Architecture of West Africa: A World in Dwelling* (New York: Routledge, 2011).

Chapter Two

Themes, Part I

Contributions to the Region and the Nation

If others fail to appreciate the merit of the colored man, let us cherish the deserted shrine. The names which others neglect should only be the more sacredly our care. Let us keep them for the hoped-for day of full emancipation, when, in the possession of all our rights, and redeemed from the long night of ignorance that has rested over us, we may recall them to memory, recollecting, with gratitude, that the stars which shone in our horizon have ushered in a glorious dawn.—William C. Nell. *The Colored Patriots of the American Revolution* . . . (1855)[1]

I have tracked my bleeding countrymen through the widely scattered documents of American history; I have listened to their groans, their clanking chains, and melting prayers, until the woes of a race and the agonies of centuries seem to crowd upon my soul as a bitter reality.—George Washington Williams. *History of the Negro Race in America from 1619 to 1880* . . . (1882)[2]

Although common themes emerge in the historiographic and cultural work of the museums examined here, each museum has a bond with its specific geographical location and identifies its own mission. In doing so, they all strive to amplify and often to obvert—reorient and challenge—an existing body of knowledge. Each museum also benefits from and can contribute to further research in multiple academic disciplines. Scale, presentation of textual and visual narratives, use of objects, and relative importance of a theme to each museum's program vary, and their framing orientations communicate a unique signature and draw on the strengths of their collections. These unique qualities remind us that, while regional museums can be studied as a collective effort to bring African American history and culture to the fore-ground, much will be lost if the analysis becomes totalizing or essentialist.

The major thematic categories that have emerged in my field work include: Settlement—the instrumental role of African Americans in the founding and development of cities and regions, including the establishment and flourish-ing of all-black communities; Historical Eras and Events—key movements and/or individuals in political, social, and military history; and Cultural Achievements—the "fine" arts, music, and popular culture. I take up the first two themes here and consider cultural achievements in chapter 3. Several other thematic categories, which I consider in chapter 4, offer a harsher per-spective on the triumph over adversity and struggle and they stand in stark contrast to the celebratory representations of settlement, citizenship, patrio-tism, and cultural contributions. They include: the realities of Slavery—the African, transatlantic, and American slave trade, and the long history of slav-ery as an institution in the United States; Africa—the continent and individual countries and regions—as the locus of origins and traditions, as the scene of separations, and as points of recent, current, or future return; and Activism and Human Rights—including antebellum rebellions, Jim Crow uprisings, the civil rights movement, and contemporary protest movements.[3] These themes are also present at the National Museum of African American History and Culture in Washington, DC, where they tend to be explicitly contextual-ized within the broader frame of national American history and are conveyed on a larger literal and symbolic screen.[4] That broader national message is present to a lesser and varying extent at regional museums.

SETTLEMENT NARRATIVES

The founding and early development of the nation, specific regions, and major cities are common themes in mainstream history museums, but exhibi-tion narratives and examples are rarely racially or ethnically inclusive. This exclusion has gradually been addressed in recent years and can continue to be inspired by the work of the museums I examine here. They foreground the col-lective and individual contributions made by African Americans and present them as significant and worthy of extended attention. They are not absorbed within what historian Thomas J. Davis has aptly described as the "they, too, were here" syndrome. Davis explains that this syndrome "reveals itself in static, undifferentiated, impersonal exhibitions that sweep across time with the aim of showing that black people, like whites, were also here." He argued thirty years ago that exhibitions on the Afro-American experience should "press beyond the images and objects of motionless black bodies standing in monolithic poses that express little or nothing of the change, contrast, and individuality that set black life and culture apart and infused it with its own shape and substance."[5] Narratives of African American life—represented as dynamic and proactive, rather than static and reactive—have begun to appear in mainstream museum exhibitions, but the corrective mission has always been and remains a necessity and priority for African American museums.

A Nation of Nations: The People Who Came to America as Seen Through Objects and Documents Exhibited at the Smithsonian Institution, an exhibition mounted in 1976, provides a major case in point of under-representation, despite the effort to be inclusive. That exhibition has recently been reappraised, however, in an ongoing exhibition entitled *Many Voices, One Nation: Material Culture Reflections on Race and Migration in the United States* at the Smithsonian's National Museum of American History (2017–). I will return to this exhibit later in this chapter.[6]

Settlement and early development are placed in the foreground at the Museum of African American History (Boston), the African American Museum in Philadelphia, the Reginald F. Lewis Museum of Maryland African American History and Culture (Baltimore), the DuSable Black History Museum and Education Center (Chicago), the Charles H. Wright Museum of African American History (Detroit), the Birmingham Civil Rights Institute (Alabama), and the California African American Museum (Los Angeles). In seeking to enlighten and educate, these museums function as a corrective to longstanding gaps and misrepresentations in both the historical record itself and prior exclusionary museum representations. A brief (and highly selective) overview can illustrate this point.

Boston's longstanding tradition of social and political activism is documented at the Museum of African American History through the achievements and contributions of blacks to the city, the region, and the nation. The website explains that it is "New England's largest museum dedicated to preserving, conserving and interpreting" those contributions; its exhibitions, public programs, and education activities "showcase the powerful stories of black families who worshipped, educated their children, debated the issues of the day, produced great art, organized politically and advanced the cause of freedom." The website also emphasizes that this regional history, which spans the colonial period through the nineteenth century, is actually "national in scope and significance," and that the Museum presents "remarkable and vivid historical accounts about the lives of free African Americans and white abolitionists whose efforts changed a nation."[7]

In addition to documenting key actors in the abolitionist cause, the museum's local historical lens focuses on the fight to integrate Boston public schools, which succeeded in 1855. The involvement of African Americans in the social, political, and legal history of the region and the nation is embodied in the museum's physical location. The African Meeting House (1806) and Abiel Smith School (1835) establish the site as a literal embodiment of a community dedicated to education, religion, and activism. The museum also works in collaboration with the Boston African American Historic Site to sponsor a walking tour of the "Black Heritage Trail" which includes other notable homes and public buildings in the surrounding Beacon Hill neighborhood.

The spirit of place is strong in the Meeting House. As a museum pamphlet explains, it was "built by free black laborers in 1806" and is considered "the oldest surviving black church building in the United States." It was recently restored to its 1855 state and still contains two of the original pews. The building was closed for renovation on my first visit to the museum. When I returned and was able to enter the newly restored space for the first time I was struck by its aura, fully aware that Frederick Douglass had walked on the floorboards, that William Lloyd Garrison, Maria W. Stewart, and William C. Nell, among others, had stirred audiences to action here through debates and public speeches (*Figure 2.1*). Spatial memory is arguably revived and extended here, making the past present.

On one visit to the restored space, for example, I attended a public programming event featuring archaeologist Cheryl La Roche, who explained that

Figure 2.1. Museum of African American History, Boston/African Meeting House.
Source: Author's Photo

"much of our built environment is gone" and that archaeology is "our last line of defense." Roche recited a lineage of actions devised and debated on this site and directed listeners, many of whom appeared to be under twenty-one, to take a minute to "imagine those thunderous protests." In terms of carrying this knowledge into the future, she insisted that the youth of our country must know this history.[8]

The museum doesn't rely solely on the aura and resonance of these buildings, however. Uniformed members of the National Park Service are there to greet visitors (as they enter the Abiel Smith School) and then direct them to the third floor to view a fifteen-minute video titled "Building on a Firm Foundation." The video's major themes are "struggle, resistance, and change." The roles of free black nineteenth-century Bostonians—the primary focus—are played by young nonprofessional actors. "Denise," the primary narrator/character, brings an energy and immediacy to a partially dramatized overview of social and legal history. This historical perspective is brought into finer focus by the documents and illustrations on view in the galleries. In the video's final scene Denise poses the question: "Do you see yourself reflected here?" That self-reflexive strategy transfers the ongoing responsibility of a citizen/activist to the viewer. The video becomes an interactive aspect of the museum experience, and active engagement continues with a brief discussion facilitated by the National Park Service staff.

While African Americans are the primary focus, the museum communicates an explicit message about cooperation and collaboration between black and white members of the Boston community. Object cases and wall texts surround the large space in which visitors view the introductory video. These exhibition elements speak of aspects of daily life, as well as public, political, and cultural history. Those aspects are immediately visible here and are represented in greater detail in the major gallery space on the second floor. The third-floor exhibits feature a case containing small items, books and shoes, for example, that illustrated a "Hidden History on Nantucket," as well as paintings and sculptures. The second- and third-floor galleries contain "Treasures from the Collections" which document social and political history with a focus on abolition and the fight for equality.[9]

The African American Museum in Philadelphia is currently located in a busy commercial area on 7th and Arch Streets, but a move to the former Family Court building (which is still in the planning stages) will bring it closer to Philadelphia's "Museum Mile" on the Benjamin Franklin Parkway.[10] Unlike the historic buildings at the MAAH (Boston) the museum building itself is not "historic" but, like the MAAH, the museum stands in close proximity to Independence Hall, the Liberty Bell, and the American Philosophical Society. It capitalizes on the generally well-known background of the city— which, like Boston, figured prominently in colonial history and the history of the early Republic—as a context for introducing the lesser-known dimensions of African American history. Exposure to this history comes first through an interactive multi-media exhibition entitled *Audacious Freedom: African Americans in Philadelphia 1776–1876 (Figure 2.2)*.

Visitors are directed or accompanied by a staff member to the exhibition, but the individual activation of and interaction with the material takes place without docent intervention. We are left in a large room where, with the push of a button, a montage of murals becomes visible. At first they appear to be static images—portraits, documents, cityscapes—but they do not remain static. They become animated by the visitor's interaction with a touch screen. The visitor's touch activates a voice-over announcement: "We are people of African ancestry." Individual stories follow: of skilled labor, of defending the nation in times of war, of fighting "tirelessly for freedom." A timeline at the base of the montage affords more information and allows a deeper engagement if the visitor chooses to approach and read the details. This framing device can be intriguing—some visitors move quickly through the narrative options, while others linger, look, listen, and then read—and it functions effectively as an exposition to underscore key themes: Family,

Figure 2.2. African American Museum in Philadelphia/*Audacious Freedom: African Americans in Philadelphia, 1776–1876.***
Source: Author's Photo**

Work, Religion, Culture, Law, and Politics. These themes are then amplified in other permanent and special exhibitions.[11] The exhibit design initiates an interactive relationship between the visitor and museum content, a strategy that continues throughout the museum.

A ramp connects this gallery to three others including *Philadelphia Conversations* on the second floor (*Figure 2.3*), where ten full-length portraits—which are in fact video projections—stand ready to become animated when the visitor pushes a button. The subject of each portrait, a single individual set against a period-room background of paintings and objects, begins to speak about his or her life. By appearing to make eye contact with the visitor, they share their story directly with us. Some of the speaking subjects have made their mark on history and may be known to (a limited number of) visitors. These subjects include activist and philanthropist James Forten (1766–1842) whose financial support aided William Lloyd Garrison in founding *The Liberator*[12]; the internationally acclaimed singer Elizabeth Taylor Greenfield (1819–1876), known in the press as the "Black Swan"; and artist David Bustill Bowser (1820–1900) whose subjects included John Brown and whose regimental banners were carried by the US Colored Troops during the

Figure 2.3. African American Museum in Philadelphia/*Philadelphia Conversations* (Detail), James Forten.
Source: Author's Photo

Civil War. There are also "ordinary" people represented here, a sailmaker, for example, and a 106-year-old woman who, according to her oral performance, has "seen it all from the beginning." The visitor may also make choices from a list of discussion questions and the subject stands ready to elaborate.

At the Reginald F. Lewis Museum in Baltimore the settlement/development theme is foregrounded in a permanent exhibition on the third floor; on the way, visitors may view a video introduction to the museum in the theater on the second floor. The main exhibition is divided, yet not distinctly separated into three parts. The design is fluid and, in comparison to other institutions, the R. F. Lewis tends to minimize the didactic and emphasize mobility and achievement. Each thematic part is introduced by a brief video and then developed through wall texts and objects displayed in vitrines. Some are taken from the museum's collection; many are on loan from private collectors and other institutions.

Building Maryland, Building America develops the theme of work. In "Labor That Built a Nation," an explanatory wall text establishes the arrival of free blacks in Maryland in the 1630s and focuses on various forms of work.[13] At the same time it addresses the realities of slavery and ongoing racism. Free-standing vitrines contain tools, a horse collar, a seed planter, a stove back, and steel-toed boots. A muted photo reproduction of Baltimore Harbor is also a reminder of the importance of the fishing industry on Chesapeake Bay. The multiple focus of the *Things Hold, Lines Connect* section is Family, Community, Public Sphere, and Citizenship.[14] In *The Strength of the Mind* section the initial emphasis is on naturalist and inventor Benjamin Banneker and then broadens to include arts and culture. An extensive wall text develops the key concept of "The African American Mind." The achievements and contributions represented here are balanced between the well-known and the little known, both in terms of individuals and in terms of events. Striving in the everyday world is as central to the narrative as is succeeding in the public sphere. Slavery is addressed in the introduction to each theme, but that subject is immediately followed by the turn to productive reactions to oppression and, as the NMAAHC narrative might explain it, "Making a Way out of No Way." In each case the exposition establishes the fact of slavery and then contextualizes its importance by employing a qualifier—"in spite of" or "despite" or "yet"—which rhetorically reorients the focus toward achievement.[15]

In *Building Maryland, Building America*, for example, after introducing the reality of "slavery and exploited labor" (and how this "enriched" the state and nation), we find a turn to the fact that enslaved Africans adapted "native skills" to their situation, developed trades, and persisted in their efforts to achieve freedom, self-determination and success. In *Things Hold, Lines Connect* we learn that the disruption and separation of families and communities created strong and persistent efforts to "renew and sustain" the bonds of family, church, and social organizations. In *The Strength of the Mind* section the acknowledgment of a "displaced and disenfranchised" condition yields to an emphasis on the continuity of African cultural and artistic traditions. A Resource Center on the fourth floor provides opportunities for educators and independent researchers to access (on site and online) the catalogue of library holdings and a reference guide to publications on many aspects of Maryland's social, political, and legal history. Close relationships with educators, and a commitment to serving the needs of Baltimore's K–12 curriculum, is a key aspect of the museum mission.

Although the DuSable Black History Museum and Education Center in Chicago does not signal its cultural identity through architectural statements, the engraved stone tiles bearing the names of "Chicago History Makers" that are set into the exterior walkway literally pave the approach to the museum. Once inside the entry, identified as Founders Hall, visitors are immediately surrounded by African American local, national, and global history. The founders include community leaders who helped Margaret and Charles Burroughs establish the Museum. They are represented in small but arresting mosaic murals by Chicago artist Thomas Miller, along with a mural depicting Jean Baptiste Pointe DuSable, "the first non-Native American settler and father of the place known as Es-chi-ka-gou (Chicago").[16] Small mosaic portraits are set into the walls at ceiling height; larger murals frame the gallery entrance doors and adorn the pediments (*Figure 2.4*).

A continuous narrative above one of the pediments encompasses an array of sailboats, the museum building, and a map of Africa. In addition, larger mixed media murals commemorate Chicago's first African American mayor, Harold Washington, and the city itself. Occupying the center of the Hall are a *DuSable Bust* and *Trading Post Replica* by Chicago sculptor and activist Marion Perkins. Taken together, these visual representations establish a specific as well as general historical frame for the museum's exhibitions.

HISTORICAL ERAS AND EVENTS— MAKING POLITICAL, SOCIAL, AND MILITARY HISTORY VISIBLE

The contributions made by African Americans to the nation's history exceed the frame of any single museum—or any book about museums. With reference to several cases in point, I will take up one major topic here: the active participation of African Americans in the military, beginning with the American Revolution. The theme of military service—with an emphasis on *the patriot*—is a recurring figure in African American museum exhibitions,

Figure 2.4. DuSable Black History Museum and Education Center/Founders Hall.
Source: Author's Photo

where it is brought to the foreground as a significant element in the larger national narrative. A *patriot,* according to the first definition in the *Oxford English Dictionary*, is "A person who loves his or her country, *esp.* one who is ready to support its freedoms and rights and to defend it against enemies or detractors." However, the *OED* also provides this connotative definition: "(orig. *U.S.*). A person actively opposing enemy forces occupying his or her country; a member of a resistance movement, a freedom fighter."[17] African American patriots have arguably conformed to both definitions—explicitly and implicitly. While they fight for their country they also fight as members of a resistance movement. (I put this in the present tense to emphasize the ongoing nature of their compromised status when it comes to full recognition.) In an effort to secure the very freedoms denied by the nation they are undoubtedly "freedom fighters." While the word *patriot* often functions as a literal designation for actual men (and women), as I go on to discuss later in this section the figure of the African American patriot also functions as evidence in support of a recurrent major claim in early African American history texts: that honors and rewards are long overdue to these defenders of the nation and its principles.

The 54th Regiment of the Massachusetts Volunteer Infantry, the first all-black unit formed by the Union army in the Civil War, is remembered on the Boston Common with a massive memorial designed by Augustus Saint-Gaudens and Charles F. McKim. It is generally identified as the "Shaw Memorial" (a reference to the work's apparently central figure and the regiment's white leader, Colonel Robert Gould Shaw).[18] The high-relief, bronze statue depicts Colonel Shaw on horseback with his black infantry soldiers on foot marching beside him. The names of these soldiers are inscribed at the statue's base.

While the iconic memorial on the Boston Common foregrounds Colonel Shaw, minutes away on Joy Street the Museum of African American History contains individual vitrines and entire exhibits that display "The Legacy of Black Military Service" and "Black Massachusetts Regiments." The exhibitions emphasize that, while freedom was "redefined in America" in 1863 with the Emancipation Proclamation, the battle began with the American Revolution. The participation of blacks in that War of Independence—and in each subsequent "national" war effort—remains an undertold story, yet it is one that *was* addressed by the first black historians and continues to be brought to light in African American museums. A special exhibition entitled *Freedom Rising* opened at the museum in 2013 on the 200th anniversary of the Emancipation Proclamation and continues online as an interactive Digital Collections Project. The exhibition elements include a copy of William Cooper Nell's *The Colored Patriots of the American Revolution*, published in 1855. Nell, a local hero, notes in the preface that he "was born on Beacon Hill." He attended Boston public schools and is often credited as the first black public historian.[19] Other objects include Colonel Robert Gould Shaw's uniform—including a frock coat, hat, and sword—and an "Army of the James" medal (1864), the "only official military medal ever commissioned expressly for black troops" (Museum label). In stark contrast to this celebration, an ongoing rotating exhibition entitled *Treasures from the Collections* draws on the museum's more than 3,500 objects to offer a comprehensive view of the realities of slavery—a fact that cannot be overshadowed by the celebration of black achievement. These objects include: a bill of sale dated November 13, 1848, for Tom, an eleven-year-old boy; a slaveship diagram from *The European Magazine*; and an abolitionist discourse pamphlet.

Representing the history of military service has also been an ongoing focus at the DuSable Black History Museum. *Making a Way for Democracy: Citizen Soldiers of the Fighting Eighth in World War I*, for example, currently zeroes in on a particular period. However, the museum's prior long-term exhibition, *Red White Blue and Black: A History of Blacks in the Armed Forces*, carved out a much broader canvas. A well-supported, object-based exhibition, it included informative wall texts and photographic reproductions in addition to vitrines devoted to specific individuals and/or groups such as the Tuskegee Airmen. The timeframe spanned the Revolutionary War, the Civil War, the Spanish American War, and World Wars I and II. The conditions of service were noted and juxtaposed in the same vitrine with a slave bill of sale (1794), a musket ball, and a wall text outlining "laws of convenience and circumstance." The Civil War vitrine included weapons, ammunition, and portraits. Also included was the uniform of Chicago-born Major Robert Henry Lawrence Jr., the first black astronaut. Lawrence was selected for the Manned Orbital Laboratory Program in 1967 but was killed in a crash only five months later while serving as an instructor for a flight test trainee.[20]

At the California African American Museum, the representation of military history is also well supported by artifacts from the collection. At one point, however, the museum made use of a space in their schedule by mounting a temporary exhibition of photographs entitled *African American Military Portraits from the American Civil War: Selected Images from the Library of Congress Collections* (2013). Located in a large gallery off the museum's main entrance, the exhibition was both reverent and informative. The introductory wall text informed visitors that the "sampling of photographs" represented "just a few of the many soldiers whose names, in most cases, have been forgotten to history." Visitors were encouraged to see the exhibition in a larger context as a "window of reflection into one of the most seminal periods of this country's history" and evidence of "a profound resolve" to fight for their individual freedom and "the freedom of an entire people."[21] Although the images were only reproductions of original tintypes, they were framed, hung, and supported as originals might have been: the floors were carpeted; muted shades of paint covered the walls; carefully curated background music created a sense of appreciation for those who had served the nation. In addition, original objects, some of which were on loan to the museum for the exhibition, included a pension certificate for Private Lewis I. Conover—H Company, 127th Regiment, United States Colored Volunteer Infantry (April 1907); a Grand Army of the Republic member's hat (c.1920) (private collection); and an original photograph and personal items belonging to Joseph "Uncle Jo" Clovese, the "last surviving African American veteran of the American Civil War."

The work being done by the museums I have highlighted above is but a sample of the consistent appearance of the figure of "the patriot" and all that this entails. As a material "figure" it can embody the actual through objects and literal traces of the past. As a rhetorical figure it can make an argument for recognition and deep reflection on what it has meant—and what it means now—to fight for the nation itself and its putative egalitarian principles.

CONTEXTS AND THEORY:
THE "DIVERSITY DEFICIT," COURSE CORRECTIONS,
AND RHETORICAL HISTORIOGRAPHY

All too often national histories present themselves as based on given or neutral narratives based on secure empirical facts or scientific theories.—Mark Bevir. "National Histories: Prospects for Critique and Narrative"[22]

The exhibition *A Nation of Nations: The People Who Came to America as Seen through Objects and Documents Exhibited at the Smithsonian Institution* stands as a model of how the nation represented itself to itself—before and after the bicentennial. Both the exhibition, mounted in 1976 by the Smithsonian's National Museum of History and Technology, and the catalogue that survives as its supplement advocated for greater attention to "the material world." Yet the exhibition elements, along with the catalogue and its descriptive essays, revealed the need for a more expansive collection strategy at the Smithsonian and a more inclusive, comprehensive study of the subject matter. *A Nation of Nations* is a valuable historical artifact, however, given its presentation of African American history and culture and what it reveals about collection and exhibition categories at the Smithsonian at the time of the nation's bicentennial.[23] It also stands as part one of a two-part question about the nature of our national (unifying) settlement narrative: Are we best represented as *A Nation of Nations*? or as *Many Voices, One Nation*?

Very few of the objects in *A Nation of Nations* were identified with African and/or African American makers, materials, or formal influences, or the facts of trade, slavery, and imperialism.[24] Of the more than 450 objects listed in the catalogue, less than two dozen indicated a link to African or African American makers or subjects. As Brooke Hindle, director of the National Museum of History and Technology (now the National Museum of American History), noted in the introduction to the catalogue: "There was consistent pressure to conform, to be assimilated into the culture of the majority. These pressures had very real force and effect, but at the same time all sizable minorities, except for the suppressed blacks, celebrated—often exuberantly—their cultural background and differences."[25]

The exception made by Hindle for "suppressed blacks" was not developed as an issue in his introduction. However, C. Malcolm Watkins, senior curator in the Smithsonian's Department of Cultural History, offered a related critique of the state of the discipline in his catalogue essay entitled "A Plantation of Differences—People from Everywhere": "Until recently it has been one of the verities of historians that slaves, uprooted from their tribal communities . . . , became deculturated." Watkins went on to qualify this statement, noting that there was "a growing body of evidence that the social isolation of blacks may have strengthened memories and encouraged the handing down of cultural traits."[26] These observations and the issues they address still inform professional museum practice and scholarly discourses, although there are more African American voices taking part in the conversation. In addition, there are many more culturally specific collections, exhibitions, and institutions on the museum landscape, including the Smithsonian's National Museum of African American History and Culture.

In 2017, when *Many Voices, One Nation: Material Culture Reflections on Race and Migration in the United States* opened at the National Museum of American History, its precursor (*A Nation of Nations*) became a critical reference point. Contributors to the catalogue for *Many Voices* repeatedly looked back to the themes, intentions, achievements, and shortcomings of the bicentennial exhibition. Like its precursor, this ongoing exhibition seeks to be inclusive. Unlike *A Nation of Nations*, however, *Many Voices* contains numerous objects that contribute to the exhibition's goal of inclusivity. The accompanying catalogue also includes many essays that foreground the contributions of African American makers and address critical details concerning creation, use, and circulation.[27]

This is especially evident in the prefatory material. Gary Gerstle writes in the foreword, for example, that: "One can still experience that 1976 exhibit by studying the book. . . . Anyone doing that will be struck, however, not just by what that exhibit accomplished but by how much its interpretation has aged, and how much we need a new reckoning with the peopling saga." Margaret Salazar-Porzio and Joan Fragaszy Troyano explain in the introduction that the goal of *Many Voices* is to provide "a more textured history" which draws on "decades of historical scholarship that critically examines the complicated relationships among migration, race, nation, and our norms of 'E Pluribus Unum.'" They go on to emphasize that *Many Voices* is "an important point of departure from *A Nation of Nations*, which provided a relatively inclusive history but did not feature key debates that have confronted our nation over the years. Who is free? Who is equal? Who is welcome? And how do these questions impact what it means to be American?" Salazar-Porzio and Troyano also note that *Many Voices* "spotlights key debates about freedom, equality, and belonging that influenced the context in which people produced and used their artifacts and images."[28]

The exhibition retrieves underrepresented elements of American history through objects and scholarship, and the catalogue's scope embraces Native Americans and other indigenous pre-settlement populations. In the epilogue, "Our Polycultural Past and Future Century," Scott Kurashige restates one of the exhibition's major goals. Using the keywords *multiplicity, diversity, heterogeneous*, and *intersectional* he expresses the hope that the project "will help to redress the 'diversity deficit' within our national institutions." The success of the larger long term project will depend in part on the interventions of those who collect, curate, and write the labels, wall texts, and catalogue essays which reinforce these messages; it will also depend in part on the individual viewer's engagement with the objects and historical truths they encounter during their museum visits.[29]

The "diversity deficit" identified by Kurashige in the catalogue for *Many Voices, One Nation* has been addressed at the regional level by African American museums for at least fifty years and, for at least 150 years, it has been addressed by African American historians. In looking at the tradition of that explicitly "rhetorical" history it is necessary to ask, along with Stefan Berger, "what is 'national history'?" In his introduction to *The Past as History: National Identity and Historical Consciousness in Modern Europe* Berger offers a disarmingly straightforward answer, claiming that national history is composed of "the 'great works' on the national past" that "synthesize the knowledge of their time as well as the political and social world views and expectations of their authors." On a "more abstract" and less neutral level, Berger adds that in the "broad genre of historical representation, the "national" is regarded as "the most important dimension of history writing and [is] differentiated from other spatial . . . and non-spatial (ethnic/racial, class, religious and gender) histories despite the fact that it inevitably interacts with those other histories." Adding yet another level, Berger notes that national history is "the meta-or master narrative of historical writing"; it is "normally teleological and serves legitimatory functions."[30] While "national history" might serve as an unquestionable and necessary version of events (Berger's first sense) it too often prioritizes one among multiple (spatial and nonspatial) versions.

National history is clearly neither singular nor neutral insofar as it exerts a selective and exclusionary force with a clear trajectory and a "progressive" argument. Berger's subject is the construction of European national histories, but his observations also pertain to the "national" dimension of African American history, especially as written by African American historians since the nineteenth century. One of their goals—to obvert the prevailing (national) history of the United States—was both "teleological" and "legitimatory." These historians clearly saw the need to present different origins and different trajectories. They had to dislodge what Mark Bevir identifies as the "secure empirical facts or scientific theories" common to traditional national histories.[31]

William Cooper Nell and other early historians made a crucial contribution to the development of an inclusive national and strategically *rhetorical* African American history. While we might agree that history writing in general is a "discursive practice" and an "argumentatively formed narrative," as Bruce Bronbeck observed in "The Rhetorics of the Past," some history writing may be seen as particularly purposive and pragmatic (consequence oriented) when "used to argue outside the narrative itself as evidence for some social or moral lesson."[32] Historians like Nell clearly fall into this category. One of their overarching arguments was that, while they were being deprived of their rights of citizenship, blacks continued to contribute to the development and—in the case of military service—the protection of the nation. The link between objects and texts—as material *traces* and *sources* of information—is a crucial element in the consequential work of African American history as a subject and the African American museum as a space for the representation of that history.

While early African American history texts documented actual events, they also created what Pierre Nora terms sites of memory.[33] Nora distinguishes between the real environments (*milieux de mémoire*) in which events occur and the sites (*lieux de mémoire*) we later create and invest with memory. Monuments and museums have often been discussed in the context of *lieux de mémoire* but, as Elizabeth Rauh Bethel notes, written histories also function as memory sites. Bethel uses Nora's classifications to identify the work of several early African American historians as *lieux de mémoire* and finds that: "While the *milieux de mémoire* [the people and events] are varied—Africa, the American Revolution, transnational heroes—the *lieux de mémoire* [the texts which introduce, analyze, and critique] uniformly address American issues: full and unconditional citizenship; economic, political, and cultural equity and equality."[34]

I want to echo Bethel's point and suggest that the history text itself may serve several functions: as a material object that can be read *and* displayed in a museum, as an archive of collective memories, and as a factual basis for argumentation. Finally, history texts may function as symbolic substitutes for material traces of identity and history. Nineteenth-century African American histories thus have an exponential value—as material artifacts of the discipline, as factual repositories, as memory places, and as masterworks of rhetoric. They inform and they seek to persuade. When the book itself is exhibited in a museum, as Nell's book is in Boston, it embodies the groundbreaking work of the historian as well as the events/environments they document.

This tradition of rhetorical historiography precedes the rise of African American museums. A comprehensive treatment of the subject is beyond the scope of this study but a selective review of the first generations of African American history texts reveals that they were explicitly rhetorical and that their arguments were later taken up by African American museums. As the early historians addressed gaps in the historical record they also introduced and responded to misconceptions about origins, values, lifeways, capabilities, and fitness for full citizenship.[35] And they shed light on the status of African Americans within the broader, typically exclusionary national narrative. In doing so they provided an important source for the representation of African American history and culture in the museums of the future.

A very early example of the tendency to critique as well as inform can be found in *A Text-Book on the Origin and History, &c. &c. of the Colored People* by Reverend James W. C. Pennington (1841). It begins with a question: "Who and whence are the colored people?" Pennington responds first with the Biblical origins, then employs this lineage to address the claim (used by whites to justify injustice) that blacks are the cursed sons of Canaan and thus doomed to be enslaved.[36] His final move—an anatomy of prejudice—is repeated with variation in subsequent texts where this critique is the opening—the prologue to the history—rather than the epilogue.

The physical copy of William Cooper Nell's *Colored Patriots of the American Revolution* (1855) on exhibit in the *Freedom Rising* exhibition at the Museum of African American History in Boston marks the intersection of history writing and museum exhibitions. The book's display explicitly attests to the individual importance of the text and implicitly addresses the importance of African American historiography. With the aid of the "museum effect" visitors may be drawn to and impressed by the age, materiality, and aura of an original edition of the book. The preservation and exhibition of the text also honors and calls attention to the need for an inclusive record at a particular time in national history. Nell devotes individual chapters to eighteen states, beginning with Massachusetts and the first casualty of the war, Crispus Attucks. He offers an overview of the actions of notable "colored patriots" and integrates developments in the political and legislative spheres (related, for example, to voting rights or the Fugitive Slave laws) that involve and, in most cases, negatively affect those patriots.[37] The text concludes with a *Survey of the Conditions and Prospects of Colored Americans*, a seventy-page critique supported by quotations from primary sources. Here Nell reviews the deplorable status of the colored Americans' so-called "Citizenship," celebrates their persistent efforts toward "Elevation," and offers a performative farewell: "So sure as night precedes day, war ends in peace, and winter wakes spring, just so sure will the persevering efforts of Freedom's army be crowned with victory's perennial laurels!"[38]

During the Civil War, William Wells Brown published *The Black Man: His Antecedents, His Genius, and His Achievements* (1863). In the introduction he states his purpose: "If this work shall aid in vindicating the Negro's character, and show that he is endowed with those intellectual and amiable qualities which adorn and dignify human nature, it will meet the most sanguine hopes of the writer."[39] In addition to providing biographical portraits that include Benjamin Banneker, Nat Turner, Toussaint L'Ouverture, Crispus Attucks, Phillis Wheatley, Denmark Vesey, Frances Ellen Watkins Harper, Martin Delany, Frederick Douglass, and Charlotte Forten, Brown includes a self-portrait that traces his own childhood, his escape from slavery, and his work as an antislavery lecturer. By including himself as an example of the aptitude and determination of *any* person of color, Brown supports his main argument.[40] We might recall here the *Philadelphia Conversations* exhibit at the African American Museum in Philadelphia where life-size figures of prominent African Americans become animated and give voice to their experiences and accomplishments.

Pennington had argued in his 1841 "Text-Book" that prejudice was the hallmark of those who "hate the truth." George Washington Williams expanded on that argument in 1883 with a two-volume comprehensive *History of the Negro Race in America from 1619 to 1880. Negroes as Slaves, as Soldiers, and as Citizens; Together with a Preliminary Consideration of the Unity of the Human Family, An Historical Sketch of Africa, and an Account of the Negro Governments of Sierra Leone and Liberia.* This expansive title underscores several key themes that will prove vital to the missions of African American museums and the themes they foreground. In the preface he identifies that corrective purpose by establishing the need for the text, in part because "in every attempt upon the life of the nation, whether by foes from without or within, the Colored people had always displayed a matchless patriotism and an incomparable heroism in the cause of Americans." He explicitly expresses the hope that "such a history would give the world more correct ideas of the Colored people, and incite the latter to greater effort in the struggle of citizenship and manhood."[41] As they did in Nell's *Colored Patriots*, the major themes of slavery and patriotism appear throughout the two volumes.

Williams devotes volume II to the period between 1800 and 1880 and often quotes at length from primary documents: letters, meeting minutes, and legislation. In a brief prefatory "Note" to volume II, dated December 28, 1882, he explains that he is writing at a time when "the American slave" has become "an American citizen": "How wondrous have been his strides, how marvelous his achievements!" Yet he also makes the stark observation I quoted at the beginning of this chapter, in which he underscores the fact that pathos, blood, and suffering are evident in the documents that inform his history. Williams maintains his dual focus on pathos and patriotism in volume II. He attends to the antislavery movement, "national legislation" on slavery, slave rebellions, and "the John Brown movement"; as well as the Emancipation Proclamations, he presents detailed accounts of military service: "Negro Troops in the War of 1812"; "Negroes in the Navy"; and "The Negro in the War for the Union." Moreover, he documents attitudes in the North and South on "Employment of Negroes as Soldiers" and "the sufferings Negro troops endured as prisoners in the hands of the Rebels." The official documents we find in museums, attesting to military service, pension awards, repeated requests for and denials of benefits, offer material evidence of the conditions Williams describes.

Edward A. Johnson's *A School History of the Negro Race in the United States, from 1619–1890* (1894), primarily a teaching text written in accessible prose with abundant illustrations, also deserves recognition in this brief overview of corrective projects. The text was later expanded to include a *History of the Negro Soldiers in the Spanish-American War* and *A Short Sketch of Liberia* (1911). Johnson uses the preface to address readers who will be educating the young (and perhaps other adults): "I respectfully request that my fellow-teachers will see to it that the word *Negro* is written with a capital *N*. It deserves to be so enlarged, and will help, perhaps, to magnify the race it stands for in the minds of those who see it." Johnson has a strong underlying argument familiar to those who have read the nineteenth-century texts I include here: that blacks have unequivocally demonstrated their worth and therefore they should be given equal credit, equal rights, and equal opportunities. He includes the accomplishments of "Some Noted Negroes" but, like Williams, his emphasis is on military achievement. There are chapters devoted to: "Negro Soldiers in Revolutionary Times"; "Negro Heroes of the Revolution"; The War of 1812; and the "Employment of Negro Soldiers." However, he does not stop at a summary of the contributions to these war efforts. When he turns to a "History of Negro Soldiers in the Spanish-American War and Other Items of Interest" he includes direct testimony by white officers regarding the unusual bravery and skill of the Negro soldiers, and he devotes an entire chapter to the fact that "President McKinley Recognizes the Worth of Negro Soldiers by Promotion." He also transcribes an article from the *New York Independent* which attests to the fact that Negro soldiers are "Competent to Be Officers—The Verdict of General Thomas J. Morgan, After a Study of the Negro's Quality as a Soldier."[42]

One final example of early radical rhetorical histories represents a disciplinary turn and establishes a link to the corrective histories that gradually fill the regional and finally the national museum landscape. *A Social History of the American Negro, Being a History of the Negro Problem in the United States* was published in 1921 by Benjamin Brawley. In the preface he acknowledges his precursors and, for example, cites Williams and Nell as sources. However, in a statement of his method and purpose, he strives to set himself apart: wanting to "give fresh treatment to the history of the Negro people in the United States . . . from a distinct point of view, the social." Brawley marks this disciplinary turn by tracking the founding of organizations, the establishment of churches, a record of collective action, and the "actual life of the Negro people in itself." Brawley stops to note that leaders in the antebellum period "were by no means impractical theorists but men who were scientifically approaching the social problems of their people. They not only anticipated such ideas as those of industrial education and of the

National Urban League of the present day, but they also endeavored to lay firmly the foundations of racial self-respect."

In spite of the mounting evidence of patriotism, intellectual accomplishment, and artistic talent that had been documented in Pennington's *Text-Book on the Origin and History* (1841) and repeated by historians throughout the nineteenth century, the argument still had to be made. For Brawley the "problem" of being a Negro in the United States still demanded attention—it was a problem not only for blacks but for the nation, as Frederick Douglass had warned his readers in the first *Narrative*. Brawley traces that history from its African origins up to "The Negro in the New Age" post World War I. The final chapter, "The Negro Problem," levels a fierce critique: "The Negro is so dominant in American history not only because he tests the real meaning of democracy, not only because he challenges the conscience of the nation, but also because he calls in question one's final attitude toward human nature itself."[43] The self-reflection these historians demanded from their readers prefigures the self-reflection that African American museums encourage in their visitors.

NOTES

1. William C. Nell, *The Colored Patriots of the American Revolution, with Sketches of Several Distinguished Colored Persons: To Which Is Added a Brief Survey of the Conditions and Prospects of Colored Americans* (Boston: Robert F. Walcutt, 1855. Reprint. Ayer Co., Publishers, Inc. Salem, NH, 1986), 379. digital-research-books-beta.nypl.org/read/14238779?source=catalog.

2. George Washington Williams, *History of the Negro Race in America from 1619 to 1880. Negroes as Slaves, as Soldiers, and as Citizens*, two volumes (New York: G. P. Putnam's Sons, 1882, volume II, iii. Project Gutenberg: www.gutenberg.org/files/21851/21851-h/21851-h.htm).

3. National surveys conducted in 2008 and 2016 reveal that: "The most common themes . . . are local and regional history, famous individuals, African art and history, slavery and abolition, national history including civil rights, as well as art and music." Jeff Hayward and Christine Larouche, "The Emergence of the Field of African American Museums," *The Public Historian* 40, no. 3 (August 2018), 168–69. This research confirms in very broad terms what I have discovered in my field work.

4. The National Museum of African American History and Culture exceeds its precursors in terms of size (more than 100,000 square feet of exhibition space). This allows for *multiple* installations of large objects, such as a slave cabin and a segregation-era Southern Railway Car, and extensive use of multimedia and interactive technologies. (Several of the regional museums are able to do this on a smaller scale, as I will go on to explain.) Questions about what the new national museum does differently and what it does more or less effectively than its regional precursors

will have to be addressed over time with the benefit of sustained attention to its expansive space of representation. The top floor is dedicated to the *Culture Galleries*—encompassing the visual arts, music, drama, performing arts, and other forms of artistic expression (level 4). On the floor below, the *Community Galleries* are devoted to sports, military history, the "Power of Place" (with a focus on major cities and smaller local regions), and "Making a Way out of No Way," representing various local and national movements, including the first A.M.E. Church in Los Angeles and women's organizations including the National Council of Negro Women (level 3). The second floor is devoted to classrooms, a library, an interactive gallery, a Center for African American Media Arts, and a Family History Center. At the foundational/ bedrock position—literally and symbolically—are the history galleries that occupy three levels beneath an underground concourse. The museum building itself, including the visitor's approach and passage beneath a large courtyard or porch, constitutes the primary framing experience. The entrance at street level is dominated by a thorough security screening process. The expansive Heritage Hall, which includes the information center and museum store, functions as a gathering place, a starting point, and a space where visitors may return to rest and reorient themselves. There is also a separate area—a *Contemplative Court*—for reflection. For an extensive history of the development of the NMAAHC see Mabel O. Wilson. *Begin with the Past: Building the National Museum of African American History and Culture*.

5. Thomas J. Davis, "'They, Too, Were Here': The Afro-American Experience and History Museums," *American Quarterly* 41.2 (June 1989): 329, 332, 339. Davis offers a comparative review of exhibitions mounted between 1987 and 1988 by the National Museum of American History (Washington, DC), The National Afro-American and Cultural Center (Wilberforce, Ohio), The Valentine, The Museum of the Life and History of Richmond, Virginia, and The Balch Institute for Ethnic Studies (Philadelphia). He notes, for example, that "instead of the Valentine's survey approach, the Balch pursued an in-depth or monographic approach that concentrated on illuminating the shape and substance of a confined and well-defined experience."

6. The title "A Nation of Nations" was inspired by the work of Walt Whitman, our national poet of inclusiveness, and quotations from Whitman introduced each of the catalogue's four parts. The Smithsonian's National Museum of American History has now mounted an exhibition and published a companion volume of essays in which the gaps in that bicentennial exhibition are explicitly addressed. See Margaret Salazar-Porzio, Joan Troyano, Lauren Safranek, eds. *Many Voices, One Nation: Material Culture Reflections on Race and Migration in the United States* (Washington, DC: Smithsonian Institution, 2017).

7. www.maah.org/about.

8. This lecture, delivered on 6/20/13, was part of the museum's Lowell Lecture Series. Also see the related monograph: Cheryl Janifer LaRoche, *Free Black Communities and the Underground Railroad: The Geography of Resistance* (Urbana-Champaign: University of Illinois Press, 2014). See Leland Ferguson, *Uncommon Ground: Archaeology and Early African America, 1650–1800* (Washington, DC: Smithsonian Books, 1992) on the role of archaeology in uncovering history. See Paul R. Mullins on "what race and racism 'look like' in the material world."

Mullins finds that archaeology "paints a picture of very complex lines of difference and an intricate political mosaic that created the contemporary cityscape" but that "some community constituents seem to desire something less equivocal." Paul R. Mullins, "African American Heritage in a Multicultural Community: An Archaeology of Race, Culture, and Consumption," in *Places in Mind: Public Archaeology as Applied Anthropology*. eds. Paul A. Shackel and Erve J. Chambers (New York: Routledge, 2004), 58–59.

9. Gallery installations, of course, may vary over time.

10. Aaron Moselle, "Philly's African American Museum moving to the Ben Franklin Parkway," *WHYY.org*, August 11, 2022. The move is expected to take five years.

11. Exhibits have included, for example: *381 Days: The Montgomery Bus Boycott Story*, which develops the theme of political activism, and *Artful Intentions: Area Artists Expressions of Life*, which offers evidence of artistic legacies and cultural achievements.

12. For an overview of the still underrepresented contributions of Forten and others, see Richard S. Newman and Roy E. Finkenbine, "Black Founders in the New Republic: Introduction," *William and Mary Quarterly* 3rd Series, LXIV, no. 1 (January 2007).

13. Fath Davis Ruffins notes that the R. F. Lewis retrieves the little known "history of settlement and enslavement, and the growth of free black churches, schools, and communities" and that the exhibition "elements flow together seamlessly." "A Community Revealed: The Reginald F. Lewis Museum of Maryland African American History and Culture," *Curator* 49.1 (Jan. 2006): 84, 86.

14. Ruffins makes a connection to poet Lucille Clifton, who asserts that things do hold; "African American communities do not fall apart." For Ruffins that "point . . . is critical to the museum's mission: to express the social cohesion, religious determination, struggle against the odds, and contributions to history" ("A Community Revealed," 86).

15. Marcus Wood sees the choices made by the R. F. Lewis as "not so much a turning away from the horror of the Middle Passage" but "a desire to turn towards the forging of slave cultures and African American social life." He notes "the almost unrelenting positivism with which the Reginald Lewis approaches the narrative of African American social and cultural development in Maryland," the "spectacularly abstracted and physically silenced approach to the memory of the Middle Passage," and the absence of a "guiding voice" to interpret a large photomural at the entrance to their exhibition galleries. Marcus Wood, "Slavery, Memory, and Museum Display in Baltimore: The Great Blacks in Wax Museum and the Reginald F. Lewis," *Curator* 51.1 (January 2009): 155–57.

16. DuSable Museum pamphlet.

17. "patriot, n. and adj." *Oxford English Dictionary Online*. June 2018. Oxford University Press.

18. The Shaw Memorial as well as the Museum's African Meeting House and Abiel Smith School are included in the National Park Service's "Black Heritage Trail." For a detailed discussion of the design and reception of the Shaw Memorial, which was unveiled in 1897, see Kirk Savage, *Standing Soldiers, Kneeling Slaves: Race, War,*

and Monument in Nineteenth-Century America (Princeton: Princeton University Press, 1997). The "Shaw campaign," Savage notes, "introduced the element of black recognition into the more conventional worship of white heroism" and, after "a long process of revision and experimentation," it resulted in the "first monument representing bone fide black soldiers in proper uniform" (197, 200).

19. As Margot Minardi explains, "The research of William Cooper Nell and other early African American historians disrupted the prevailing narrative of a 'free' New England simply by putting enslaved and formerly enslaved people onto the landscape of memory." This process of historical recovery included "research into black Revolutionary heroes." "Making Slavery Visible (Again): The Nineteenth-Century Roots of a Revisionist Recovery in New England," in *Politics of Memory: Making Slavery Visible in the Public Sphere*, ed. Ana Lucia Araujo (New York: Routledge, 2012), 96–97.

20. Andrea Burns notes that, in its first incarnation during the civil rights movement of the 1960s, what would become the Charles H. Wright was named the International Afro-American Museum (IAM). The IAM carried out its mission of education in part through the use of a mobile exhibit van which focused not only on Africa and African history but on "Africans in American History." Like the DuSable, Burns explains, the IAM van "connected audiences with the African 'past' and the African American present." The latter included an emphasis on "achievements in art, the military, agriculture, and the contributions of figures like Crispus Attucks, Benjamin Banneker, and Phillis Wheatley." Andrea Burns, *From Storefront to Monument: Tracing the Public History of the Black Museum Movement*, 78–85.

21. Wall text for *African American Military Portraits from the American Civil War* at the California African American Museum, 2013.

22. Mark Bevir, "National Histories: Prospects for Critique and Narrative," *Journal of the Philosophy of History* 1, no. 3 (September 2007), 312. Used with permission of Brill, permission conveyed through Copyright Clearance Center, Inc.

23. The Smithsonian-sponsored *Festival of American Folk Life* (1976) did focus on "Black American culture from the viewpoint of the diaspora," and included a small but valuable volume of essays and documentation of the events. It contains an excellent essay by John Vlach, for example, on "Phillip Simmons: Afro-American Blacksmith." See *Black People and Their Culture: Selected Writings from the African Diaspora*, ed. Linn Shapiro (Washington, DC: Smithsonian Institution, 1976).

24. A report published in 1988 by the Geffrye Museum (London) pointed to similar problems of under-representation and offered suggestions that seem applicable not only to the Geffrye but to other museums that seek to excavate and exhibit the "Black Contribution to History." Early in their Report, Peter Fraser and Rozina Visram, who carried out the study, noted that "the belongings of the well-to-do survive better than those of the poor" (3). In their concluding summary of recommendations, they insisted that "the Black contributions to the history of the United Kingdom should be properly integrated, not treated as an alien intrusion" (81). These two points effectively frame the conditions under which many other inclusive histories would be undertaken. The Geffrye is a small museum made up of period rooms, Almshouse buildings, and gardens that primarily represent British upper middle-class life from

1600–1939. The formulation of an "Anti-Racist Policy" and implementation of its values in the museum's exhibition spaces occasioned the study. Their observations and recommendations, which could be translated to bear upon American museums, included the need for greater attention to evidence of: international trade and stylistic influences, working-class life, women's lives, and literature and the arts. On a wider stage—beyond domestic interiors and to an extent beyond the existing Geffrye collections—they identified relevant contexts which might be introduced through object interpretation and archival work; they included: political activism, the struggle against slavery, the Pan-Africanist movement, the "tradition of radical women," and the presence of black men and women in the medical and legal professions. See Peter Fraser and Rozina Visram, *Black Contribution to History. Report Commissioned by CUES Community Division and the Geffrye Museum* (London: Geffrye Museum, 1988).

25. Brooke Hindle, Introduction, in *A Nation of Nations: The People Who Came to America as Seen through Objects and Documents Exhibited at the Smithsonian Institution*, ed. Peter Marzio (New York: Harper & Row, 1976), xv.

26. C. Malcolm Watkins, "A Plantation of Differences—People from Everywhere," in *A Nation of Nations*, 73.

27. *Many Voices, One Nation: Material Culture Reflections on Race and Migration in the United States*, ed. Margaret Salazar-Porzio, Joan Fragaszy Trovano, with Lauren Safranek (Washington, DC: Smithsonian Institution Scholarly Press, 2017). In "Unsettling the Continent, 1492–1776" (pages 27–43) Barbara Clark Smith analyzes an African cowrie shell necklace and a rice fanner basket which speak to the currency of the slave trade and the endurance of "African agricultural methods," respectively (30, 35). In "Contesting the Nation, 1900–1965" (pages 137–63) Fath Davis Ruffins offers an overtly political history. As Smith "unsettles" the continent from 1492–1776, Ruffins trains her unwavering gaze on the twentieth-century activist "movements, organizations, and individuals" that agitated for change (139). With references to portraits of W. E. B. Du Bois and Dr. Carter Woodson, and objects including a Ku Klux Klan hood and the double-sided signage used to identify segregated areas of a railroad car, Ruffins demonstrates in print what we may expect to experience in the museum. Other object-centered approaches include "Communities of Refuge in Frontier Illinois" (101–109) in which Nancy Davis focuses on Free Frank McWorter, a once-enslaved man who had purchased his freedom and went on to establish the first known town (New Philadelphia, Illinois) to be "founded and platted" by an African American. While the land itself retains few marks of the original settlement, Davis explains, the surviving "objects stand as records of the ideas and concepts" of the "unique communities" that once occupied the physical place. In this case the objects include a photograph of the founder's son, Solomon McWorter, and a child's rocking chair made by Solomon and saved by the McWorter family (108). In "African American Expression in Antebellum America: The Story of Dave Drake" (111–21) Kym Rice explores the life and works of "Dave the Potter." His surviving pots "not only offer insight into the practices embodied in an antebellum plantation and industrial slavery," they also speak to his ability to discover and maintain his "self-identity" and communicate through what may be seen as a "subversive" form of self-expression in his poems as well as the pots they decorate (111, 116).

28. Margaret Salazar-Porzio and Joan Fragaszy Troyano, Introduction, in *Many Voices, One* Nation, 12–14.

29. Scott Kurashige, "Epilogue: Our Polycultural Past and Future Century," in *Many Voices, One Nation*, 271.

30. Stefan Berger with Christoph Conrad, *The Past as History: National Identity and Historical Consciousness in Modern Europe* (Basingstoke, UK: Palgrave Macmillan, 2015), 1–2.

31. Bevir advocates a "shift from developmental historicism" to a "radical historicism" that "lends itself to perspectival critique and decentered narratives" (293, 296). While his focus is the work of professional historians, Bevir's descriptions and prescriptions are also applicable to museum-centered historiography. A good example of the decentering of civil rights history, for example, can be found in Jeanne Theoharis, *A More Beautiful and Terrible History: The Uses and Misuses of Civil Rights History* (Boston: Beacon Press, 2018) where she argues that: "A story that should have reflected the immense injustices at the nation's core and the enormous lengths that people had gone to attack them had become a flattering mirror. The popular history of the civil rights movement now served as testament to the power of American democracy" (x).

32. Bruce Bronbeck, "The Rhetorics of the Past: History, Argument, and Collective Memory," in *Doing Rhetorical History: Concepts and Cases*, edited by Kathleen J. Turner (Tuscaloosa, AL: University of Alabama Press, 1998), 47, 49, 53.

33. See Pierre Nora, "Between Memory and History: *Les Lieux de Mémoire*," *Representations* 26 (Spring 1989), 7, 17. Nora begins by claiming that we now have very few extant "remnants of [past] experience"; thus we gravitate toward—even construct—sites "where memory crystallizes and secretes itself." We have *"lieux de mémoire*, sites of memory," he explains, "because there are no longer *milieux de mémoire*, real environments of memory." He finds that memory "attaches itself to sites, whereas history attaches itself to events." This seems especially relevant if we consider that much of the *"milieux"*—real environments—of enslaved individuals and communities was not preserved, thus making the construction of texts as *lieux* an urgent undertaking.

34. Elizabeth Rauh Bethel, *The Roots of African-American Identity: Memory and History in Free Antebellum Communities* (New York: St. Martin's, 1997), ix–x, 186. Bethel identifies several historians in this context, including J. W. C. Pennington, William Cooper Nell, William Wells Brown, and William Still. She argues that "the *lieux de mémoire* they constructed "would inform African-American community-building into the twentieth-century."

35. (Some have been reprinted and are widely available—thus they are not only museum pieces.) Pero Gaglo Dagbovie contends that there might be doubt as to the disciplinary qualifications of William Cooper Nell, James W.C. Pennington, William Wells Brown, and even W. E. B. Du Bois, who (based on their methods and sources) may/not deserve to be considered "the 'first' genuine" black historians. See *What Is African American History?* (Cambridge, UK: Polity, 2015), 2.

36. Pennington goes on to trace the origins of slavery—not to Africa but to this continent—to Spanish colonists in South America and the practice of aboriginal

slavery. In arguing against the claim that "Africans first suggested the idea of slavery," he insists that "slavery was bred, born and nurtured in the will of Charles the Fifth [of Spain]." He goes on to refute the claim that blacks are inferior by enumerating their achievements and offering examples that date back to ancient Egyptian arts and sciences. Finally, he attends to the nature of prejudice in America and attributes it to selfishness, ill will, "blindness of mind," and those who hate the truth. Reverend James W.C. Pennington, *A Text-Book on the Origin and History, &c. &c. of the Colored People* (Hartford: L. Skinner, 1841), 7, 42–45, 74–90.

37. Henry Louis Gates credits Nell's text as "the first assessment of the African American military role in the nation's struggle for independence and in the War of 1812." Henry Louis Gates, *Life upon These Shores: Looking at African American History 1513–2008* (New York: Knopf, 2011), 107. Gates also observes that Nell "became a pioneer in collecting black oral history and memorabilia."

38. William Cooper Nell, *The Colored Patriots of the American Revolution*, 381.

39. William Wells Brown, *The Black Man: His Antecedents, His Genius, and His Achievements* (Boston: James Redpath, 1863), 6.

40. Gates notes that, "At a time when northern whites considered African Americans to be incapable of sustained thoughts, the large number of publications by black abolitionists, and especially former slaves, became powerful antislavery acts." See *Life upon These Shores*, 106.

41. George Washington Williams, *A History of the Negro Race in America* (New York: Bergman Publishers, 1968. 1883. Reprint), Project Gutenberg: www.gutenberg .org/files/21851/21851-h/21851-h.htm. Vol. I. Preface, v, vi, viii and Volume II and "Notes," iii–iv.

42. Edward A. Johnson, *A School History of the Negro Race in America from 1619 to 1890 Combined with the History of Negro Soldiers in the Spanish-American War, Also Other Items of Interest* (Revised Edition, 1911, Reprint New York: AMS Press, 1969).

43. Benjamin Brawley, *A Social History of the American Negro, Being a History of the Negro Problem in the United States, Including a History and Study of the Republic of Liberia* (New York: Macmillan, 1921. Reprint. Johnson Reprint Corp., 1968), ix, 165, 242, 374.

Chapter Three

Themes, Part II

Cultural Achievements—The Art Exhibition as a Rhetorical Space

... those forces labeled cultural may at times have a deeper and more wide-spread impact on most of our lives than political or economic forces.—T. V. Reed. *The Art of Protest: Culture and Activism from the Civil Rights Movement to the Streets of Seattle*[1]

When works of art are exhibited in a museum they typically benefit from the "museum effect," a strategy of display that encourages visitors to look closely and regard the work as worthy of intense scrutiny.[2] The thematic narrative of the exhibit may also support a specific way of seeing. This is often the case in African American museums, where the exhibition of art offers a crucial extra-aesthetic benefit: proof of the existence of vital cultural traditions as well as individual artistic achievements. Before visiting an African American museum, for example, some visitors may have encountered—but not noticed or questioned—the marginalization of black artists and their subjects, the repetition of demeaning stereotypes that fail to represent a full range of lived experience, and/or the preference for genres that emphasize subservience and abjection. In encountering works of art by African American artists (and by reading explanatory wall texts and object labels), these visitors may gain a more comprehensive and expansive view of African American life and culture. That corrective dimension may be communicated more subtly in art exhibitions than in exhibitions dedicated to historical events or achievements in science or industry, but the argument is no less significant.[3] As social scientist James C. Scott notes, artistic expression, including visual works, songs, tales, and ritual performances, may serve as "hidden transcripts" that offer direct and indirect resistance to domination.[4]

In considering how the exhibition (as well as the original creation) of art might serve the dual function of an aesthetic form and a form of political action, the distinction between the "projective space of the museum" and the "reflective space" of the art gallery is instructive. Art historian Christopher Marshall proposes that in the museum's "projective space" the "exhibitionary elements have been knitted together . . . to reach out beyond themselves and "articulate" a broader, sometimes didactic message conveyed by "explicit" and "informationally overloaded displays." He suggests that, in the gallery's more self-contained "reflective" space, works of art do not "reach out beyond their own frame" but instead encourage a "slow space effect" and slow looking. However, he does note exceptions such as the US Holocaust Memorial Museum in Washington, DC, which uses innovative, gallery-inspired techniques in their "deployment of art and art-inspired displays."[5]

If reflective space and projective space are combined to create a single dually effective space, the work of art can be an end in itself and a "rhetorical" element in a larger argument. This is a key component of many African American museums.[6] These dually effective and affective spaces afford an opportunity to exhibit permanent and special exhibitions of what may long have been separated into the categories of "fine," "vernacular," and "decorative" art. As John Vlach explains in *The Afro-American Tradition in Decorative Arts,* there has been a "tendency in Afro-American art history to obscure the efforts of the early black artisan, to lose sight of the roots of the Afro-American tradition." Looking more broadly at cultural production, Robert G. O'Meally insists that we must not exclude, as (perhaps merely) vernacular, the "patchwork of forms and colors"—and the actual performance of the blues, for example—that constitute African American art forms. O'Meally notes that *"vernacular* art and artifacts convey" a "fast-changing and invisible history" that "cannot be told in any other way."[7] African American museums make this history evident in ways that extend well beyond what some see as the "compensatory" efforts of mainstream museums.[8]

ARTICULATION: MAKING THE VISUAL ARGUMENT

At the DuSable Black History Museum and Education Center, the California African American Museum, the Museum of African American History (Boston), the Harvey B. Gantt Center, the Museum of the African Diaspora, and the National Underground Railroad Freedom Center, for example, the exhibition of art is a prominent feature. As we see in exhibitions devoted to settlement and development, exhibitions of art also serve to obvert a long tradition of visual and textual underrepresentation and misrepresentation (of both artists and subject matter). Works of art—exhibited as ends in themselves—also educate viewers in a broader sense; they become means to an end by bringing artists and subjects to the foreground, by filling in the gaps created by longstanding exclusions, and by correcting and critiquing visual and narrative stereotypes.[9]

The extensive visual arts collection at the DuSable Museum includes both African American and African art as well as material culture. The cofounders, Dr. Margaret Burroughs—an artist, teacher, and art historian—and her husband, Charles, were serious collectors. The museum opened in 1961 as the Ebony Museum of Negro History and Art but, with several changes in name and location over time, the word "art" was eliminated.[10] The museum's holdings now include "more than 150,000 pieces including paintings, sculpture, print works and historic memorabilia."[11] A monumental (9-foot x 8-foot) wooden bas-relief mural titled "Freedom Now" by Robert Witt Ames is a permanent exhibition element.[12] As an accompanying interactive kiosk explains, the mural was unveiled in 1965 at the Massachusetts State House, "seat of the abolition movement." Sponsored by the Illinois Humanities Council, it is "dedicated to five martyrs, Medgar Evers, Michael Schwerner, James Chaney, Andrew Goodman, and James J. Reeb." Its narrative scope includes "diverse aspects of life on the African continent prior to European colonization," the arrival of Africans in North America in 1619, the fact and effects of the Middle Passage, and the role of African Americans in the settlement and development of the "American landscape."[13] It also includes key figures in the struggle for civil rights, including Frederick Douglass, W. E. B. Du Bois, and educator and activist Mary McLeod Bethune, as well as historical events spanning several centuries.

The mural thus encompasses many of the major themes foregrounded at the DuSable and other African American museums. Located in the multipurpose Ames Auditorium, it is surrounded by portraits of "Black Americans in Illinois."[14] In keeping with an emphasis on Africa as both a point of origin and a constant influence, the exhibition of African art and artifacts is often a focal point of the temporary galleries. A special exhibition gallery on the lower level is devoted to contemporary artists. Like the California African American Museum, the Museum of the African Diaspora in San Francisco, The Harvey B. Gantt Museum, and other African American museums, the DuSable often facilitates the exposure of new creative achievements alongside those that have attained critical (and market-wide) attention.

The California African American Museum collection includes work by Robert Scott Duncanson, Edward M. Bannister, Sargent Claude Johnson, Betye Saar, and David Hammons, and less familiar artists of the nineteenth and twentieth centuries. The work of contemporary artists—with a "small but growing" number from the Caribbean, Haiti, and Brazil—speaks of migration and the diaspora. The museum underscores the importance of art to the broader understanding of the talent, intellect, and contributions of African Americans, and public programming connected to special exhibitions enhances that mission. *We Wanted a Revolution: Black Radical Women, 1965–1985*, for example, an exhibition of the work of black women artists organized by the Brooklyn Museum that traveled to the California African American Museum (October 2017–January 2018), included a closing symposium during which artists, curators, and academics came together to discuss the exhibition and its main themes.[15] Here we can see that 1) art and historical events are integrated in the exhibition content, and 2) the exhibition/symposium has the potential to become a "historic event" with its own (activist) future.

The Museum of African American History in Boston has a collection of over 3,500 items and, as noted in the discussion of settlement narratives, some of those holdings are featured in rotation in a permanent exhibit: *Treasures from the Collection*. The collection includes documents (newspapers, abolitionist pamphlets, slave ship diagrams, inventories, and bills of sale, for example), first editions of books—including Nell's *The Colored Patriots of the American Revolution* (1855), clothing (William Lloyd Garrison's morning coat, top hat, and hat box; Robert Gould Shaw's uniform, frock coat, hat, and sword; and Paul Robeson's hat), toys, and items of everyday domestic use. The visual arts are equally well represented and well integrated in this multigenre display.

The museum's visual arts collection is strong in sculpture, particularly the work of women artists including Elizabeth Catlett, Meta Warrick Fuller, and Edmonia Lewis. The collection includes 1,000 plate glass negatives representing the work of photographer, lawyer, Massachusetts state representative, abolitionist, and business owner Hamilton Sutton Smith (1857–1924). The varied subjects of these primarily large format images include family portraits, landscapes, iconographic locations (including Niagara Falls and Harpers Ferry) and historical events (including the first inauguration of Woodrow Wilson in 1913). Documentation of the middle class is preserved in the negatives of another African American photographer, Hubert Collins (1882–1966) whose studio was located in Lower Roxbury.[16] These images provide an invaluable look at the everyday lives (genre scenes) and memorable events of those who would not be known through the "historical" chronicles of public life *or* through fine art representations (often stereotypes) of black life by white artists.

The Harvey B. Gantt Center "has primarily built its collection" from works by African American artists "that have been gifted to the institution."[17] Most prominent among these is the John and Vivian Hewitt collection of fifty-eight works, first acquired by the Bank of America and then pledged to the museum. This includes the work of Romare Bearden, Elizabeth Catlett, Ernest Crichlow, and Henry Ossawa Tanner. The ongoing exhibition,

FuturePresent: Acquisition Highlights from the Permanent Collection, combines examples of the museum's current holdings with works by contemporary artists—works that may eventually form part of its legacy in the future. Reverence for great artists of the past is matched by great expectations for the future. We find that forward-looking focus in the website description for *FuturePresent*, where artists like Stacy Lynn Waddell and Radcliffe Bailey are said to "push the boundaries of the traditional canvas and frame," and Phillip Thomas is identified as an artist who "explores landscapes and societal themes through a contemporary lens."

The Museum of the African Diaspora in San Francisco also foregrounds and actively supports "local, emerging and mid-career visual artists and art collectives." It does so in part through its Emerging Artists Program, which accepts proposals "for solo exhibitions that reflect the cultural and artistic richness of the African Diaspora." Since the start of the program in 2015 the museum has showcased twenty local artists and art collectives[18] and contributes to a dialogue between well-established and newly emerging artists through symposia linked to special exhibitions. (I will discuss these efforts and other public programs in chapter 5.) A very recent example in the Emerging Artists series is the work of Richard-Jonathan Nelson: Interlacing Distributed Intelligence/ Noir Care (June 22, 2022–September 18, 2022). The website description emphasizes the visionary power and corrective dimension of the work: "Through the hybridizing of traditional craft practices like embroidery, weaving, and quilting along with digital art, the Black body is reimagined as a place for futuristic progress. Thereby creating images of the Black Diaspora far removed from continued historic depiction as servile and without agency, but instead as visual and culturally complex individuals."[19]

The National Underground Railroad Freedom Center, while not primarily an arts-collecting institution, devotes abundant reflective *and* projective space to temporary exhibitions of the arts. The highlight for many visitors to the Freedom Center is the reconstructed "slave pen" (which I discuss in detail in chapter 4). It dominates a high-ceilinged exhibition space and is fully supported by explanatory text panels, an artifact case, and muted background music. Adjacent to the slave pen, however, are spaces for permanent and temporary exhibits of the work of contemporary artists. While they do not necessarily offer themed exhibitions in the traditional sense, these spaces include work in a variety of media that is, explicitly or implicitly, in dialogue with the major theme of the institution: the struggle for freedom and the "Courage," Cooperation," and "Perseverance" this entails. In close proximity to the slave pen, for example, we find a place that affords the reflective "slow space effect" and encourages slow looking. Here visitors can stand or sit on benches—in an area dedicated to "Perseverance"—and dwell on these multilayered representations of African American history and everyday life. [20]

The COVID-19 pandemic resulted in closings across the spectrum of museums. Virtual alternatives slowly appeared, and in some cases have remained in place even after the museums reopened. Online exhibitions and access to collections has also proved to be an effective form of outreach— potentially a new way to attract visitors to the physical space of the museum. As the summer 2022 exhibition offerings approached their closing dates, however, it was clear that the museums examined here had resumed a robust schedule that included live exhibitions of visual art.

The Harvey B. Gantt Center mounted three on-site art exhibitions in 2022. As already noted, *FuturePresent: Acquisition Highlights from the Permanent Collection* featured selections from the John and Vivian Hewitt collection of major nineteenth- and twentieth-century African American artists along with works by "future masters and creative leaders of African-American art and art history" in an exhibition that "visualizes the future of art at the Gantt Center and beyond." *Painter's Refuge: A Way of Life—A Solo Exhibition of Recent Work by Reginald Sylvester II* was devoted to a painter and assemblage artist whose work is "rooted in social realities and guided by his spirituality." *Billie Zangewa: Thread for a Web Begun* featured the work of the Malawi-born textile artist whose silk paintings "illustrate gendered labor in a socio-political context, where the domestic sphere becomes a pretext for a deeper understanding of the construction of identity, questions around gender stereotypes, and racial prejudice." The range of work exhibited by the museum at this particular moment encapsulates the ongoing mission of the Gantt and other African American museums: to establish the field by underscoring a legacy of artistic achievement, and to look at contemporary/new developments that foretell a legacy of the future.[21]

Underscoring the legacy, for example, was a prominent aspect of the 2022 exhibition offerings at the R. F. Lewis Museum. They included: *Elizabeth Catlett: Artist as Activist*; *Romare Bearden: Visionary Artist*; and *Maryland Collects Jacob Lawrence*.[22] In support of a potential future legacy, the Museum of the African Diaspora continued the Emerging Artists Program. In another solo exhibition, *David Huffman: Terra Incognita*, Afro-Futurist themes are foregrounded as Huffman demonstrates his "interest in science fiction, formalist abstraction, and social justice movements" through multimedia constructions called "Traumanauts." These "futuristic beings . . . travel the galaxy in constant search for home." The focus on social justice and inclusion was also brought to the literal forefront—the museum entrance—in a site-specific installation by Sam Vernon entitled *Impasse of Desires*. Here the artist draped the entrance and first-floor gallery with sheets of fabric and found objects to create a sense of the experience of "queer subjecthood." [23]

The African American Museum in Philadelphia is a good case in point of the possibilities of combining temporary on-site exhibitions and multiple online offerings. A recent on-site exhibition was devoted to the work of contemporary artist Derrick Adams; another focused on recent additions to the permanent collection and the museum's ongoing conservation mandate. *Derrick Adams: Sanctuary* was "inspired by the "Negro Motorist Green Book'" and featured "approximately 50 pieces of mixed-media collage, assemblage on wood panels, and sculpture presented in an installation designed by the artist that reimagines safe destinations for the Black American traveler during the mid-twentieth century." *Taking Care: Recent Acquisitions & Conservation* presented works acquired since late 2019 as well as several newly conserved works. In addition, online offerings included: *Anna Russell Jones: The Art of Design* (drawing from the museum's permanent collection of this multi-disciplinary, prolific artist and "first African American graduate of the Philadelphia School of Design for Women"); *Rendering Justice* (featuring public art projects, primarily by formerly incarcerated artists); and *Through His Eyes: Youth Activism in the Civil Rights Era in Philadelphia* (drawing from the museum's extensive Jack T. Franklin photographic collection).[24] The display and rhetorical use of the visual arts can challenge the commonplaces of art history and the content of mainstream museum exhibitions, and thus allow the African American museum gallery to function as a corrective space. However, the art-centered corrective project, like the rhetorical history text, must be mobilized on multiple fronts: by mounting exhibitions *and* by creating catalogues and art-historical texts dedicated to the subject of African American art. The latter helps to position the subject in the academic field of art history, and to reveal and subvert misrepresentations of that subject matter.

ESTABLISHING THE FIELD: EXHIBITIONS AND CATALOGUES

The visual arguments made by art exhibitions, often supplemented by textual explanations, present evidence of African American artistic traditions, the creative ability of black artists, the complex nature of black life as subject matter, and the fact that black artists work in a wide variety of genres and styles. These arguments, as articulated in exhibitions, address gaps and exclusions in art history scholarship. They also critique conventions and prejudices in traditional representations of the subject matter that misrepresent and oversimplify black life. The question of "a black aesthetic"—its existence and its characteristics—also emerges as a consistent theme in exhibitions, reviews, catalogue essays, and book-length studies.

The Civil War in Art and Memory (2016) is an excellent case in point of a corrective text positioned at the intersection of military history and art history. This anthology of essays includes an analysis of the *Robert Gould Shaw and Massachusetts 54th Regiment Memorial* in Boston by Augustus Saint-Gaudens (discussed in chapter 2)—a monument to its white abolitionist Colonel and the African American soldiers who served in one of the first black regiments in the Civil War—but it also examines less well known examples: the "visual records" of interracial marriage, representations of black troops in engravings printed in American and British newspapers, visual representations of "embodied black devotion," and "visual and cultural constructions of black deference and comity."[25] Edited by Kirk Savage, the collection foregrounds visual evidence of African American participation in the war effort in spite of the fact that public recognition of these contributions was uncommon at the time. Delayed recognition became the duty of photographers, artists, historians—and eventually museums.

Along similar lines, *The Civil War and American Art* (an exhibition and catalogue) was produced by the Smithsonian American Art Museum in 2013; it too presents evidence of the presence and contributions of black soldiers. Yet, while the enlistment of blacks in the Federal army began in 1862, comparatively few paintings or photographs record their presence or represent their roles.[26] Images of the "colored Infantry" occasionally attest to this change: Thomas Waterman Wood's "A Bit of War History: The Contraband, The Recruit, and The Veteran" (1866) encapsulates that historical overview through the appearance of the same figure in three successive states of being. "A Burial Party, Cold Harbor" (1865), a photograph by John Reekie, is another exception. It captures a group of black gravediggers—soldiers and contraband—in the act of interring bodies that had been left unburied or partially buried on the battlefield for almost a year. As curator Eleanor Jones Harvey explains, this is a "rare instance of a photograph focusing on blacks' involvement in the war."[27]

Collections and exhibitions have begun to fill the gaps in the historical record that prevent full understanding of the contributions made by African Americans to the settlement of the nation and its defense through military service. Museum exhibitions also fill gaps in the art historical record to allow fuller appreciation of achievements by African Americans in art and in all aspects of culture. This is an archeological undertaking that may once have seemed insurmountable. For example, as philosopher and cultural critic Alain Locke lamented in *Negro Art: Past and Present* (1936): "We will never know and cannot estimate how much technical African skill was blotted out in America," although "Negro craftsmen were well-known as cabinet-makers, wood-carvers and iron-smiths."[28]

However, in *The Negro in Art: A Pictorial Record of the Negro Artist and of the Negro Theme in Art* (1940) Locke did end an essay on "The Negro as Artist" with a more optimistic prediction:

> We must not expect the work of the Negro artist to be too different from that of his fellow-artists. Product of the same social and cultural soil, our art has an equal right and obligation to be typically American at the same time that it strives to be typical and representative of the Negro; and that, indeed, if the evidence is rightly read, we believe it already is, and promises even more to be. The American Negro, it begins to seem clear, is destined to make as distinct a contribution to the visual arts as he has made in music.[29]

Here Locke emphasizes the "changing social conception of the Negro" over time, the drive toward "self-delineation" and "racial self-expression" and away from those who viewed the "art of the Negro as a ghetto province," and the removal of the "barriers of racial prejudice."[30] Yet those barriers continued to be in evidence in mainstream art histories and museum exhibitions well into the twentieth century—with some notable exceptions.[31]

The commitment to the visual and verbal documentation of African American art functions as a kind of ground bass, a structural melodic element that insists on contradicting the blindness, erasure, and denial of that history. The work of individual artists, continuity with African traditions, and analysis of objects which may have been noticed but not categorized as "fine art" are gradually being brought to the foreground.[32] The culturally specific art-historical text and the culturally specific exhibition are key participants in that project; they establish the field by identifying artists and works and they supply the art-critical contexts in which they should be considered.

This also requires attention to a history of exclusion, and Locke was certainly not the first scholar to offer an acute critical statement on that subject. In an early attempt to establish the field, Freeman Henry Morris Murray self-published *Emancipation and the Freed in American Sculpture: A Study in Interpretation* (1916). A heavily annotated critical survey of individual sculptors and their work, Murray's study addressed the contexts in which artists were working, supplied a cogent history of their reception, and offered a brief but rigorous analysis of primary and secondary sources. He described and analyzed works by white artists, such as Hiram Powers, who would have been well known to his audience, and black artists, including Edmonia Lewis and Meta Vaux Warrick Fuller, who might not have been known to the readers of his time.

Murray's tone, while highly controlled, conveyed a scathing critique of racialized and racist representations and the attitudes that informed them. While analyzing the iconic neoclassical sculpture *The Greek Slave* by Hiram

Powers, which had been exhibited at the 1851 International Exposition in London, Murray noted that it "may be regarded . . . as American art's first anti-slavery document in marble" but "then, as now, a 'white' slave would attract more attention and excite far more commiseration than a black one or one less white than 'white'"[33] Other revisionist curatorial and textual projects gradually answered the demand for recognition. Art historians began to examine the role that reductionist and racist art had played in the social construction of identity and the denial of equality based on race. In addition to presenting a comprehensive counter-history, alternatives to Eurocentric art history and mainstream exhibition practices raised questions about the unexamined prejudices that extended well beyond the realms of art and reception.[34]

A brief overview of counter-movements dedicated to inclusion—through exhibitions, catalogues, exhibition reviews, and art history texts—reveals the depth and complexity of the revisionist project. Writing at the end of the twentieth century, curator and art historian Sharon Patton insisted that: "Anyone newly introduced to African-American art must divide their attention between three types of [textual] sources: American art history, African-American cultural history, and African-American art." The first source—American art history—has a longstanding record of exclusion which is now being modified. The second and third sources—African-American cultural history and African-American art—include scholarly texts, exhibitions, and related programs.[35]

The goal of bringing African American artists to the foreground was achieved in part through exhibitions and in part through the publication of scholarly texts. An early example of the latter is *Seventeen Black Artists* (1971), in which artist Elton C. Fax offered a biographical treatment of his subject based primarily on taped interviews with artists and/or their families. He identified the "Forerunners"—including Joshua Johnston, Scipio Moorehead, Robert Duncanson, Edmonia Lewis, Meta Warrick Fuller, and Henry Ossawa Tanner—and devoted sections to the life and work of Elizabeth Catlett, Romare Bearden, Jacob Lawrence, Roy De Carava, Faith Ringgold, Benny Andrews, and John Biggers.[36]

Two decades later, with the need for recognition still not sufficiently addressed, Romare Bearden and Harry Henderson produced *A History of African American Artists from 1792 to the Present* (1993). This study contained individual chapters on more than thirty artists, all of whom were born by 1925 and had been at work prior to the civil rights movement. In an introduction (written after Bearden's death) Henderson described the origins of the project. Bearden had been asked by the Museum of Modern Art in 1965 to speak to students "about the history and development of black artists in America." He found that he knew "only a dozen artists before his own generation" and of those few his knowledge was limited. Clearly blindness and ignorance persisted, and Henderson and Bearden began a project of "discovery" that lasted over fifteen years. This led to the publication of the book in 1993, five years after Bearden's death.[37]

Another important contribution to the field is *African American Visual Arts: From Slavery to the Present* (2008) in which Celeste-Marie Bernier focuses on the "aesthetic issues and experimental practices" of twenty artists in a wide range of media. Her unifying context is their "ongoing search for agency" and a tendency to push "the boundaries of media and materials in the search for a visual language which would represent the difficult realities of African American struggles for existence." (The exhibition program of the Museum of the African Diaspora, among other museums examined here, clearly attests to these developments.) Bernier is writing a stringent corrective in which she faults longstanding white resistance to both the possibility and the clear evidence of black creativity, and she admonishes black artists and critics who, in her view, have been insufficiently critical of the prevailing white art-historical master narrative.[38] Once volumes dedicated to African American art began to appear in well-established art history series, mainstream institutional acknowledgment of the subject's status seemed to be underway.

Rigorous attention to the long but previously unacknowledged history of African American art now includes Sharon Patton's *African-American Art* (1998), an addition to the *Oxford History of Art* series that can be added to her comprehensive bibliographic essay on prominent and heretofore "'invisible'" art historians. Looking back to the start of her teaching career, Patton confesses that she lacked sufficient knowledge of the tradition she now documents. She admits that: "All of us young black art historians at mainstream universities were studying everything except black (including African) art." Like the volume itself, her bibliographic essay and detailed timeline fill the gap that compromised her own art historical education. Again and again among black as well as white art historians and artists, a confession is followed by a turn to corrective action—including corrective scholarship. Patton admits that her project is still under construction. It is dependent on an archeological reclamation of unknown and/or undocumented artists and other archival work, including the inclusion of key position statements by artists and critics.[39] She also emphasizes the increasing influence of activist politics in general, and the Black Panther Party in particular, explaining that art becomes "more abrasive" and often documents prior events including lynchings and riots.

In a subchapter entitled "Defining Black Art" Patton includes a lengthy quotation from curator Edmund Barry Gaither in which he describes "two kinds of black art": the first is "usually realist" and depicts historical events, heroes, and ideas," while the second, a form of "Neo-Africanism," offers new interpretations of traditional African art. The emphasis on continuity with African sources is consistent with the reinterpretation of African forms that we find in the work of African American architects. Patton begins in the 1640s and traces a timeline of artistic achievement and (often delayed) recognition. The earliest points in a history which remains under construction (and is often dependent on ongoing archeological and archival work) include a slave-made drum (c. 1640s) and earthenware from Virginia and South Carolina (c. 1670). She includes landmark exhibitions spanning more than sixty years (1930–1994), many of which were mounted at culturally specific museums and galleries devoted to African American art. Important examples also appear and slowly grow in number at mainstream museums. National and local fairs and expositions, beginning with the Texas Centennial's Hall of Negro Life (1936), also prove to be important venues for the exhibition of African American artists.[40]

In *African American Art: A Visual and Cultural History* (2017) Lisa Farrington carries the corrective critical tradition forward and contextualizes artists and movements within their contemporaneous aesthetic and political spheres. In terms of the intersection of politics and cultural production, for example, she examines the importance of the Black Arts Movement of the 1960s–1970s, the protests mounted against mainstream museums for their exclusion of black artists in established collection and exhibition practices, the formation of the Black Emergency Cultural Coalition (BECC) in 1969, and subsequent exhibitions of African American art in major mainstream museums in the 1970s.[41]

In terms of exhibitions, the participation of mainstream institutions was needed in order to communicate the corrective message. Collaborative exhibitions undertaken by culturally specific and mainstream institutions played a role in an ongoing consciousness raising project.[42] *The Evolution of Afro-American Artists: 1800–1950*, for example, which opened at the Brooklyn Museum (1967) and then toured other museums, was a joint effort by the City University of New York, the Harlem Cultural Council, and the New York Urban League. In a catalogue essay we find Carroll Greene Jr., codirector with Romare Bearden of the exhibition committee, advancing a performative and now poignant prophecy: "Let us hope that if a similar exhibition is assembled at the century's end, surveying the next fifty years of Afro-American artists, such an exhibition will not only reveal genuine artistic progress, but will also be indicative of a new freedom in a productive age, in what must be our nation's total commitment to equality."[43]

Another important contribution was the exhibition *New Black Artists* (1969), a collaboration between the Harlem Cultural Council and The School of the Arts and the Urban Center of Columbia University. In his Foreword to the exhibition catalogue Edward K. Taylor, executive director of the Harlem Cultural Council, noted that the primary goal was to "present an exhibition of Black artists, in which the word Black has meaning." Taylor commented on the "reluctance of the art world to deal in categories other than those established in the Western art-historical continuum" and proposed an overview of "certain qualities" that might unite these artists. At the same time, however, he acknowledged the "complex" and "controversial" nature of the "question of the relation of black identity to works of art."[44]

Sharing Traditions: Five Black Artists in Nineteenth-Century America (1985), a traveling exhibition organized by the Smithsonian's National Museum of American Art, drew mainly on the museum's collection of the works of Joshua Johnson, Robert Scott Duncanson, Edward Mitchell Bannister, Edmonia Lewis, and Henry Ossawa Tanner supplemented with additional loans. In his Foreword to the exhibition catalogue, Director Charles C. Eldredge noted how difficult it was "to identify an early tradition of Afro-American art which is distinct" because the artists "adopted an artistic vocabulary of subjects and styles derived from European examples." In spite of this, he also went on to explain that black artists, in general, "lacked not only academies, museums, and patrons, but also social and economic opportunities for advancement."[45] In a lengthy catalogue essay, curator Linda Roscoe Hartigan noted that "for almost a century, the life and work of the "first free black portraitist" Joshua Johnson "were lost in historical oblivion" and that the reclamation of this history "exemplifies the challenges associated with researching the early chapters of Afro-American art." In an analysis of the reception of the work of Henry Ossawa Tanner, perhaps the most widely known of the featured artists, Hartigan's critique of prevailing attitudes is especially severe: "The white American art press frequently attributed his use of color, rhythmic design, and religious sentiment to his heritage, qualifying his accomplishment as those of the country's 'foremost Negro artist.' Such backhanded praise effectively precluded serious evaluation of his work in relation to either American or European art."[46]

The need for a course correction in the world of art exhibitions and art histories was clear to those who broke ground and announced the achievements of African American artists. Yet the acknowledgment and acceptance of these announcements was slow to materialize.

CONTEXTS AND THEORY: AN "AFRICAN AMERICAN AESTHETIC," COURSE CORRECTIONS, RHETORICAL ART HISTORIOGRAPHY

Art world hierarchies cannot be underestimated, and their role in limiting what we can see and understand must be acknowledged. They may appear disguised as "objective standards" or cloaked as the "historical record," when in fact they represent the conventions of cultural dominance.—Elizabeth Broun. Preface. *Free within Ourselves: African-American Artists in the Collection of the National Museum of American Art* (1992)[47]

In his catalogue introduction to *Afro-American Artists, New York and Boston* (1970), curator Edmund Barry Gaither had made a salient prediction: "The 'new black show' is a valuable educational and cultural experience for both black and white viewers and artists. It will remain so as long as the racial attitudes out of which it grew remain, although it will no longer be the black artist's only outlet.[48] While the foundational corrective project of mounting exhibitions and establishing the groundwork for an African American-focused art history continued, a parallel textual project was being undertaken that stated the facts and consequences of misrepresentation. *The Image of the Indian and the Black Man in American Art, 1590–1900* by Ellwood Parry (published in 1974), for example, provided a comprehensive survey of the "prejudices and preconceptions at work in the predominantly *White male* [sic] artists who created these visual statements at different moments in the history of American art." Parry offered a summary of the roles and positions characteristically assigned to blacks in works by white artists. In the seventeenth century "pictures of black slaves or servants in America were virtually nonexistent, save for a very minor figure or two in the lower corner of a decorative European map of the New World"; "the only Blacks in colonial portraiture were household servants, endlessly waiting at the feet or at the elbow of their white masters." By the end of the eighteenth century, Parry explained, "a few American painters, working in London, managed to incorporate Black figures into semiheroic compositions or history paintings . . . ; otherwise, Negroes were usually forced to play comic parts in American genre scenes and political cartoons well into the 1800s." Parry concluded that "It was not until the height of the Abolition movement in the 1850s, followed by the Civil War and then Reconstruction, that images of Black men began to change drastically in content as they multiplied rapidly. . . . Burgeoning interest in the legal end of slavery and the new life of the Negro thereafter resulted in a major reversal of roles."[49]

A significant study of the representation and reception of blacks *as subjects* was undertaken in *The Image of the Black in Western Art*, an exhibition launched by the Smithsonian Institution Traveling Exhibition Service (SITES) in 1980. The ten-page illustrated booklet produced to accompany the original exhibition moves chronologically and thematically, beginning with "Ancient Egypt" and ending with "The Age of Discovery" (the fifteenth and sixteenth centuries). In the final commentary, the anonymous author noted:

> Representations of Blacks have appeared in Occidental Art for centuries. Politics, religion, economics, and myths about African and Africans have affected the position Blacks have held in the imagination and concerns of the Western world. As a result, the image of the Black in Western art has oscillated between the servant and the saint, the captive and the king.[50]

By this point several volumes of the book series *The Image of the Black in Western Art* had appeared. Volume IV, published in 1989, turned from a largely Western European base to a more specific focus on American art. In an analytical and descriptive commentary, editor Hugh Honour addressed the racist attitudes in both the creation and reception of works by white artists and critics, and he acknowledged some rare departures from those typically biased norms. Honour's critical perspective emerged as he alerted his readers to the prevailing "assumption of white supremacy—in intellect, morality, and physical beauty," the "mania for categorization," and the "urge to impose order on the world."[51] By the time volume IV (which covered "The American Revolution to World War I") had appeared it was almost impossible to ignore the perpetuation of racist stereotypes contained in this and previous volumes.

In a review of this volume art historian Albert Boime found that the editorial and critical commentary by Hugh Honour did not sufficiently examine the evidence of race prejudice revealed in the art itself.[52] Boime was both laudatory and critical: he credited the series itself as a "monumental" undertaking and "magisterial achievement," and found that Honour both "makes a fundamental contribution not only to art history but to popular history" and "establishes a method for filling in the blind spots"; yet he also noted that Honour sometimes "misses the complexities of the visual and historical context."[53] Soon after, in a critical project of his own, *The Art of Exclusion: Representing Blacks in the Nineteenth Century* (1990), Boime investigated the "visual encoding of hierarchy and exclusion." He went back to credit Freeman Murray's study and to implement Murray's rigorous methods and activist message,[54] as he probed iconic works to reveal their underlying prejudice and inclination to subordinate blacks while appearing to honor, or at least to advocate for, them.[55]

The most recent volume in the series marks a departure in title and focus, widening the frame to address *The Image of the Black in African and Asian Art* (2017). This survey takes us back to the beginnings of art making and forward to new approaches to art history. In the preface the editors, David Bindman, Suzanne Preston Blier, and Henry Louis Gates Jr. address the contents and contexts for the book, including the original *Image of the Black in Western Art* series published between 1976 and 2014. Their reflections on that series provide a microcosm of the historical, political, and cultural contexts in which those earlier volumes were produced. They note, for example, that the "stated objective" of the original series, which had been conceived in the 1960s by Dominique and Jean de Menil, was to contribute "to ending segregation by providing an alternative to the corrupt visual stereotypes that supported it." From the perspective of the deMenils at a crucial point in the civil rights movement, the representation of blacks in Western/European art could be used to "demonstrate that relations between peoples of African and European descent had not always been governed by the enslavement of the former by the latter." For these ardent collectors and patrons, "the great art of the past gave glimpses of a possibility of mutual respect and renewed understanding."[56] The editors also explain that the aim of *The Image of the Black in African and Asian Art* is to do "justice . . . to the African presence in art worldwide." They note that the catalogue essays are "in essence a set of studies of how Africa sees and personifies itself through art" and they acknowledge the ongoing debate among both artists and scholars about issues of continuity with African traditions, artistic individuality, and the roots and development of syncretic styles. This project represents both a continuation of and yet a significant departure from the five-volume Western-focused series (to which it is related as a "companion volume"). It redirects our gaze, although both Africans and Asians are still, at times, being represented by a racial other.[57]

As works of art by African American artists slowly entered the lists of art history, and progress was being made in achieving equality and accuracy of representation, the existence of an "African-American aesthetic" continued to be a subject of debate. As art historian Richard Powell has observed, the characteristics of that "aesthetic" have long been debated among the "critical rank and file" and yet the questions raised "are still left unanswered.[58] Powell contributed to the discussion in his comparative analysis of *Black Art and Culture in the 20th* Century (1997) where he took a thematic "object-based approach" to the representation of "diasporal cultures" and focused on "black subjectivity across . . . regional and racial boundaries." Powell organized his comparative history under thematic categories: the "souls of black folk"; the "persona of the 'New Negro'"; a "black proletariat"; "race pride and cultural assimilation"; "aesthetic variants on the concept of blackness"; and "aesthetic commerce in black cultural identities." He also surveyed a broad range of new media, including "computer-assisted imagery" and "body-centered performance art." [59]

The terms of this debate were already discernible in *The Black Aesthetic* (1971), an important interdisciplinary anthology.[60] In "Some Observations on a Black Aesthetic" poet/activist Adam David Miller observed that "When we write about ourselves from a point of view that takes black life seriously, that views it in scale, with human dimensions, then we are creating a black aesthetic." In "The Negro Artist and the Racial Mountain" (originally published in 1926) Langston Hughes argued for free choice in the making of "black art." Hughes admitted that he was "ashamed . . . for the colored artist who runs from the painting of Negro faces to the painting of sunsets after the manner of the academicians because he fears the strange un-whiteness of his own features. An artist must be free to choose what he does, certainly, but he must also never be afraid to do what he might choose." In "Black Cultural Nationalism" Africana studies scholar and writer Ron (Maulana) Karenga insisted that "Black art must expose the enemy, praise the people and support the revolution." "If we must paint oranges and trees," Karenga demanded, "let our guerillas be eating those oranges for strength and using those trees for cover."[61] Social realism and cultural activism consistently appear in these descriptions of subject, mission, message, and medium.

Another snapshot of the debate about characteristics can be found in Holland Cotter's analysis of "Black Artists: Three Shows" (1990) in which he observed that the exhibitions under review raised a "number of questions . . . about black art itself." Cotter addressed the fact that black artists were (still) not adequately represented in mainstream museums and galleries and he concluded that "a 'black art' show remains practically the only venue in which many of these artists can get a museum showcase." One of the primary issues here was whether or not the work of black artists must be political. Cotter found that the curators of the shows "appeared to be proposing" that "political consciousness and spirituality" were "primary concerns of African-American art."[62] He identified *Art as a Verb: The Evolving Continuum* as the exhibit "most directly" concerned with "politics as content." This exhibition was developed by the Maryland Institute, College of Art in 1988 and exhibited there and subsequently at two locations in New York. Based on the surviving exhibition catalogue we can see that, in addition to feminist and activist politics, the politics of form and substance were part of the focus; the works included videos, performances, installations, multimedia constructions, and paintings.[63]

Cotter's review also included *The Appropriate Object*, which opened at the Albright-Knox Art Gallery (Buffalo, NY) in 1989 and traveled to other venues including the Detroit Institute of Arts. It featured seven contemporary artists; Richard Hunt, Oliver Jackson, Alvin Loving, and Betye Saar were among them. In the foreword to the catalogue, Douglas G. Schultz, director of the Albright-Knox, noted that, although these artists demonstrated a "shared interest in multicultural imagery," the subject had not received adequate attention in either exhibitions or critical analyses.[64] The well-illustrated catalogue, with commentaries by Schultz and Wright and interviews with each artist, suggests how some artists operate within and yet manage to prevail over enduring categories.

The third exhibition reviewed by Cotter, *Traditions and Transformations: Contemporary Afro-American Sculpture*, was mounted at The Bronx Museum of the Arts (1989) and featured the work of eleven sculptors, spanning a period from 1973–1988. In the introduction and acknowledgments to the exhibition catalogue, Philip Verre presented an extensive list of the "inquiries" undertaken by the works on view. This list makes a significant contribution to the debate concerning what constitutes "black art." The elements he included were: an "emphasis on ritual" and "pronouncement of political and social issues"; "a geometric vocabulary"; the "use of narrative and myth"; biography; "adaptation of African and Afro-American cultural traditions"; a "dialogue between low and high art"; and a "wide array of formats . . . materials . . . and techniques." In a catalogue essay, artist and art historian George Nelson Preston emphasized the use of African mask styles, the "motif of personification," and the importance of architectural elements, including chthonic mounds and the "agglutinative construction of architecture found on the savannas of West Africa."[65]

In reviewing the exhibition Cotter found that many of the works invoked "the notion of ritual as cultural continuum." If we compare his observations to points made in the 1971 anthology *The Black Aesthetic*—where social realism and cultural activism emerged as key elements—we find a consistent theme: political consciousness. However, Cotter's comprehensive review also reveals additional elements that characterize and enrich the "black aesthetic" while continuing to make it resistant to characterization. For example, the continuity with African traditions—beliefs, rituals, forms, materials, and themes—may mark a defining characteristic. Yet the variety of possible traditions and the complicated nature of the diasporic experience also make the borderlines of "an African American aesthetic" that much harder to locate.[66]

In the last decade of the twentieth century several mainstream exhibitions made important contributions to the expanding field of equal representation. They included *Free within Ourselves: African-American Artists in the Collection of the National Museum of American Art* (1992–1994) which opened at the Wadsworth Atheneum in Hartford, Connecticut, and then traveled to four other cities. The project, initially conceived as a curriculum guide for teachers in the Washington, DC, area, resulted in a traveling exhibition and a major book publication. The story of the museum's acquisitions, outlined in the preface by Elizabeth Broun and the introduction by Regenia

Perry, speaks of closely held private collections, last-minute rescues, and fortuitous gifts.[67] Elizabeth Broun communicates a brutal accuracy in her assessment of the consequences of institutional prejudice.

Acts of representation—and misrepresentation—have consequences that often exceed the size or scope of the single act on its own. The stakes of truth-telling are high. In the introduction to the exhibition catalogue for *Facing History: The Black Image in American Art, 1710–1940* curator Guy McElroy argued that images of blacks had long sustained the notion of "the inherent inhumanity of black people" and that this contributed to "a visual record of African-Americans that reinforced a number of largely restrictive stereotypes of black identity."[68] We might be reminded of the corrective project undertaken by black historians beginning in the nineteenth century. As McElroy noted, those representations satisfied the aesthetic demands of the art market as well as the prejudices of the sociopolitical status quo. The exhibition, which opened in 1990 at the Corcoran Gallery in Washington, DC, and traveled to the Brooklyn Museum, is an excellent case in point of the distance between intention and reception.[69] It is not surprising that an exhibition which sought to document a tradition of misrepresentation would run the risk of appearing to contribute to the continuation of that tradition. *Facing History* exposed itself to critique by seeming to repeat these historical offenses while also falling short of the presentation of a full range of black artists, black identities, and black lives. However, the exhibition catalogue contained an incisive critical essay by Henry Louis Gates Jr. in which he identified the categories to which blacks had been restricted: "The majority of images included in this book represents blacks as, first, slaves, and, second, ciphers, whose semblance to actual historical persons cannot be recognized." Here in "The Face and Voice of Blackness" he allows *readers* of the catalogue (as opposed to *visitors* to the exhibition) to think through the complexities of both the creation and the staging of these works (in the museum).[70]

Keeping in mind the caveat that "art world hierarchies" can be a profound influence, as Elizabeth Broun insists, we can still hope that the exhibition of art offers a more subtle form of education than the exposure to accepted historical "facts" and the evidence that supports them. In fact, works of art can wield a rhetorical/argumentative power equal to the most cogent presentation of other forms of factual evidence. Moreover, when multiple works of art inhabit a single space—be it a gallery or an exhibition catalogue or an illustrated volume—they can provide influential, perhaps irrefutable evidence of achievement, creativity, and excellence. The keyword of course is "exposure," and the prediction made by Edmund Barry Gaither in 1970 remains relevant; museum exhibitions, catalogues, and rhetorical/theme-based art history texts continue to be a valuable source for attitude correction.

NOTES

1. T. V. Reed, *The Art of Protest: Culture and Activism from the Civil Rights Movement to the Streets of Seattle* (Minneapolis: University of Minnesota Press, 2005), p. xviii. Copyright 2005 by the Regents of the University of Minnesota. Reed also cautions against assuming easy alliances between "politically committed artists" and specific works of art: "aesthetic texts are always both ideological and in excess of ideology, and their role in and around movements can be to remind activists, who often are tempted by the pressures of political struggle into ideologically reductive positions, that the full lived complexity of cultural life cannot be reduced to any ideological system"). See xviii, 302–3.

2. Svetlana Alpers describes the "museum effect" as the treatment of an object/artifact in a way that encourages a particularly "attentive" way of looking, "turning all objects into works of art." Svetlana Alpers, "The Museum as a Way of Seeing," in *Exhibiting Cultures: The Poetics and Politics of Museum Display*, eds. Ivan Karp and Steven D. Lavine (Washington, DC: Smithsonian Institution Press, 1991), 26. My point here is that some of the objects in question were in fact "works of art" but they were rarely recognized as such in the dominant mainstream (white Western art-oriented) culture. Thus, they needed the "museum effect" to bring them to light.

3. In 1941 anthropologist Melville J. Herskovits, a former student of Franz Boas, published *The Myth of the Negro Past*, a key example of sustained corrective in the field of anthropology. The "myth" to be refuted in this case was the false notion that, as a result of race-based inferiority, a "Negro past" did not—could not—exist. Herskovits rejected that myth on principle and offered original ethnographic field research to support his counterargument. In the process he found the concepts of "retention and reinterpretation" particularly useful for discovering how (not if) African traditions, customs, and values had developed in the Americas. *The Myth of the Negro Past* (New York: Beacon Press, 1941, reprinted in 1958 and 1990).

4. For extensive development of this idea with respect to power relations—including those between masters and slaves—see James C. Scott, *Hidden Transcripts: Domination and the Arts of Resistance* (New Haven: Yale University Press, 1990).

5. Marshall wonders if these "competing effects and associations of art" can be "resolved" in other museum spaces and suggests that one of "the principle strengths" of some contemporary museums is their ability to use an "art element" to "break free of the museum's institutional voice" and preserve "the viewer's freedom to make his or her own connections." Christopher R. Marshall, "When Worlds Collide: The Contemporary Museum as Art Gallery," in *Reshaping Museum Space: Architecture, Design, Exhibitions*, ed. Suzanne MacLeod (London: Routledge, 2005), 170–71, 176–77, 179.

6. For a detailed explication of this phenomenon see Gregory Clark, "Rhetorical Experience and the National Jazz Museum in Harlem," in *Places of Public Memory: The Rhetoric of Museums and Memorials*, ed. Greg Dickinson et al (Tuscaloosa: University of Alabama Press, 2009), 130–33. Clark enlists John Dewey and Kenneth Burke to explain how a museum may (like jazz itself) be found to do "civic

work"—in that it brings people together to experience "an aesthetic expression and a rhetorical assertion of democratic culture."

7. See John Michael Vlach, *The Afro-American Tradition in Decorative Arts* (Cleveland: Cleveland Museum of Art, 1978), and Robert G. O'Meally, "On Burke and the Vernacular: Ralph Ellison's Boomerang of History," in *History and Memory in African-American Culture*, eds. Geneviève Fabre and Robert G. O'Meally (New York: Oxford University Press, 1994).

8. Richard Sandell notes that "non-specialist" museums may make "compensatory" efforts by mounting "small-scale, sometimes temporary interventions," or they may create "celebratory" and perhaps highlighted exhibitions which "demand a greater degree of accommodation or organizational change and planning." In cases where a more highly committed, structural revision is undertaken, a nonspecialist museum may also demonstrate a "pluralist" commitment to "integrate cultural difference within a unifying interpretive framework"; this may include "proactive collecting initiatives, a fundamental redisplay of collections and even radical reallocations of gallery spaces." Richard Sandell, "Constructing and Communicating Equality: The Social Agency of Museum Space" in *Reshaping Museum Space: Architecture, Design, Exhibitions*, ed. Suzanne MacLeod (London: Routledge, 2005), 190–91.

9. There are, of course, many nonrepresentational works of African American art that may be instrumental in raising the viewer's historical and political consciousness. For an analysis of the longstanding debate regarding the merits of realist—therefore "socially engaged black art"—*versus* that of nonrepresentational (yet still arguably referential) modes, see Phillip Brian Harper's *Abstractionist Aesthetics: Artistic Form and Social Critique in African American Culture* (New York University Press, 2015). For example, Harper notes that Kara Walker's work, including her minimally representative silhouettes, "potentially expands our sense of political possibility, in that it opens unrestricted onto the world at large and invites us to imagine what we might do to transform it." Such expansion of vision and attendant action is less predictable, perhaps, in abstract works than in what we may think of as "realistic" representations.

10. See Eugene P. R. Feldman, *The Birth and the Building of the DuSable Museum* (Chicago: DuSable Museum Press, 1981) for a detailed early history by one of the principal developers. Amina Dickerson's *The History and Institutional Development of African American Museums* (American University; MA thesis, 1988) offers additional details.

11. DuSable Museum Membership pamphlet, undated.

12. The DuSable website notes that the Ames mural is "one of several [objects] in the DuSable's fine art collection that features minority subject matter created by non-African Americans."

13. DuSable self-guided tour pamphlet.

14. The pamphlet for the Museum's self-guided tour notes that they "are part of 23 paintings commissioned by the State of Illinois for the 1963 Centennial of the Emancipation Proclamation to illustrate African American history as it related to Illinois."

15. A similar symposium was held at the Brooklyn Museum (4/21/17). In addition to the California African American Museum and Brooklyn Museum, other venues

for this exhibition included the Albright-Knox Gallery (Buffalo) and The Institute of Contemporary Art (Boston).

16. The Museum also has a strong collection of the work of photojournalist Don West, photographer and educator David Herwalt, and photographer/editor Herb Snitzer, whose work often covered the jazz scene.

17. See *FuturePresent: Acquisition Highlights from the Permanent Collection*, ganttcenter.org/exhibitions/futurepresent/

18. See the Museum of the African Diaspora website for details.

19. www.moadsf.org/what-we-do/moad-emerging-artists-program.

20. Two examples of the Freedom Center's exhibition of its permanent (commissioned) collection in this space are Aminah Brenda Lynn Robinson's two-panel mural *Journeys I and II* and several pieces from Malaika Favorite's twenty-part *Washboard Stories* (2004). A very recent exhibition of contemporary art entitled *Marking Time: Art in the Age of Mass Incarceration* (April–August 2022) included the work of more than thirty artists that aimed to "shift aesthetic currents, offering new ways to envision art and to understand the reach of the carceral state on life today." See freedomcenter. org/markingtime-copy/.

21. For full descriptions and in some cases online access to these Harvey B. Gantt exhibitions see www.ganttcenter.org/exhibitions/futurepresent/; www.ganttcenter.org /exhibitions/painters-refuge-a-way-of-life/; www.ganttcenter.org/exhibitions/billie -zangewa-thread-for-a-web-begun.

22. For descriptions and in some cases online access to these R. F. Lewis exhibitions see: www.lewismuseum.org/exhibitions/.

23. For descriptions and in some cases online access to these Museum of the African Diaspora exhibitions see: www.moadsf.org/exhibitions/interlacing-distributed -intelligence-noir-care; www.moadsf.org/exhibitions/david-huffman-terra-incognita; www.moadsf.org/exhibitions/impasse-of-desires.

24. For full descriptions and in some cases online access to the exhibitions at the African American Museum in Philadelphia see: www.aampmuseum.org/current -exhibitions.html.

25. Kirk Savage, ed., *The Civil War in Art and Memory* (Washington, DC: National Gallery of Art, 2016). The book is the result of a 2013 symposium at the National Gallery of Art. See in this collection: Gwendolyn Dubois Shaw, "The Freedom to Marry for All: Painting Interracial Families during the Era of the Civil War" (5–14); James Oakes, "The Summer of 1863: Lincoln and Black Troops" (53–64); Richard J. Powell, "The Wounded Zouave and the Cyrenian Paradigm" (65–80). Powell analyzes "The Wounded Zouave"—an iconic photograph "usually attributed to the Brady National Photographic Art Gallery," Winslow Homer's "Contraband," and Horace Pippin's "Zachariah." In "Unknowns: Commemorating Black Women's Civil War Heroism" (212–26) Micki Mcelya summons visual evidence (photographs, flags, and monuments) to recuperate the contributions of black women to the war effort, a story that has been "flattened over time into a supporting role shaped by normative gender constructs, the glorification of patriarchy, and the equation of manhood with militarism." Also see Steven Conn for an analysis of "Narrative Trauma and Civil War History Painting, or Why Are These Pictures So Terrible?" *History and Theory* 41, no.

4 (2002). Conn is primarily focused on the limits of history painting to "make sense of the world as it once had."

26. In the exhibition catalogue, curator Eleanor Jones Harvey begins a chapter titled "Abolition and Emancipation" by noting that, before the Civil War, genre painters "who depicted blacks in America had long tended to invoke ethnic caricatures" that "were consistent with the embedded prejudices of the day, North and South." However, Harvey finds that during the War the representation of blacks "as an inferior race" changed, moving from "caricature to empathy," as "a trajectory of racial awareness . . . became visible," particularly in the paintings of Eastman Johnson, Winslow Homer, Thomas Waterman Wood, and Thomas Moran. In fact, as Harvey argues, Homer and Johnson "changed the way blacks were represented in American art between 1857 and 1877. Their subjects included daily life in the North and South which encompassed the southern cornfields and the explicit horrors of slavery—for example Johnson's "A Ride for Liberty—The Fugitive Slaves" (1862) and Moran's "Slave Hunt, Dismal Swamp, Virginia" (1862). Eleanor Jones Harvey, *The Civil War and American Art* (Washington, DC: Smithsonian American Art Museum, 2013), 173, 221.

27. Harvey 96 and n.45 p.255.

28. Alain Locke, *Negro Art: Past and Present*. Bronze Booklet No. 3 (Washington, DC, The Associates in Negro Folk Education, 1936).

29. Alain Locke, "The Negro as Artist," in *The Negro in Art: A Pictorial Record of the Negro Artist and of the Negro Theme in Art*, ed. Alain Locke (New York: Hacker Books, 1968), 10.

30. Alain Locke. Foreword. *The Negro in Art*, 3.

31. Black artists are represented in *The Pluralist Era: American Art, 1968–1981* by Corinne Robins, although one subchapter segregates them as "Some Black Art and Artists." Robins finds that the "pluralist alternative" was open to "many things and many spirits" and thus appears to have been a more expansive period in practice as well as in theory. She surveys the work of Betye Sarr, Alma Thomas, Benny Andrews, Howardena Pindell, and Romare Bearden. When the book appeared, these artists might have been well known to art historians, curators, collectors, and others with an appreciation of African American art, but they were likely little known or unknown to a general audience; their inclusion marked a corrective step toward a more inclusive art history. Corinne Robins, *The Pluralist Era: American Art, 1968–1981* (New York: Harper & Row, 1984), 7.

32. Vlach has explained that basketry, musical instruments, wood carving, quilting, pottery, boatbuilding, blacksmithing, architecture, and graveyard decoration constitute "expressions of black American art that as yet lie unrecognized." He surveys each category individually in *The Afro-American Tradition in Decorative Arts*. Also see "Negro Craftsmanship in Early America" by Leonard Price Stavisky (*The American Historical Review* 54.2, Jan.1949, 315–25) for a carefully researched study that emphasizes economic perspectives on the suppression and reemergence of the work of blacks from the colonial period through the early years of the Republic and into the nineteenth century.

33. Freeman Henry Morris Murray, *Emancipation and the Freed in American Sculpture: A Study in Interpretation* (Washington, DC: Press of Arthur Murray Brothers, Inc., 1916), 3.

34. Sharon Patton notes an exhibition in 1920 of "nearly 200 works of African-American Art" at the New York Public Library branch on 135th Street which would later become the Schomburg Center for Research in Black Culture. Sharon F. Patton, *African American Art* (New York: Oxford University Press, 1998). See the comprehensive timeline; 303–9.

35. Patton. *African-American Art*, 11, 13.

36. Elton C. Fax, *Seventeen Black Artists* (New York: Dodd, Mead & Co., 1971).

37. Romare Bearden and Harry Henderson, *A History of African American Artists from 1792 to the Present* (New York: Pantheon Books, 1993).

38. Celeste-Marie Bernier, *African American Visual Arts: from Slavery to the Present* (Chapel Hill: University of North Carolina, 2008), 1.

39. Patton concedes that her attention to eighteenth- and early-nineteenth-century artists constitutes the "most threadbare" part of her study, the time when slavery suppressed but never eradicated the making of art/objects. *African-American Art*, 13.

40. Patton quotes at length from Gaither's catalogue introduction to *Afro-American Artists, New York and Boston*. See Patton 193–95 and 275 n.4.

41. Farrington, Lisa, *African American Art: A Visual and Cultural History* (New York: Oxford University Press, 2017).

42. The subject, too vast to be covered in depth here, can be reviewed in Patton's timeline.

43. The exhibition included the nineteenth- and early twentieth-century masters Scipio Morehead, Joshua Johnston, Robert S. Duncanson, Edward M. Bannister, Edmonia Lewis, and Henry O. Tanner as well as a second generation, including Meta Warrick Fuller, Hale Woodruff, Aaron Douglas, and Lois M. Jones. Representatives of the latest generation (at the time) included Jacob Lawrence, Horace Pippin, Beauford Delaney, and Elizabeth Catlett. See *The Evolution of Afro-American Artists: 1800–1950.* The catalogue includes no author or editors, no publisher or year, and no page numbers.

44. The qualities Taylor identified included: "a need for immediate communication"; the "necessity for a dramatic posture, for 'soul'"; a desire to protest the racial condition"; "simple and straightforward" forms that often show "primitive, rough, or unfinished feeling"; and a "certain involvement with the world of Ju-Ju, of ritual and witchcraft." Edward K. Taylor. Foreword, *New Black Artists* (New York: Printed by Clarke & Way, 1969). The catalogue lists no author or publisher and is not paginated.

45. Charles C. Eldredge, Foreword, in *Sharing Traditions: Five Black Artists in Nineteenth-Century America* by Linda Roscoe Hartigan (Washington, DC: Smithsonian Institution Press, 1985), 7.

46. Linda Roscoe Hartigan, *Sharing Traditions: Five Black Artists in Nineteenth-Century America* (Washington, D.C.: Smithsonian Institution Press, 1985), 39 and 111–13.

47. Elizabeth Broun, Preface, in *Free within Ourselves: African-American Artists in the Collection of the National Museum of American Art*, by Regenia Perry

(Washington, DC: Smithsonian Institution, and Pomegranate Artbooks, 1992), 11. Reprinted with permission of the Smithsonian American Art Museum, Smithsonian Institution.

48. Edmund Barry Gaither, Introduction, *Afro-American Artists, New York and Boston* (Boston: The Museum of the National Center of Afro-American Artists, The Museum of Fine Arts and The School of the Museum of Fine Arts Boston, 1970).

49. Ellwood Parry, *The Image of the Indian and the Black Man in American Art, 1590–1900* (New York: George Braziller, 1974), xi–xiii.

50. See *The Image of the Black in Western Art* (Washington, DC: Smithsonian Institution Press, 1980) (no author, no page numbers).

51. Hugh Honour, *The Image of the Black in Western Art*, vol. IV, "From the American Revolution to World War I" (Cambridge: Menil Foundation, Harvard University Press, 1989), 11–12. The book was a finalist for the Pulitzer Prize in History (1990).

52. The preface to a new edition of *The Image of the Black in Western Art* by David Bindman and Henry Louis Gates Jr. includes the observation that: "*Image* no longer appears to be a neutral term but begs the question of the context and ideological stand point of each representation." See David Bindman and Henry Louis Gates Jr., Preface, *The Image of the Black in Western Art*, volume II, part 2 (Cambridge: Harvard University Press, 2012), xi. The new edition of volume IV, parts 1 and 2, retains Honour's text.

53. Albert Boime, "Invisible in the Foreground," Review of Hugh Honour's *The Image of the Black in Western Art. New York Times Book Review*, April 2, 1989. The title of the review relates to a discovery Boime made in reading Joseph T. Wilson's *The Black Phalanx: A History of the Negro Soldiers of the United States, In the Wars of 1775–1812, 1861–1865* (Hartford, American Publishing Company, 1888.) In the course of a well-documented military history, Wilson quotes "an authority" who observed that John Trumbull, "'in his celebrated historic picture of the battle [of Bunker Hill] introduces conspicuously the colored patriot'" (Wilson, 38). Having read Wilson's account, Boime admits that he had seen reproductions of the painting ("The Death of General Warren at the Battle of Bunker's Hill") many times and yet "did not recall ever seeing a black figure in it." That figure was, thus, "invisible" to him.

54. Boime candidly reveals his "lingering ambivalence . . . [as] a white scholar doing a study from the perspective of the black victim." In "bringing to light" the work of Albert Murray (whom he credits as the "first black American art historian"), Boime addresses but cannot resolve that conflict. See *The Art of Exclusion: Representing Blacks in the Nineteenth Century* (Washington, DC: Smithsonian Institution Press, 1990), xv.

55. Boime observes that William Sidney Mount's *The Bone Player* (1856) "reveals a particular fascination for toothy grins in his depiction of black people" and that Thomas Ball's *Emancipation Group* (1874) memorializes a "towering Abraham Lincoln bidding a kneeling slave to rise." Boime notes how, in Ball's work, "[o]nce again the conventional geometries have been deployed for ideological purposes." *The Art of Exclusion*, 88, 16–17.

56. Preface, *The Image of the Black in African and Asian Art*, ed. David Bindman, Suzanne Preston Blier, and Henry Louis Gates Jr. (Cambridge: The Belknap Press of Harvard University Press, 2017), vii.

57. Preface, *The Image of the Black in African and Asian Art*, vii, x.

58. Richard J. Powell, "Art History and Black Memory: Toward a 'Blues Aesthetic,'" *History and Memory in African-American Culture*, eds. Geneviève Faber and Robert G. O'Meally (New York: Oxford University Press, 1994), 228.

59. Richard J. Powell, *Black Art and Culture in the 20th Century* (London: Thames and Hudson, 1997), 18–19.

60. *The Black Aesthetic*, ed. Addison Gayle Jr. (New York: Doubleday, 1971).

61. Adam David Miller, "Some Observations on a Black Aesthetic" in Gayle, *The Black Aesthetic*, 404. Ron Karenga, "Black Cultural Nationalism," in Gayle, *The Black Aesthetic*, 34. Langston Hughes, "The Negro Artist and the Racial Mountain," in Gayle, *The Black Aesthetic*, 180.

62. Holland Cotter, "Black Artists: Three Shows," *Art in America* 78, no. 3 (March 1990): 170–71. The exhibitions included: *Art as a Verb: The Evolving Continuum* (Maryland Institute College of Art and The Studio Museum in Harlem, 1988–1989); *The Appropriate Object* (Albright-Knox Gallery, Buffalo, NY, and other venues, 1989); *Traditions and Transformations: Contemporary African-American Sculpture* (Bronx Museum, 1989).

63. Cotter, 166. *Art as a Verb* featured thirteen artists. Eleven were women, including Howardena Pindell, Adrian Piper, Faith Ringgold, Betye Saar, and Joyce Sullivan. Charles Abramson and David Hammons were the only males. The small exhibition catalogue included individual essays by cocurators Leslie King-Hammond and Lowery Stokes Sims as well as a coauthored introduction. Here they explain that each artist "struck out independently" in their choice of form "because of a dissatisfaction with what they perceive to be the limitations of western art media." They also point out that these artists "focus on the dilemmas of their existence within the technological society of the United States at the end of the twentieth century. See Leslie King-Hammond and Lowery Stokes Sims, Introduction, *Art as a Verb: The Evolving Continuum: Installations, Performances, and Videos by 13 African-American Artists: November 21, 1988–January 8, 1989*, Maryland Institute, College of Art. (Baltimore: The Maryland Institute College of Art, 1988) (no page numbers). The exhibition moved to The Metropolitan Life Gallery and The Studio Museum in Harlem (January–June 1989). In an exhibition review Arlene Raven noted that: "A verb is an active part of speech. The artists . . . , called first generation by the curators, lived through segregation and desegregation, Berkeley's Free Speech Movement, and Black Power." See Arlene Raven, "Mojotech," *The Village Voice* (March 28, 1989), 93. For a well contextualized appreciation of the exhibit see Patricia Failing's "Black Artists Today: A Case of Exclusion," *Art News* (March 1989): 124–31.

64. The use of African materials and gestures in the work of Richard Hunt and Oliver Jackson can be examined in the context of multiculturalism, and as curator Beryl Wright noted in the catalogue's introduction their work also bears comparison to "medieval armor and Greco-Roman statuary." Wright pointed out that the way these artists "use visual language challenges aesthetic formulas that prescribe this or that"

and that the work does not seem to follow feminist, black art, or minimalist principles. Wright also noted that all of the "objects" in the exhibition (which included sculpture, large- and smaller-scale installations, and paintings) hold the viewer because "they function as holistic, though variegated entities resonant with interpretive possibility." See the foreword by Douglas G. Schultz and introduction by Beryl Wright. *The Appropriate Object* (Buffalo, NY: Buffalo Fine Arts Academy, 1989), 6, 9, 11.

65. Philip Verre, "Introduction and Acknowledgements" and George Nelson Preston, "Traditions and Transformations" in *Traditions and Transformations: Contemporary Afro-American Sculpture* (The Bronx Museum of the Arts, 1989).

66. Bringing the matter of tradition and continuity to the foreground, *Black Art—Ancestral Legacy: The African Impulse in African-American Art* (Dallas: Dallas Museum of Art, 1990) traveled from the Dallas Museum of Art to the High Museum of Art in Atlanta, the Milwaukee Art Museum, and the Virginia Museum of Fine Arts between 1990 and 1991. Its purpose was to engage in an "exploration of the connections between 20th-century African-American artists and their African heritage" (11). The catalogue survives as a record of the powerful work of formally trained and self-taught artists.

67. Regenia Perry, *Free Within Ourselves: African-American Artists in the Collection of the National Museum of American Art* (Washington, DC: Smithsonian Institution, 1992).

68. Guy McElroy, "Introduction: Race and Representation," *Facing History: The Black Image in American Art 1710–1940* (New York: Chronicle Books, 1991), xi.

69. In an incisive and well-balanced review, Michael Brenson noted that curator Guy McElroy "lets the record speak for itself." See "Black Images, American History," *New York Times* April 20, 1990: C30.

70. Henry Louis Gates Jr., "The Face and Voice of Blackness" in *Facing History: The Black Image in American Art 1710–1940*. In a critical exhibition review entitled "Defacing History" Michelle Wallace acknowledged the "larger intellectual project" but thought it "lost track of the more complex and challenging issues" and perhaps deliberately cleansed or defused the unsightly history it sought to represent. While Wallace commended the catalogue, she concluded that the exhibition itself was "ambivalent about drawing upon the very considerable resources of the 'other' and bringing what currently lies outside the museum inside." Michelle Wallace, "Defacing History," *Art in America* 78, no. 12 (December 1990), 121, 123, 185. In "Are Art Museums Racist?" Maurice Berger also leveled a stringent critique of the exhibition and the "underlying resistance of the art world to people of color." Although he credited the exhibition as a "sign of improvement," Berger also found that the show's "iconographical approach sidestepped the broader institutional and patronage issues contributing to the formation of racist representations." See *Art in America* 78, no. 9 (September 1990): 70, 73. Berger's interviews with central figures in the debate also appear in this issue in "Speaking Out: Some Distance to Go," *Art in America* 78, no. 9 (September, 1990).

Chapter Four

Themes, Part III

Representing Difficult History in an Activist Present

I posit "sites of slavery" as the objects, texts, figures, places, and narratives from the American past that provide tangible links between present-day Americans and American chattel slavery. Like Nora's sites of memory, the sites of slavery on which I focus produce discourses about how best to remember American democracy and to construct national identity.—Salamishah Tillet. *Sites of Slavery: Citizenship and Racial Democracy in the Post-Civil Rights Imagination*[1]

The exhibitions of "difficult" history I address in this chapter represent the realities of the slave trade, the violent rupture with established roots in land/ family/religion/and culture and its long-term effects, and the struggle to obtain basic human rights. These exhibitions often strive to make direct contact with the visitor, to evoke a visceral reaction, and to transfer the burden of knowledge and responsibility. As Jennifer Bonnell and Roger Simon explain in "Difficult Exhibitions and Intimate Encounters":

an exhibition might be judged as difficult if it is experienced as eliciting the burden of "negative emotions," those unpleasant and troublesome feelings of grief, anger, shame, or horror that histories can produce, particularly if they raise the possibility of complicity of one's country, culture, or family in systemic violence such as the seizure of aboriginal land, the slave trade, or the perpetration of genocide.[2]

Like many of the exhibitions I have discussed in previous chapters, these exhibitions connect the past to the present and to the future. However, they are arguably more challenging; their strategies are more immersive; they demand a kind of absorption that differs from, for example, close looking at works of visual art.[3] They must translate what has survived as written documentation into another medium of instruction. A visitor may have some familiarity, for example, with the firsthand account of the Middle Passage in *The Interesting Narrative of the Life of Olaudah Equiano*: "The closeness of the place, and the heat of the climate, added to the number in the ship, which was so crowded that each had scarcely room to turn himself, almost suffocated us. . . . The shrieks of the women, and the groans of the dying, rendered the whole a scene of horror almost inconceivable."[4] A visitor's formal education may have included a few of the scrupulous details offered by historians like Stephanie Smallwood, who explains that: "Some three hundred or more people were intended to occupy the space of a slave ship. Only the long, flat surfaces formed by the decks were suitable for storage of so many, and those only after the addition of platforms between decks to double the available surface area."[5] Yet the encounter with difficult history in a museum may exceed the effects of the written account. It may reach beyond the boundaries of the text and make the reality hard to ignore. This enduring abolitionist project has multiple objectives. "The success of the abolitionist movement," as Marcus Rediker explains, "lay in making real for people in Britain and America the slave ship's pervasive and utterly instrumental terror, which was indeed its defining feature."[6] The same may be said for representations of slavery in the twenty-first century.

SLAVERY

The collections, exhibitions, and specific programs of every museum bear a reciprocal relationship to the mission-related and localized thematic dimensions of the institution. In the museums I examine here, the attention devoted to the history and explicit realities of slavery is affected by each museum's collections, mission, and focus. In some cases, when slavery-related themes and objects are foregrounded, they are often juxtaposed with or surrounded by material that introduces physical, political, and cultural forms of resistance. This strategy often takes us beyond the confines of chattel slavery and its legacies. Moreover, if the museum's goal is to overcome the emphasis on victimization, it may seek to replace that master plot with a teleology of achievement.[7] In relation to trauma as "unclaimed history," the relative placement of (and/or lack of space afforded to) slavery, the slave trade, the diaspora, and other aspects of forced or necessary migration, may also suggest that these realities present an "affront to understanding" and/or are resistant to the "platitudes of knowledge."[8]

In looking at the ways in which African American museums give voice to this far-reaching subject we find a range of practices and underlying beliefs about how much time and space—and which narratives—warrant exhibition. Fath Davis Ruffins suggested in 2006 that an "exhibitionary silence about American slavery" has been "forcefully broken," yet traces of hesitation still linger in exhibition practices and in the wide-ranging debate among museum professionals, scholars, and visitors about the status of slavery in representations of African American history and culture.[9] At roughly the same time that Ruffins made that observation, and ten years before the actual opening of the museum in Washington, director Lonnie Bunch noted the challenges that must be faced as museums strive to explore "the full range of African American experiences" including "the difficult, the controversial and the defeats." The consequential nature of that mission rang out clearly in his rationale: "Until we use the past to better understand the contemporary resonance of slavery, we will never get to the heart of one of the central dilemmas in American life—race relations." In addition to overcoming ignorance and oversimplification, Bunch explained, facing and learning to embrace "ambiguity" is one of the greatest challenges for museums and visitors. He argued that museum visitors often come "in search of uncomplicated narratives" but that the ambiguities and complexities of slavery and race do not lend themselves to the comforts of clarity and closure.[10] Bunch revisited the point in an interview for the *New York Times* in 2020, speaking now as the newly appointed secretary of the Smithsonian Institution, and he continued to defend the need to exhibit "difficult history," insisting that "the challenge is to use history to help the public feel comfortable with nuance and complexity."[11]

The Charles H. Wright Museum and the National Underground Railroad Freedom Center have chosen to foreground the actual mechanisms of slavery—the former by taking visitors on a journey into the suffocating bowels of a slave ship, and the latter by placing an empty slave pen at the visual and spatial center of the institution's design. I want to examine these two examples of thematic foregrounding first and then consider the strategies often used by other museums to integrate, or in some cases to subsume rather than centralize the theme of chattel slavery. Finally, with Ruffins and Bunch in mind, I want to recognize two very recent exhibitions—at the DuSable Black History Museum and the Reginald F. Lewis Museum—that suggest a new mandate (perhaps unspoken) to represent the subject of slavery in our time. In both cases the approach is innovative and creative.

INSTALLATIONS I. THE SLAVE SHIP/
THE CHARLES H. WRIGHT MUSEUM

The visitor's direct confrontation with slavery and arrival at the threshold of the Middle Passage is strategically delayed at the C. H. Wright Museum. Slavery is neither the beginning nor the end of the expansive long-term exhibition *And Still We Rise*. The approach to the explicit slavery theme is gradual and deeply contextualized. The goal of the entire exhibition is to offer "a comprehensive look at the history of African-American resilience."[12] In the first of several separate gallery environments, a large interactive globe presents the twelve million square miles covered by the continent of Africa. In an exposition narrative conveyed mainly through wall texts, the visitor finds an introduction to African creation myths and cosmic beginnings. Moving on, visitors enter a "Regal City: The Kingdom of Benin" and encounter a series of galleries in which the sights and sounds of a thriving market become the background for an overview of the structure of Benin society and its values. The vitality of the scene changes, however, in the next gallery, "Trouble on the Horizon," where a display of shackles supports the cautionary theme. Shackles are a ubiquitous iconic symbol in museum exhibitions as they offer material evidence of chattel slavery and function more broadly as a synecdoche: they establish a part-for-whole relationship to the experience of enslavement.[13]

Visitors who follow the intended trajectory of the exhibition design soon find themselves in "A Place of No Return" where a tableau vivant complete with life-size figures and ambient voiceover depicts the slave trade. The traders are clearly identified as both European and African, thus establishing the complicity of Africans in both the socioeconomic structure of slavery and its ordinary daily transactions. Equally important in combatting unexamined assumptions about inferiority, visitors learn that the Africans who will be "traded" are valuable—that they are "skilled and experienced." When we move on, through a dark passage and up a flight of stairs, we find ourselves in a space identified only as a West African slave fort.

In attempting to describe this small pen inhabited by four life-size figures I need to shift to the first person: any claim to objectivity (indicated by the use of "one" or "we" or "the visitor") seems out of place and beside the point. The sense of enclosure is deliberately and horribly effective; but this is not my final destination. Another passage leads me to the deck of a slave ship, a generalized replica with the names of 2,500 actual slave ships marked on its bow.[14] This replica stands as a representative icon of the uncommon brutality which was common practice in crossings of the Middle Passage. As Rediker notes, the slave ship "changed relatively little between 1700 and 1808"; it remained "a strange and potent combination of war machine, mobile prison, and factory" (in which the "sailors 'produced' slaves within the ship"). He points out that abolitionists made effective use of minutely detailed images of these ships—the slave ship *Brooks* was the subject of a widely distributed antislavery pamphlet—in order to represent the "miseries and enormity of the slave trade."[15] Like these pamphlets, but arguably with greater performative force, this installation brings me in direct contact with the excruciating details.

Prominent gallery signage identifies the space and the moment, "Boarding the Captives." I soon arrive in a construction of "The Beast's Belly" where forty life-size figures are crammed into three pens.[16] The scale of the exhibit is massive, yet the feeling of compression is intense. Voices moan and cry out in many languages.[17] There is no place to hide, no safe distance. In my experience, I enter the "proximate space of oppression" that some critics felt was lacking in the original installation.[18] There are no didactic distractions, no wall texts or labels. The compressed shelving of anonymous human cargo is shocking; the association with iconic images of the Nazi death camps seems unavoidable.[19] On a second visit, the following day, my experience is multiplied by my apprehension; I know what I am about to confront. (For some reason I take no pictures.) Once I climb out of the belly of the beast I find myself in a very different environment, both in terms of geographical place and museological methods. A gallery titled "A Working Life, African American Occupations" describes life on the plantation, mainly via didactic wall texts and few objects. The next gallery, "Slavery in Detroit," also depends heavily on wall texts and photographs, with few objects. [20]

INSTALLATIONS II: SLAVE PEN—THE NATIONAL UNDERGROUND RAILROAD FREEDOM CENTER

Initially the property of John W. Anderson of Mason County, Kentucky, the slave pen on exhibit at the National Underground Railroad Freedom Center in Cincinnati was found in an old tobacco barn by the current owner, farmer Raymond Evers, who then donated it to the museum. The structure became the centerpiece of the museum's interior, where it dominates a large open exhibition area on the second floor and rises to the floor above (*Figure 4.1*).

Once the artifact was acquired, midway in the Freedom Center's design phase, it became necessary for key elements of the interior design to be revised to accommodate the looming presence of the 20 x 30-foot (roughly 1½ story) hewn-log structure. John Meadows, one of the lead architects on the project, notes that slave pens "served as holding cells for slaves being force-marched . . . to be sold at auction." Although they were once ubiquitous, few survive. This relic from the early 1800s was preserved intact,

Figure 4.1. National Underground Railroad Freedom Center/Slave Pen Exterior.
Source: Author's Photo

"concealed in a barn, protected from the weather" and with the "chains still attached to the walls, shafts of light falling through age-blackened clapboards of sycamore and walnut."[21] As one of the museum labels explains: "The slaves endured brutal conditions, chained together, often strangers to each other, shackled in place, sometimes forced to relieve themselves where they were. In this way, the Slave Pen recalled the dark holds of the slave ships that brought the slaves' African ancestors through the Middle Passage to America 100–150 years before."

The almost empty enclosure (*Figure 4.2*) stands as a material—if silent—witness to the horrors of chattel slavery and its domestic commercial operations (transport, detainment, sale/resale). Material and textual evidence of the strategies and escape routes that constituted the Underground Railroad and its "phantom-like workings"[22] continues to be discovered by archaeologists, archivists, and historians. The object-centered approach to representation must often find support in other types of primary—and secondary—sources, and this is not limited to the Underground Railroad.[23] The Freedom Center's slave pen stands as a reminder of the need for that lifeline to liberty, in the past, and the need to preserve and interpret it for the future. As a visitor, I found myself captivated by the stark emptiness of the pen and then drawn to

Figure 4.2. National Underground Railroad Freedom Center/Slave Pen Interior.
Source: Author's Photo

investigate the informative displays that surround it. Like others, I remained in the exhibition space for close to an hour to experience the full dimensions of the installation.[24]

Although much is left to the imagination, the pen itself is supplemented by abundant ancillary materials (*Figure 4.3*). These include a five-panel, free-standing narrative text titled "Emancipation and Its Legacies" and wall texts that outline "The Internal Slave Trade" in multiple regions of the United States. Coming much closer to home, two wooden text panels contain details of the original owner's slave-trading operation. These details include portions of a letter from the owner, John Anderson, to Thomas Marshall of Natchez, Mississippi dated November 24, 1832, in which Anderson spells out the current prices for "Negroe" men, women, and children and issues a general purchase order to Marshall for the coming season. On the reverse side of the exhibit panel is a list of the (first) names of the enslaved persons who were part of Anderson's probate inventory in 1834. The text is carved into—rather than printed on—the wooden panel's surface, giving the raw data a depth and immediacy that would be hard to realize on a flat plane.

An explanatory touch-screen video stands nearby, narrated by the Freedom Center's Senior Historian Carl B. Westmoreland.[25] The video underscores

Figure 4.3. National Underground Railroad Freedom Center/Slave Pen Interior and Surrounding Ancillary Materials.
Source: Author's Photo

key exhibition themes, including discovery, archaeology, and reconstruction of the slave pen. Using stop-motion and still photography, the video presents an *in situ* record of the project's development—as the team worked to "reassemble [the] temple of pain." The video also includes a reading of a poem by Westmoreland titled "Tell It" that includes the lines: "Tell the historian/Tell the ugly truth" and "Don't let it happen again." The poem is also inscribed on one of the wooden text panels *(Figure 4.3)*. An adjacent two-sided artifact case includes everyday objects excavated from the area near the barn where the slave pen had been concealed and preserved. Muted and somber background music marks the space as part of the larger installation. The elaboration of the slave pen story in this supplemental environment helps to awaken historical consciousness, yet it does not compete with the structure itself as the mute witness to history.[26]

In keeping with the Freedom Center's focus on mechanisms of escape from slavery—past and present—the slave pen is visible from multiple vantage points. It functions as a reminder of the conditions of captivity as well as the fate of those who escape, those who may be recaptured, and those who will become enslaved for the first time. Although not always in view, the pen proves inescapable. Visitors repeatedly encounter it as they navigate the three separate pavilions—Courage, Cooperation, and Perseverance—that comprise the Center's exhibition spaces.

Relevant details of the slave trade in the region where the Freedom Center slave pen was discovered can also be found in a variety of primary sources. These valuable documents are likely not on the reading lists of most visitors, however, and this museum encounter may be their first, perhaps only, exposure. In the *Narrative of His Sufferings . . . During a Captivity of More Than Twenty-Five Years*, Lewis Garrard Clarke describes a Kentucky slave trader named Bill Myers who "went to a large number of auctions and purchased women about forty years old with their youngest children in their arms." The women, he explains, "are sold cheap" (since their child-bearing years are coming to an end). "The children he took and shut up in a log pen"—which was likely similar to the one installed at the Freedom Center. Clarke explains that Myers "gathered the women in a large drove, and carried them South and sold them." He then describes the fate of the children, who are left behind in the slave pen. However, Myers "was detained there [in the South] for months longer than he expected, and winter coming on, and no proper provision having been made for the children, many of them perished with cold and hunger, some were frost bitten, and all were emaciated to skeletons."[27]

The direct connection between the use of "slave pens" and the interstate sale of persons in the upper South—including the state of Kentucky—has been established by historian Walter Johnson: "Taken together, the interstate traders, large and small, urban and itinerant, accounted for as many as two thirds of a million forced migrations in the decades before the Civil War, half of those involving the separation of an enslaved family." He notes that the "people they purchased were gathered in . . . slave pens and jails, where they sometimes waited as long as two months before being shipped south." Johnson includes the example of William Cotton, "who owned a slave depot during the early 1830s" and "spent his summers in Kentucky buying slaves." Johnson also draws on the firsthand testimony of William Still, who served on the Philadelphia Vigilance Committee at the "northern outlet of the Underground Railroad." Still collected and subsequently published narratives of people who, as Johnson notes, "dated their decision to run away to the time when they heard they were to be sold for debt or punishment." As Johnson explains: "Facing both social death and literal death in the killing fields of the lower South," those who chose to escape "had nothing left to lose; isolation, hunger, exposure, tracking dogs, and the threats of violent capture and sadistic punishment . . . could no longer provoke enough fear to keep these men from running away."[28]

As a "site of conscience" the Freedom Center's mission is to relate a "uniquely American history to contemporary issues," and to address the "persistence of modern forms of slavery today." Thus another permanent exhibition, *Invisible: Slavery Today*, is devoted to global "forms of exploitation" and efforts to combat those practices. In a recent statement by Jamie Glavic and Dion Brown of the Freedom Center, available in a collection of "Twenty Perspectives from Museum Leaders," we learn that when it opened in 2010 this was "the world's first permanent museum gallery dedicated to modern-day slavery and human trafficking."[29] In 2014 the Freedom Center also launched the website "endslaverynow.org" where virtual visitors can learn about contemporary forms of slavery—including forced labor, child labor, sex trafficking, and domestic servitude—as well as current forms of activism. In 2017 the *Open Your Mind: Understanding Implicit Bias Learning Lab* was installed on site. In partnership with the Kirwan Institute for the Study of Race and Ethnicity at The Ohio State University, it is "designed to assist the public in understanding and recognizing bias and other forms of discrimination, as well as to explore recent debates in the realm of implicit bias research."[30]

INTEGRATION AND/OR INCORPORATION?
MAKING ROOM FOR SLAVERY

Each institution's location, collections, and mission influence its attention to the topic, but chattel slavery and its supporting regimes of power cannot be limited to a regional—as opposed to a national or global—disgrace. Moreover, the extended effects of slavery have no temporal, psychological, or generation-specific end point. It seems that discrete geographical locations and finite timelines might now have a different but still significant role to play in exhibitions and narratives. Kristin Gallas and James DeWolf Perry, the editors of *Interpreting Slavery at Museums and Historic Sites*, propose these "Six Components of a Comprehensive and Conscientious Interpretation of Slavery": Comprehensive Content; Race and Identity Awareness; Institutional Investment; Community Involvement; Visitor Experiences and Expectations; and Staff Training. In the context of "Comprehensive Content and Contested Historical Narratives" they argue that "The United States suffers from . . . collective amnesia about much of our history of slavery, and especially about its breadth and depth throughout our society and across the country." The solution would be to give attention to "the full geographical extent and economic importance of US slavery and . . . the great diversity of experiences of slavery . . . and active resistance." The Northeastern states, of course, would have to be included here.[31]

If museums are thematically focused—like the National Underground Railroad Freedom Center and the Birmingham Civil Rights Museum—the relationship between chattel slavery and other human rights issues will influence their narratives and design strategies. In such forward-looking institutions, contemporary examples of enslavement and other attacks on human rights are emphasized, and the slave trade that existed from the fifteenth through the nineteenth centuries opens onto twentieth- and twenty-first-century iterations that command equal exhibition space.

Slavery, as a historical fact and a narrative theme, is present in other African American museums but it does not necessarily receive equal or sustained attention. However, a recent temporary exhibition at the Reginald F. Lewis Museum (October 2021–January 2022) indicates this museum's decision to focus more directly on the subject. *Bodies of Information: Understanding Slavery through the Stearns Collection* offered visitors the chance to engage with slavery-related archives and to scrutinize documents from the nineteenth-century antebellum period.[32] In the past, visitors to the Reginald F. Lewis were suggestively reminded of the treacherous Middle Passage by a large, digitized photomural of the open sea reproduced on one wall on the third floor. It carried no title or informative label. Marcus Wood has argued, in fact, that the fairly abstract image constitutes "a refusal to enter the space of terror that the Middle Passage occupies within the archive of American slavery."[33]

At the DuSable Black History Museum, where Africa is emphasized as a source of origins and traditions, explicit attention to slavery has been less evident. A notable exception has been the *Freedom Now* mural, in which the dense historical canvas refers to the start of the Atlantic slave trade in 1619, plantation life, Nat Turner's slave revolt (1831), and the achievements of Frederick Douglass and Harriet Tubman.[34] However, a new multimedia exhibition draws on the power of Instagram Stories to foreground the subject. *Equiano.Stories*, a joint project undertaken with the Stelo Stories Studio, dramatizes Olaudah Equiano's boyhood and brings to life the Igboland village of Essaka where he was born. The epic story is captured as a self-recorded, first-person account, within the format of Instagram Stories, using video, still images, and text.[35] The museum's extensive collection of African art and artifacts supports the dramatic video narrative. An interactive website offers access to these objects and provides background information. A key message here, as expressed on the main web page for the exhibition reminds us that "*Equiano* is our origin story which does not begin in enslavement. It begins in FREEDOM."

At the California African American Museum, the permanent exhibition, *The African American Journey West*, has indirectly addressed slavery with an emphasis on the diaspora and migration. Slavery has also been explicitly addressed in special exhibitions, such as *Slave Trade: From Africa to the Americas, 1650–1870* (2011) which included small but powerful installations of a slave ship and slave cabin. Then in *Slavery on the New Frontier, 1848–1865* (2018–2019), the museum explored the subject in even greater depth and brought home the point that California was not a "freedom frontier." This major exhibition of objects, images, and explanatory wall texts ran for seven months and included extensive public programming. It now remains available on the museum's website as a slideshow, along with ancillary videos and a tour led by the curators.[36]

In museums that foreground resistance to slavery, the theme of activism may triumph over the representation of atrocity. At the Museum of African American History in Philadelphia, for example, slavery is embedded but not foregrounded in the permanent exhibitions *Audacious Freedom* and *Philadelphia Conversations*. In the "Family" section of *Audacious Freedom* we learn that "slavery often tore families apart." In the "Law" section we learn that George Washington owned nine slaves; and in the "Politics" section we are exposed to examples of political activism as well as efforts to address slavery and inequality in general. At the Museum of African American History in Boston, the abolition movement receives substantial attention, as we might expect given its geographical location and abolitionist history, and objects like a "Bill of Sale" and a notice for a "Runaway Slave" are exhibited/contextualized in vitrines as evidence of the urgency of the movement.[37] The museum's social history orientation emphasizes contributions made by African Americans from Colonial times to the present, and explanatory texts clearly indicate that The African Meeting House (one of the museum's two historic buildings) was built by free black laborers. There are references throughout the museum to the abolitionist meetings held there and the presence of Frederick Douglass, among many other prominent figures.

Slavery may haunt the representation of history in many museums without necessarily emerging into the spotlight. The Museum of the African Diaspora in San Francisco is one example. Although it focuses primarily on the work of contemporary visual artists, and slavery may not be an explicit topic of their exhibitions, slavery is undeniably linked to the diaspora and is arguably a latent presence that emerges in specific individual works and in exhibition themes. For example, in a special exhibition in 2007 titled *Slave Narratives* (which included an online component), audio/visual portraits of Olaudah Equiano, Mary Prince, and Fountain Hughes, among others, were represented along with opening and closing remarks by Maya Angelou.[38]

AFRICA: A POINT OF ORIGIN AND POINT OF RETURN

Where is Africa on the topographical map of the African American museum? There is no single or simple answer to that question. When it is represented in the museum, "Africa" is both a literal physical place *and* a symbolic topological reference point, a marker for the traditions and themes embodied there and carried elsewhere via the diaspora. Historian Robin D. G. Kelley points out this important reciprocal influence, noting that US history will not be the same if we place it in a "diasporic framework."[39] As a result, the way we understand the present might also be informed by previously ignored contexts. Museologically, the engagement with Africa can also be performative, as art historian and curator Ruth B. Phillips explains: "To the degree that new exhibitions about Africa, or any other region of the world, engage with post-colonial critiques of the museum, they will serve as transformative spaces where outworn and dangerous stereotypes are countered by images and representations that make diverse cultural groups recognizable not only to others but to themselves."[40]

Geographically the African continent covers almost twelve million square miles. Politically, it is now composed of fifty-four sovereign states plus non-sovereign territories whose inhabitants belong to and strongly identify with many different ethnic groups. Culturally, the continent resonates as a source of multiple traditions and belief systems. Perhaps, as Stuart Hall contends, Africa is no less than "what we have made of it": "the name of the missing term, the great aporia, which lies at the center of our cultural identity and gives it a meaning which, until recently, it lacked." Hall finds that these "symbolic journeys are necessary for us all—and necessarily circular. This is the Africa we must return to—but 'by another route': what Africa has <u>become</u> in the New World, what we have made of 'Africa': 'Africa'—as we retell it through politics, memory, and desire."[41] Given the wealth of associations that may arise when Africa is represented or invoked in a museum, it has the potential to become an enigmatic space that insists on re-cognition. The museum can provide a home for that project of retrieval.

Theorists from a range of disciplinary perspectives continue to suggest that individual and collective links to Africa may be affected by a combination of literal histories, personal and collective memories, and contemporary realities. Being African, notes philosopher and cultural theorist Kwame Anthony Appiah, may be but "one among many salient modes of being, all of which have to be constantly fought for and rethought."[42] African ancestry when "combined with American nativity" created a "dilemma" in the antebellum period, as historian Elizabeth Rauh Bethel explains, and this dual affiliation presents a "continuing challenge to identity for African Americans."[43]

In African American museums we find that Africa—in all its variety and complexity—resonates as a point of origin and potentially a point of return. As we have seen, the realities of chattel slavery are given extensive treatment in some but not all the museums I have included in this study, and the African origins of the slave trade are sometimes represented as part of that larger narrative. Some museums, however, emphasize Africa as a point of origin, a source of cultural traditions, and a potential point of return. Rather than foregrounding enslavement, displacement, and the diaspora, they focus primarily on the land, the people, and the cultures of Africa as a source of and an ongoing resource for the formation of African American identities.

At some museums the traumatic ruptures created by enslavement hover in the background, where they may be latent but not directly addressed. Africa is represented instead as a source of cultural traditions (rather than the scene of traumatic separation), and continuity with those traditions becomes a significant aspect of the exhibition narrative. Museums that do not foreground Africa in their permanent exhibitions may use special exhibitions as an opportunity to explore African-centered themes. Finally, in museums built upon a human rights foundation—with slavery as their starting point and ongoing examples of abuse as a key focus—specific countries or regions in Africa may be represented as some among many points on a global map of activist concerns.

For example, *Africa Speaks* and *Great Kings and Queens* (two formerly permanent exhibitions at the DuSable Museum) made material connections to points on a physical map. It began with a scene-setting quotation from W. E. B. Du Bois: "The spell of Africa is upon me." Notably object-rich, these permanent exhibitions featured multiple galleries and benefited from the curatorial staff's collection-focused trips to Africa. *Africa Speaks* was also supplemented by objects on loan from other institutions, including the University of Chicago's Oriental Institute Museum. Wall texts and detailed object labels supported the theme of Africa's "spell-binding" magnetism. Two video screens provided historical background on African history and explained that Africans now living in urban areas seek to retrieve their African heritage and transmit it to their children, often by revisiting their rural homelands. Large wall texts established general geographical areas—East Africa, Southern Africa, West Africa, and North Africa—and each one was brought into focus through wall-mounted object-filled vitrines. In the North Africa section, for example, a vitrine displayed a single funeral figurine from Egypt dating to the Twenty-Sixth Dynasty (712–332 BCE) on loan from the Oriental Institute Museum. Another vitrine featured a single ceramic bowl from Qustul, Nubia (3000–2500 BCE), also on loan from the Oriental Institute. At the center of this expansive exhibition was a section highlighting *Central Africa: Africa at a Glance* which featured objects from the DuSable's own collection. A few steps then led visitors up to a smaller gallery devoted to *Great Kings and Queens* where large portrait panels lined each side. The gallery also included a stool made by the Bamun People, a twentieth-century sculpture that reproduces "early commemorative figures," a chair made by the Asante People, and a female figure seated on a stool (19th C).[44] In the extensive remodeling and renaming of the museum (previously the DuSable Museum of African American History) these galleries have not been reinstalled. However, as we see in the *Equiano.Stories* exhibition, the DuSable's collection of African objects is still a major element in the representation of African American history and culture.

Slavery is a central focus of the Charles H. Wright Museum's *And Still We Rise* exhibition, but an interactive globe of the African continent dominates the museum's entrance and emphasizes points of origin as well as points of forced departure. While the exhibit's trajectory insists on a gradual approach to the slave trade, visitors are initially exposed to the vastness of the African continent, to creation myths and cosmic beginnings, and to the "Regal City" of Benin. Thus, the argument is made that we cannot fully grasp the horrors of the slave trade unless we consider what those who became enslaved were forced to leave behind. The museum's Ford Rotunda also depends on Africa as its literal foundation and narrative center as the flags of African nations hang from the dome above the *Ring of Genealogy* mural and the mural itself incorporates the body of an African mother. The emphasis on Africa is consistent with the early corrective intentions of the museum and its mobile exhibition van which, as Andrea Burns explains, sought to: "[r]epair the distorted image of the African World—and image of jungle savagery, ignorance, brutality and superstition"; "[c]reate in Afro-Americans a greater sense of pride in their African heritage"; and "[i]ncrease the knowledge and respect of all Americans for Africa and Africans, past and present."[45]

Although Africa is not a primary focus in its permanent exhibitions, one example of the California African American Museum's explicit attention to Africa was the temporary exhibition *Coloring America: Selections from the California African American Museum's Permanent History Collection* (2012–2013), which included Africa in one of the four thematic sections: "West Africa & the African Diaspora"; "Local History"; "Sports"; and "Entertainment." The introductory wall text acknowledged a debt to Carter G. Woodson, who in 1927 had identified the need for "a properly contextualized black history that would offset the erasures of African-Americans in the larger American tapestry." The exhibition answered his call by offering a "testament" to "varied and diverse contributions" while providing an "overview of some relevant historical objects and artwork donated to or purchased by the museum.

In an introductory wall text for the section devoted to "West Africa & the African Diaspora" the term was associated with "dispersal of Africans and their descendants throughout the world," noting that it "has been especially applied to West and Central Africans enslaved and shipped in the Atlantic Slave Trade."[46] The pronouns in the introductory wall text identified—and identified *with*—specific subject positions ("their" and "our"). The text acknowledged "our desire to never forget our roots" and object labels reminded visitors of "our beauty, strength, and perseverance." In doing so the exhibitionary voice seemed to assume—and by virtue of the pronoun seemed to distinguish itself from—the subject position of some of its viewers. The text focused on the disruption of tradition—"millions of Africans were . . . separated from their roots"—but also emphasized continuity, adaptation, and an enduring sense of cultural identity: "they managed to maintain some African traditions, reform their identities, and establish new cultural practices." The exhibit included cultural artifacts from Nigeria as well as a map of Fort Williams ("one of the many infamous slave forts") and a Manilla (ca. 1843), a token used in the slave trade and other forms of trade in West African cultures.[47]

It would be impossible to identify, materialize, and make visible the many ties that may bind individuals, including museum visitors, to Africa. Attempts to achieve that goal in a museum can result in "representational dilemmas," as Robyn Autry points out in an analysis of the Museum of the African Diaspora in San Francisco. Autry argues that the museum offers a "fragmented view of diasporic identity" and "explores the diaspora in three primary and sometimes contradictory ways: as "a specific case of trauma and displacement . . . during the Transatlantic Slave Trade"; as "a universal symbol of human development and continental dispersal"; and as "a hybrid cultural space with clear ties to Africa." The focus on dispersal may seem to compete with—or may actually collaborate with—the focus on new, hybrid combinations. Autry finds that, at this museum "displays on cultural traditions contain the only narratives of 'return'" and "return is less about a physical return to a specific geographic place, but rather a return to African practices, which are viewed as . . . pure and uncontaminated."[48]

The museum's façade is itself a study in ambiguity. A transparent three-story curtain wall (best seen from across the street) meets and challenges the visitor's gaze as it reveals the interior of the museum and a two-story mosaic mural (which initially appears to be the image of a child). On closer inspection the image, "Face of the African Diaspora" by Robert Silvers, proves to be composed of thousands of faces. Yet another layer of identification is encouraged since the mosaic portrait is itself a regeneration of an iconic photograph, "Ms. Precious, Tamale," by Chester Higgins Jr., a compelling portrait of a young girl from Ghana whose stare is virtually impossible for the viewer to escape. The mural, described by the museum's architects as a "collage of disparate voices, histories, and traditions,[49] becomes ambiguous on at least two levels: it raises the question "What am I seeing?" compounded by the question "What is this saying?" A site-specific installation in the museum's first floor gallery, *Sam Vernon: Impasse of Desires* (2022) further complicated these questions by adding queer subjecthood to the reverberation of voices.[50]

The Museum of the African Diaspora self-identifies as a contemporary art museum that "celebrates Black cultures, ignites challenging conversations, and inspires learning through the global lens of the African Diaspora." Its broad focus is both historical and contemporary, and the work it exhibits may explore the phenomenon of diaspora from many different perspectives, communities, and cultures around the world. The museum has identified four broad overarching themes in its approach to the diaspora: Origins, Movement, Adaptation, and Transformation.[51] This comprehensive narrative mandate can yield compellingly different results in practice and affords the museum a wide spectrum to draw upon when planning exhibitions. Continuity with the past (which is a recurring issue in debates about "Afro-centric architecture" as well as in discussions about an African American "aesthetic" in the visual arts) is a key issue when the organizing theme—of an exhibition or an entire museum—is the diaspora. The assertion of a unique personal identity—and the rejection of stereotypes—is an equally important aspect of the work exhibited.

Given the multiple subject positions, the shared but not uniformly experienced historical contexts, and the competing views on the importance of Africa to the lives of those affected by the diaspora, it is unlikely that a single perspective on Africa could or should take priority in museum exhibitions.[52] Each museum is also influenced and at times limited by the content of its collections and stated mission. Moreover, as Robyn Autry notes, the "diversity of memory cultures" that contemporary "identity-driven" museums must address include: "capture and displacement from Africa, enslavement, and racial segregation," all of which are central "traumatic episodes."[53] Looking back to the early antebellum period, Elizabeth Rauh Bethel finds that "a common mythic African heritage welded from a blend of autobiographical and generational memory," was an important cultural link for free blacks. However, Bethel claims that by the 1830s these "[m]emories and reconstructed images of Africa had been replaced by a resonant national identity."[54]

Questions related to continuity, retention, and "the transformation of culture" have occupied scholars at least since the nineteenth century. As Robin D. G. Kelley explains, even "the concept of diaspora . . . falls short of illuminating all of the international dimensions and contexts of black identities."[55] Museums deal with these issues in a variety of ways: they may emphasize ongoing, perhaps material connections to Africa; they may chart lines of descent and influence that have survived in the diaspora; they may reconstruct traditions that have been lost over time; they may turn to contemporary issues and struggles that African nations and peoples share with the United States.

Where then *is* Africa on (the topographical and topological) map of the African American museum? At any given time, in any individual institution, Africa may be at the center, on the periphery, hovering just out of frame, or too far in the background to be accommodated by the museum's chosen depth of field. Yet it is always inherent in the construction "African American" and, as a modifier, its presence makes a significant difference that remains open to representation and interpretation.

ACTIVISM/CIVIL RIGHTS/ UNIVERSAL HUMAN RIGHTS

African American museums arguably maintain a human rights perspective even when the institution does not include the term "human rights" or "civil rights" in its name or exhibitions. The representation of contemporary human rights issues emerges as an explicit focus, however, in several African American museums, and the connection is frequently made between rights-related themes and conflicts in the United States and similar problems in Africa and other parts of the world.[56] The connection is a structural element—part of the overall design—at both the National Underground Railroad Freedom Center and the Birmingham Civil Rights Institute.

The message at the Freedom Center is that the struggle is not over (the past is still present) and this point is made clear in a permanent exhibition titled *Invisible Slavery Today*. The museum website describes the "overall design and feel" of the exhibition as "a dingy warehouse in an unfamiliar city, filled with wood, metal and plastic containers—shipping cartons for human beings." The brutal reality of "the five most common forms of exploitation," identified as "forced labor, bonded indenture, child slavery, sex trafficking and domestic servitude," is brought out through a narrative focus on five individuals. Each embodies one of the five forms of exploitation. There is an emphasis on activism here, and the visitor is encouraged to join this global movement. Current activist efforts were also the subject of a temporary traveling exhibition, *Women Hold Up Half the Sky* (2012–2013).[57] The subject was "injustices perpetrated against women worldwide and the ways to effect change." The developing world—African nations in particular—were the main source of examples. This was not an object-based exhibition; it relied on textile panels and wall texts, as well as excellent videos, and was heavily dependent on a culture of watching. However, there were also interactive elements that included "direct opportunities for advocacy and involvement by visitors." These included visitor talk-back cards, which could be a first step toward further activism.

At the Birmingham Civil Rights Institute, the presence of Africa is felt strongly in the representation of contemporary global human rights struggles and the links between past and present abuses. As Laura Anderson, former BCRI curator of education, explains: this is "not a museum of memories and established facts, but a living institution committed to social justice in the present through understanding of the past."[58] Looking to Africa for continuity, in terms of material culture and retention of other cultural forms, is not a collections project. Looking to Africa is a human rights project that seeks to carry forward a tradition of activism. For example, *The Front Line: Beyond the Civil Rights Movement* galleries have included the representation of a non-violent labor-related activist intervention in Nigeria during which, Anderson notes, "'women in the oil fields . . . chained themselves to fences.'"[59] The section which includes these galleries was initially identified as *Beyond Birmingham: Human Rights Around the World* (1994, redesigned in 2009) and is now *The Human Rights Gallery*. Anderson explains that the "goal of the gallery is not so much to inform visitors about human rights abuses, conflicts or victims as it is to highlight stories of human rights movements." From 2009–2011, for example, as part of a travel and cultural exchange program underwritten by the American Alliance of Museums, the museum engaged in a collaboration initiated by the Mandela House Museum in Soweto, South Africa. I will examine these and other collaborative/outreach programs in the next chapter.

CONTEXTS AND THEORY:
LIVING HISTORY, PROXIMITY, EMPATHY—
THE MUSEUM AS "GO-BETWEEN"

The bodily, psychic, and affective impact of trauma and its aftermath, the ways in which one trauma can recall, or reactivate, the effects of another, exceed the bounds of traditional historical archives and methodologies.—Marianne Hirsch. "The Generation of Postmemory"[60]

. . . it is precisely the function of public memory discourses to allow individuals to break out of traumatic repetitions.—Andreas Huyssen. *Present Pasts: Urban Palimpsests and the Politics of Memory*[61]

Historical trauma is specific, and not everyone is subject to it or entitled to the subject position associated with it. It is dubious to identify with the victim to the point of making oneself a surrogate victim who has a right to the victim's voice or subject position.—Dominick LaCapra. *Writing History, Writing Trauma*[62]

It is an understatement to say that trauma has no expiration date. The trauma of slavery and other abuses of human rights may be reactivated by contemporary social and political realities, and it may be reactivated in the provocations of a museum exhibition. Although the original occurrence may be generations removed from the present, the effects of a traumatic event can survive in communal and familial memory and, more broadly, in "epigenetic" memories that emerge in the human body during exposure to current environments. As Shannon Sullivan explains, traumatic events may be revived/re-experienced in contemporary hostile social and political environments that bear a resemblance to the original.[63] The visitor is not a blank slate, of course, and their reactions to the content will be affected by their proximity to the original source (in terms of collective and/or familial memory), their factual knowledge, and their concerns about social justice and ongoing human rights abuses.

When we find ourselves in proximity to slavery in a museum exhibition like those at the Charles H. Wright or the National Underground Railroad Freedom Center we confront the limitations of "*e pluribus unum*" as a unifying concept. The many do not dissolve into the one. The "I" and the "you" and the "we" (in museum labels and wall texts) become shifting signifiers that point in multiple directions and extend beyond the immediate space and time of the encounter. As philosopher Emmanuel Lévinas insists: "In proximity a subject is implicated in a way not reducible to the spatial sense." In terms of temporality, proximity is "a disturbance of rememberable time." What might this mean for museum representations—especially ones in which the visitor becomes a co-habitant of the exhibition? Again, with the help of Lévinas, we might say that "we" occupy an ethical space in which "we" recognize (as in knowing again—if seemingly for the first time) a responsibility for the other that precedes any specific event or "prior commitment."[64] How/can a museum experience revive latent memories, activate an empathic response, penetrate resistance to difficult history, and ask us to accept new versions of old, cherished assumptions?

Slavery installations like those at the Charles H. Wright and the Freedom Center encourage the visitor to *inhabit* a place rather than maintain a degree of receptive distance. To some extent the relationship between the exhibit and the visitor in these installations is staged as a confrontation. In a highly charged public and yet private space, an individual will react subjectively to their confrontation with the past, depending on their subject position and their openness to being challenged. The visitor's predispositions may result in a turning toward the source of suffering, a turning away, or in some other form of hesitation or resistance. Moreover, depending on how many generations removed we may be from the source of suffering, we may have more or less distance to travel in order to achieve proximity—and empathy.[65]

The suffocating sensory stimuli of the slave ship or the contrasting evacuation of space in the slave cabin may help to bridge the gap of time and/or the gap of subject position that inhibits a pragmatic (consequential) engagement. Alison Landsberg claims, for example, that "at an experiential site such as a movie theater or a museum [people] might be able, through an act of prosthesis, to take on memories of events through which they never lived." If they are also able to actively engage with these memories, it "might have a radical effect on both their worldview and their politics."[66] However, Elizabeth Spelman challenges us to admit that, depending on a culture's values and beliefs, slaves "may lack potential tragic standing" in the Aristotelian sense. Spelman notes that in Aristotle's thinking some individuals are "slaves by nature" and "have only a tiny dose of rationality." She suggests that such deeply held beliefs (which we may associate with the antebellum *slaveholding* mentality) may endure (which should be painful for a contemporary visitor to admit). In no uncertain terms, Spelman depicts the limits of an Aristotelian audience's ability to care: "As a minimally ratiocinated beast of burden, a slave is not someone to whom we can attach eventful actions of the sort which tragedy is to depict."[67] Orlando Patterson also observes that "Plato and Aristotle and the great Roman jurists were not wrong in recognizing the necessary correlation between their love of their own freedom and its denial to others."[68] An equally unsettling question is posed by András Sajó in *Constitutional Sentiments*: "why did compassion for suffering not achieve emancipation much earlier . . . and why were only specific sufferings singled out for human rights protection?" One of Sajó's more disturbing answers is that "the struggle to liberate slaves centered on the kinship of blacks ('a brother') and whites. The alleged dissimilarity of victims was one of the main barriers to the recognition of their rights, as empathy failed to operate in regard to culturally outlying persons."[69] Essentially, there are no guarantees of empathy and attendant action, no matter how egregious the offense and how dire the suffering.

Some visitors will need to be "unsettled" from routines of thought, feeling, and action before they can accept these hard truths. Exhibitions of slavery, forced migration and dislocation, and human rights abuses confront the viewer with examples of systemic/systematic inhumanity which cannot be localized (temporally or regionally). As Joshua Reeves points out, a confrontation with "an artifact of public memory" may be sufficiently unsettling to result in "a renewed pathos of community" and, if so, this may affect our future behavior toward others.[70] Or, it may not.

In his analysis of the Holocaust and of Truth and Reconciliation Commissions, Dominick LaCapra examines the process of "working through" traumatic events. Although he insists that we should mark a clear distinction between having suffered *versus* having come upon that suffering secondarily (after the fact), he argues that "the response of even secondary witnesses (including historians) to traumatic events must involve empathic unsettlement that should register in one's very mode of address." Moreover, the unsettlement we experience in the face of (the representation of) trauma may be the burden we cannot disown, relinquish, or transfer. It becomes a necessary part of our ethical position in proximity to the other:

> Empathic unsettlement also raises in pointed form the problem of how to address traumatic events involving victimization, including the problem of composing narratives that neither confuse one's own voice or position with the victim's nor seek facile uplift, harmonization, or closure but allow the unsettlement that they address to affect the narrative's own movement in terms of both acting out and working through.

For LaCapra, "historical trauma" is specific and arguably nontransferable. In contrast, "structural trauma" is not confined to a specific event; it is an "anxiety-producing condition of possibility related to the potential for historical traumatization." He insists that we must recognize and respect the distance between the sufferer and the secondary witness, between historical trauma—arising from an event—and structural trauma—arising from the fact that the event, or something like it, could happen again.[71] In this exchange hard truths emerge. As Jennifer Bonnell and Roger Simon note, those truths may become a "burdensome gift." An awareness of the burden then generates difficult questions: "the experience of difficulty resides in the efforts to make meaning that are constituted in the relationship between a visitor and the material presented in an exhibit, a relationship that is always specifically contextualized. Thus, when discussing difficult exhibitions, the obvious questions are: Difficult for whom? When? Where? In what way?"[72]

In looking at "contested historical narratives," Kristin Gallas and James De Wolf Perry note that "the cognitive and emotional difficulties experienced during the learning crisis are likely to be largely unconscious." One common difficulty is "cognitive dissonance"—a situation in which "a person receives new information that conflicts with a preexisting belief or opinion." This may then create a "cognitive dilemma"—in terms of making room for that information.[73] The pre-existing belief(s) which have been placed at risk (in the context of slavery-related exhibits) could involve our understanding of human nature—what we expect of ourselves and others—or our sense of national principles and practices.[74] We would then have to contend with the counterargument—for example, that human beings are capable of systematic brutality or that not all humans are treated as though they were in fact created equal.

Salamishah Tillet suggests that "sites of slavery"—and we might add sites that address other aspects of "difficult history"—can "produce discourses about how best to remember American democracy and to construct national identity." Yet we know that this productive dimension is a possibility—not a certainty. Andreas Huyssen reminds us that in times past (but not so long ago) "the discourse of history was there to guarantee the relative stability of the past in its pastness."[75] The preservation of the status quo may have relinquished some of its force and given way to an opposing presence: the latency of a past that just refuses to stay put. This is due in part to what Marianne Hirsch has termed "postmemory": a "structure of inter- and trans-generational transmission of traumatic knowledge and experience."[76] Consequential museum spaces also have a role to play through intentional acts of transmission.

However, our individual and collective readiness to accommodate new "knowledge" may fall short. If so, we may need what William James called a "go-between." As James explained in "What Pragmatism Means": "New truth is always a go-between, a smoother-over of transitions. It marries old opinion to new fact so as ever to show a minimum of jolt, a maximum of continuity." The jolt of recognition regarding the truths about slavery cannot be "smoothed over." What could establish "continuity" between those hard facts and the official story of this nation's founding principles and subsequent actions? According to James, "thoughts become true in proportion as they successfully exert their go-between function."[77] In terms of the museum representations under scrutiny here and the "new truths" they reveal, perhaps the "thoughts" best suited to that instrumental task might be those that emphasize a better future. Inevitably, while museums can function as the "go-between" and bestow "the burdensome gift" of knowledge and understanding, it is ultimately up to the visitor to accept the burden and act accordingly.

NOTES

1. Salamishah Tillet, "Introduction: Peculiar Citizenships." In *Sites of Slavery: Citizenship and Racial Democracy in the Post-Civil Rights Imagination* (Durham, NC: Duke University Press, 2012), 5. Copyright 2012, Duke University Press. All rights reserved. Republished by permission of the copyright holder, and the Publisher. www.dukeupress.edu.

2. Jennifer Bonnell and Roger I. Simon, "'Difficult' Exhibitions and Intimate Encounters," *Museum and Society* 5, no. 2 (2007): 67.

3. Michael Fried describes the characteristics of the "absorptive tradition" in painting as "a decisive hallmark of the 'real.'" He notes how "an absorptive thematics calls for effects of temporal dilation that in turn serve the ends of pictorial realism by encouraging the viewer to explore the represented scene in an unhurried manner" and

experience "the tangibleness but also the continuity of a perceptual field." Although there are distinctions between 1) the act of looking at a compelling work of visual art and 2) the immersive experience of a three-dimensional, multimedia installation, I suggest that the element of absorption may be common to both forms. This is especially relevant when the intended goal of the work is to represent a harsh reality, confront the viewer with the implications of that reality, and create conditions that lead to empathy. See Michael Fried, *Realism, Writing, Disfiguration: On Thomas Eakins and Stephen Crane* (Chicago: University of Chicago Press, 1987), 42–43, 64–65, 70.

4. Olaudah Equiano, *The Interesting Narrative of the Life of Olaudah Equiano, or Gustavas Vassa, the African, Written by Himself*, ed. Robert J. Allison (New York: Bedford/St. Martin's, 1995), 56. For other contemporary accounts of the Middle Passage based on testimony presented before the British House of Commons in the 18th century, see W. O. Blake, *The History of Slavery and the Slave Trade, Ancient and Modern . . . and the Political History of Slavery in the United States.* Compiled From Authentic Materials, 2 vols. (New York: Haskell House Publishers Ltd., 1969). This is a reprint of the original 1858 edition.

5. As Smallwood explains, before 1750 few ships were built for the express purpose of transporting slaves; she describes the dimensions and design of the ships, which were adapted to "accommodate human cargo." Smallwood's goal is to bring the enslaved to life "as subjects in American social history" and she does so through the use of "two interrelated but distinct bodies of archival material." One is quantitative—cargo manifests, ledgers, invoice books—and the other is qualitative—the "less visible transcript" that can be found in stories, letters, and so on. She concludes her text with an account—now available in the Bodleian Library at Oxford—of a slave named 'Sibell, as told to and transcribed in Barbados in 1799 by John Ford, probably an English traveler: "'Me no know nobody in de House, but ven me go in de Ship me find my country woman Mimbo, my Country man Dublin . . . , My Country woman Sally, and some more, but dey sell dem all about and me no savvy where now.'" ('Sibell as told to John Ford, Barbados, 1799). She compares 'Sibell's "fractured shape" to Equiano's formalized account: 'Sibell's narrative "suggests that the slave ship charted no course of narrative continuity between the African past and American present. . . . The saltwater in African memory . . . was perhaps the antithesis of a 'middle' passage, with all that phrase implies about a smooth, linear progression leading to a known end." Stephanie. E. Smallwood, *Saltwater Slavery: A Middle Passage from Africa to American Diaspora* (Harvard University Press, 2007), 204, 69, 3–5, and 202–207.

6. Marcus Rediker, *The Slave Ship: A Human History* (New York: Viking Press, 2007), 4.

7. See Charles Johnson, "The End of the Black American Narrative," *American Scholar* 77.3 (Summer 2008).

8. For an understanding of trauma in relation to personal, collective, and national history, see Cathy Caruth's introduction to part II of *Trauma: Explorations in Memory*, ed. Cathy Caruth (Baltimore: Johns Hopkins University Press, 1995), 151–57.

9. Fath Davis Ruffins, "Revisiting the Old Plantation: Reparations, Reconciliation, and Museumizing American Slavery," in Ivan Karp et al., eds., *Museum Frictions:*

Public Cultures/Global Transformations (Durham: Duke University Press, 2006), 401. Also see Alison Landsberg, who notes that the desire to forget is not limited to whites. She finds that many blacks have chosen instead "to look to Africa for a heritage of which they could be proud. But in the last several decades, both literary and mass cultural texts, like the Detroit museum, have begun the challenging project of remembering the experience of slavery." *Prosthetic Memory: The Transformation of American Remembrance in the Age of Mass Culture* (New York: Columbia University Press, 2004), 82.

10. Lonnie Bunch, "Embracing Ambiguity: The Challenge of Interpreting African American History in Museums," *Museums and Social Issues* 2, no. 1 (Spring 2007): 48, 52, 53.

11. See David Gelles, "Smithsonian's Leader Says 'Museums Have a Social Justice Role to Play,'" *New York Times*, July 2, 2020, BU 4. Also see Lonnie Bunch, *Call the Lost Dream Back: Essays on History, Race and Museums* (Washington, DC: American Alliance of Museums Press, 2010).

12. See www.thewright.org/exhibitions/and-still-we-rise.

13. Smallwood emphasizes that shackles "were an important element in the arsenal of tools used to physically disable captives" on slave ships; they were thus in high demand but were often in very short supply. As she notes: "A variety of implements served different aspects of the task: 'short irons' binding captives' wrists ensured that slaves could neither raise a hand to strike their tormentors nor seize a weapon, open a door, or scale a wall without great difficulty; 'long irons' around the ankles likewise held captives fast," *Saltwater Slavery*, 39–40.

14. In a review of the original installation, Michele Mitchell suggested that the 2,500 names "prod visitors to contemplate the extent of the slave trade." Michele Mitchell, "Of the People," *The Public Historian* 23, no. 2 (Spring 2001): 124–26.

15. Marcus Rediker, *The Slave Ship*, 9, 309.

16. Marcus Wood offers a detailed history and analysis of the creation, reception, and transformation of the original slave ship installation, which was designed to be seen from above and at a distance. In that original exhibit, rather than being surrounded or enveloped by the scene, the visitor viewed the undifferentiated (gray) bodies of the slaves—actually life-casts of Detroit children and adolescents—at a remove. As Wood explains: "Placed in the slave ship as an abject uniform group of grey human bodies for the viewer to gaze down upon, they seemed suspended in some sort of curatorial limbo." When the installation was redesigned the figures were repainted—rendering them much more life-like (and not merely life-size)—and "were lovingly taken up and reintegrated into the series of dramatic tableaux" that constitute the overall presentation. See Marcus Wood, *Black Milk: Imagining Slavery in the Visual Culture of Brazil and America* (Oxford: Oxford University Press, 2013), 350, 355.

17. Smallwood notes that many distinct languages were spoken on board slave ships, but that people were able to communicate in spite of "ethnic and linguistic diversity" (118). Sterling Stuckey emphasizes that, "during the process of their becoming a single people, Yorubas, Akans, Ibos, Angolans, and others were present on slave ships to America and experienced a common horror—unearthly moans

and piercing shrieks, the smell of filth and the stench of death, all during the violent rhythms and quiet coursings of ships at sea." However, Stuckey also explains that the ships "were the first real incubators of slave unity across cultural lines, cruelly revealing irreducible links from one ethnic group to the other, fostering resistance thousands of miles before the shores of the new land appeared on the horizon—before there was a mention of natural rights in North America." See Sterling Stuckey, *Slave Culture: Nationalist Theory and the Foundations of Black America* (New York: Oxford University Press, 1987), 3. On resistance and rebellion, see Eric Robert Taylor's *If We Must Die: Shipboard Insurrections in the Era of the Atlantic Slave Trade* (Baton Rouge: Louisiana State University Press, 2003) which includes an extensive bibliography of primary sources.

18. In a review of the original version, Dora Apel noted that visitors "cross a steel bridge" and "stand in a superior position" (looking down at the figures); she concluded that "viewers are constructed as black" and that, from their vantage point (looking down at the slave ship) they have "transcended their own history." Dora Apel, "Images of Black History," *Dissent* 48, no. 3 (Summer 2001): 92.

19. For eyewitness accounts of the horrors of the Middle Passage, some of which were read into the records of the British House of Commons in 1790 and 1791, see volume II, chapter X of W. O. Blake's *The History of Slavery and the Slave Trade. Ancient and Modern. . . . and the Political History of Slavery in the United States*, 2 vols. 1858 (Reprint, New York: Haskell House Publishers, 1969). To underscore their veracity, Blake often emphasizes the fact that these accounts of extreme suffering and extreme brutality are "allowed by all the witnesses."

20. Critical assessments of the Charles H. Wright's initial exhibition—then titled *Of the People*—found it lacking in several key areas but laudable in others. Apel criticized the museum for not addressing race as a "social construction" and noted that, rather than probing the issue of race, the narrative focus is "ultimately about class." See Apel 91, 95. Two reviews published in the same issue of *American Quarterly* addressed similar shortcomings. Christopher Clarke-Hazlett found that the "links between slavery and racism are never clearly established or explored" and that there seems to be an "inability or unwillingness to place racism in some sort of historical content." However, he praised the use of new and engaging exhibition trends, the integration of recent academic scholarship, the "confident" and "clearly African American voice," and the fact that the voice is not intended to "narrow or exclude any potential audiences" (430). He found that the (original) slave ship, an example of "powerful theater," finally "succeeds more as theater than history" (426) and noted that the exhibition overall "frequently chooses celebration over critical inquiry" (428). See Christopher Clarke-Hazlitt, "Review: Of the People" (*American Quarterly* 51.2. June 1999): 426, 428, 430. Charles Banner-Haley also identifies a need for a "serious conversation on race" but finds that the museum "goes a long way toward providing the necessary materials and documentation for the beginning of that conversation." He finds that the main theme of the museum is the Middle Passage, in the larger sense of "the movement of Africans from their homelands to the strange new world that they labored in, adapted to and helped to build." Like Clarke-Hazlitt and Apel, he sees "unused opportunities and unfortunate slants" that focus on "contribution,

struggle, and the eventual gaining of freedom" at the expense of an emphasis on victimization, "racialized slavery," radical resistance, and "the second Middle Passage" of racism. See Charles Banner-Haley, "The Necessity of Remembrance: A Review of the Museum of African American History" (*American Quarterly* 51.2. June 1999): 421–24. Michele Mitchell's 2001 review also finds that the exhibit station focused on "Urban Struggle, Urban Splendor" actually "glosses over Detroit's race riots" (26).

21. John Meadows, a member of the Freedom Center's design team, describes the artifact and the challenge of incorporating it in "From Confinement to Liberty: The National Underground Railroad Freedom Center by Blackburn Architects with BOORA Architects," *ArchNewsNow*.com, November 17, 2006.

22. This term was used by journalist S. E. Spicer as he recounted an interview with Nancy Bell of Danville, Kentucky in 1923. Bell, born in 1835, was an emancipated slave who had been sent to Liberia by her former master and then returned to the United States at the start of the Civil War. Spicer refers to the Underground Railroad as that "mysterious road which began in fear and trembling and ended where the dream of the bondsman became true—Aunt Nancy knew it minutely and the names of men who have been the makers of history were connected with its phantom-like workings." These and other documents can be found in John W. Blassingame's invaluable collection *Slave Testimony: Two Centuries of Letters, Speeches, Interviews, and Autobiographies* (Baton Rouge: Louisiana State University Press, 1977), 275–76, 514–15, 518, 533, 555–59.

23. Ruffins laments the lack of objects to support these slavery-focused themes; however, she finds reason for optimism given the contributions of "historical and marine archaeology" in changing "the number and range of possible objects studied. Fath Davis Ruffins, "Revisiting the Old Plantation: Reparations, Reconciliation, and Museumizing American Slavery" in Ivan Karp et al., eds., *Museum Frictions: Public Cultures/Global Transformations*, 413.

24. Leslie Bedford remembers that—when she encountered the slave pen—her guide pointed out "the remains of a metal loop to which slaves would have been chained" and that the "small artifact—that concrete detail" afforded "whatever resonance the installation possesses." As she also explains in a note: "There is something about leaving an object or site in its original state that enhances its dramatic power. See Leslie Bedford, *The Art of Museum Exhibitions: How Story and Imagination Create Aesthetic Experiences* (Walnut Creek, CA: Left Coast Press, 2014), 100 and n.9 page 145.

25. For an overview of his contributions, see the announcement by the Freedom Center of Carl Westmoreland's death in March 2022: https://freedomcenter .org/voice/press_release/freedom-center-mourns-the-loss-of-renowned-historian-carl -westmoreland/.

26. See the Freedom Center's excellent online exhibit "A Slave Pen Journey" for a sense of this environment: https://artsandculture.google.com/story/wAVxA -E2xxAA8A.

27. Lewis Garrard Clarke, *Narrative of the Sufferings of Lewis Clarke, during a Captivity of More Than Twenty-Five Years, among the Algerines of Kentucky, One of*

the So Called Christian States of North America. Dictated By Himself (Boston: David H. Ela, Printer, 1845), 73.

28. Walter Johnson, *Soul by Soul: Life inside the Antebellum Slave* Market (Cambridge: Harvard University Press, 1999), 48, 31. William Still served for fourteen years on the Underground Railroad/ Philadelphia Vigilance Committee and later published a volume of "numerous narratives" which are based on facts "coming within his personal knowledge" and "records of his own preserving." *The Underground Rail Road. A Record of Facts, Authentic Narratives, Letters, &c. . . . as Narrated by Themselves and Others, or Witnessed by the Author* . . . (Philadelphia: Porter and Coates, 1872. Reprint. New York: Arno Press, 1968), 4–6.

29. Jamie Glavic with Dion Brown, "National Underground Railroad Freedom Center," in *Mission Matters: Relevance and Museums in the 21st Century,* by Gail Anderson (Lanham, MD: Rowman & Littlefield, 2019), 85–87.

30. *Open Your Mind: Understanding Implicit Bias.* National Underground Railroad Freedom Center. https://freedomcenter.org/visit/permanent-exhibits/open-your-mind -understanding-implicit-bias/#:~:text=The%20Open%20Your%20Mind%20learning ,realm%20of%20implicit%20bias%20research.

31. In terms of how to design exhibitions, they suggest that individual stories "must be set in a proper context starting with the individuals, spiraling out to include the site, the neighboring community, the state, the region, and the country." Kristin L. Gallas and James DeWolf Perry, eds, *Interpreting Slavery at Museums and Historic Sites* (Lanham: Rowman & Littlefield, 2015), xv, 1–2, 5.

32. The announcement for the exhibition is available at: www.lewismuseum.org/ event/bodies-of-information-understanding-slavery-through-the-stearns-collection/.

33. Marcus Wood presents a probing analysis of the R. F. Lewis Museum's use of this image of open waters and addresses the museum's failure to represent other atrocities. Wood includes excerpts from an interview with the museum's executive director, David Terry, in which Terry explains their intention—to leave each visitor free to interpret the image. Wood contrasts what he characterizes as the Lewis's "unrelenting positivism" with more militant and direct representations at The Great Blacks in Wax Museum. See Marcus Wood, "Slavery, Memory, and Museum Display in Baltimore: The Great Blacks in Wax and the Reginald F. Lewis," *Curator* 51, no. 1 (2009): 157. Wood returns to and extends this comparative analysis in *Black Milk,* where he finds that, in addition to its representation of the slave ship, the "Great Blacks in Wax provides many other instances of the bold re-appropriation of subjects that other museums either evade altogether or present as carefully and safely closed down areas of memory" (*Black Milk,* 383).

34. Amina Dickerson notes that the DuSable's intention was "to interpret African history" as well as African American history and culture. However, the "identification with an African ancestry, while certainly not new to scholars and artists, was not as widely embraced by the general public at the time [the early 1960s] and represented an expanded vision to a stated mission for black historic preservation efforts of the era." Amina Jill Dickerson, *The History and Development of African American Museums* (MA thesis, American University, 1988), 98–99.

35. See www.dusablemuseum.org/exhibition/equiano-stories/.

36. For an extensive look at the exhibition, including an excellent video narrated by curators and scholars see: caamuseum.org/exhibitions/2018/california-bound-slavery-on-the-new-frontier-18481865.

37. As Margot Minardi notes, "The memory of slavery, and the continuing presence of people who were reminders of that past, simply didn't suit a region that, due to its influential role in the American Revolution, was touting itself as the 'Birthplace of American Liberty.'" Yet "if enslaved and formerly enslaved New Englanders were simply to be forgotten, why did anyone bother to keep" objects that represented those lives and facts?" See "Making Slavery Visible (Again): The Nineteenth-Century Roots of a Revisionist Recovery in New England," in *Politics of Memory: Making Slavery Visible in the Public Sphere*, ed. Ana Lucia Araujo (New York: Routledge, 2012), 92–93.

38. A snapshot of the *Slave Narratives* project is still available on the web: archive.ideum.com/creative-services/moad-slave-narratives/.

39. Robin D. G. Kelley, "How the West Was One: The African Diaspora and the Re-Mapping of U.S. History," in *Rethinking American History in a Global Age*, ed. Thomas Bender (Berkeley: U of California Press, 2002), 139.

40. Ruth B. Phillips, "Where Is 'Africa'? Re-Viewing Art and Artifact in the Age of Globalization," *American Anthropologist* 104, no .3 (September 2002): 944. Phillips is reviewing three exhibitions, two in London and one at the Smithsonian's National Museum of Natural History. These are "permanent reinstallations of well-known African collections" in large mainstream museums that (in their previous incarnations) had treated Africa as if it were one eternal, undeveloped, and monologic continent. The original installations "were tied to primitivism and cultural evolutionism"; the reinstallations, in her view, achieve varied success in overcoming these denigrating "representational conventions."

41. Stuart Hall, "Cultural Identity and Diaspora," in *Theorizing Diaspora: A Reader*, ed. Jana Evans Braziel and Anita Mannur (Malden, MA: Blackwell, 2003), 235, 242.

42. Kwame Anthony Appiah, *In My Father's House: Africa in the Philosophy of Culture* (New York: Oxford University Press, 1992), 177.

43. Elizabeth Rauh Bethel, *The Roots of African American Identity: Memory and History in Free Antebellum Communities* (New York: St. Martin's Press, 1997), 82.

44. The stool is a tie-in to an object owned by Chicago mayor Harold Washington, the central character in a tableau vivant in a separate exhibit nearby.

45. Andrea Burns, "When 'Civil Rights Are Not Enough': The Creation and Work of the International Afro American Museum of Detroit" in *Remembering Africa and Its Diasporas: Memory, Public History and Representations of the Past*, eds. Audra A. Diptee and David V. Trotman (Trenton, NJ: Africa World Press, 2012), 200.

46. *Coloring America: Selections from the California African American Museum's Permanent History Collection* (10/31/12–3/24/13) exhibition wall text.

47. A virtual tour is available at: caamuseum.org/exhibitions/2012/coloring-america.

48. Robyn Autry, "The Politics of Race, Space, and Memory at San Francisco's Museum of the African Diaspora" in *Remembering Africa*, ed. Diptee and Trotman, 177–78, 186–87, 191. In addition to describing the museum's architecture, its

performative façade, and its interior and exterior exhibition spaces, Autry analyzes the creation of MoAD as an aspect of the city's "controversial" urban renewal efforts; this involved the dispersal of black residents from a neighborhood south of Market Street that has become the Yerba Buena arts district, home of the San Francisco Museum of Modern Art and other cultural institutions, including MoAD.

49. Freelon Group, Museum of the African Diaspora, www.architectmagazine.com /project-gallery/museum-of-the-african-diaspora-2712.

50. Reviewing the museum shortly after its opening, Edward Rothstein complained that the mural can "only be seen fully from outside the building at a distance (and is marred by window glare)." He also found that the minimal exhibition space (about 3,000 square feet) and lack of a permanent collection resulted in "too little material for its subject and too much ground to cover." See "Anecdotal Evidence of Homesick Mankind," *New York Times*, July 20, 2006, E1. Another reading of the same facts might underscore the use of ambiguity as a provocation for further thought about the fracturing effects of the diaspora, as well as the difficulty of collecting objects that speak of endurance and change and presence. Anna M. Dempsey notes that the "museum's exterior functions as a mirror" which "frames the public sphere and inserts the reflected face of the marginalized Other onto the faces of those who view it." Anna M. Dempsey, "150 Years Later: Remembering Africa in the Museum" in *Remembering Africa and Its Diasporas,* ed. Diptree and Trotman, 237. An introduction to the related site-specific installation by Sam Vernon (2022) can be accessed at: www.moadsf.org/exhibitions/impasse-of-desires.

51. Several years ago Museum of the African Diaspora's website offered a more detailed/concrete description of how those themes are developed; the details remain valuable in understanding the thematic range of Museum of the African Diaspora's exhibitions, which include: "our shared African ancestry"; the "African roots of contemporary social, artistic and cultural forms of expression and practices that define the modern Diaspora"; "the migrations of Africans to the New World via the Transatlantic Slave Trade, and the contemporary African Diaspora that has happened since"; the "modern forms of cultural expressions that emerged from the African Slave trade, and the continuing adaptation of African traditions, beliefs, and practices"; and "how people of African descent have forged new identities, defined their place, and made their mark on new societies and communities." www.moadsf.org/about-us/our -mission. Accessed 12/28/18.

52. For a summary of selected positions on the possibility and meaning of "going home" to Africa, see: Isidore Okpewho's Introduction to *The New African Diaspora*, eds. Isidore Okpewho and Nkiru Nzegwu (Bloomington: Indiana University Press, 2009). Also see "Nation, Migration, Globalization: Points of Contention in Diaspora Studies," the introduction by editors Jana Evans Braziel and Anita Mannur to *Theorizing Diaspora: A Reader* (Malden, MA: Blackwell, 2003).

53. Robyn Autry, "The Political Economy of Memory: The Challenge of Representing National Conflict at 'Identity-Driven' Museums," *Theory and Society* 42 (2013): 57, 64.

54. Bethel, 78, 82, 130.

55. See Kelley, 136. In a subchapter of "How the West Was One" titled "The Question of Africa" Kelley offers a detailed overview of developments in the multi-disciplinary scholarship on the diaspora. Also see Tiffany Ruby Patterson and Robin D. G. Kelley, "Unfinished Migrations: Reflections on the African Diaspora and the Making of the Modern World," *African Studies Review* 43, no. 1 (April 2000). This was a special issue of the journal devoted to the diaspora.

56. See *Museums and Sites of Persuasion: Politics, Memory and Human Rights,* eds. Joyce Apsel and Amy Sodaro (London: Routledge, 2020) for evidence of these sites as a global phenomenon. See Joyce Apsel's "'Inspiration Lives Here': Struggle, Martyrdom, and Redemption in Atlanta's National Center for Civil and Human Rights" in this volume (91–115) for a close reading of exhibition strategies at the Atlanta Center.

57. The exhibition, which also traveled to NYU's Skirball Cultural Center (2011–2012) and the Illinois Holocaust Museum and Education Center (2016–2017), was inspired by the book *Half the Sky: Turning Oppression into Opportunity for Women Worldwide* by Nicholas D. Kristof and Sheryl WuDunn (New York: Knopf, 2010).

58. Laura Caldwell Anderson, "Walk with Me," 266–67.

59. Anderson was quoted by Michael Huebner, "Birmingham Civil Rights Institute's Mission of Diplomacy, Education and Human Rights Having a Global Impact," *AL.com* blog.al.com/entertainment_impact/Print.html?entry=2013/01/brimingham_civil_right. . . . 1/31/2013.

60. Marianne Hirsch, "The Generation of Postmemory," *Poetics Today* 29, no. 1 (Spring 2008): 104. Copyright 2008, Porter Institute for Poetics and Semiotics. All rights reserved. Republished by permission of the copyright holder, and the Publisher. www.dukeupress.edu.

61. Andreas Huyssen, *Present Pasts: Urban Palimpsests and the Politics of Memory* (Stanford University Press, 2003), 9. Used with Permission of Stanford University Press, ©2003, permission conveyed through Copyright Clearance Center, Inc.

62. Dominick La Capra, *Writing History, Writing Trauma* (Baltimore: Johns Hopkins, University Press: 2001), 78. © 2000 Johns Hopkins University Press. Reprinted with permission of the Johns Hopkins University Press.

63. See Shannon Sullivan, "Racist Disparities in Health Epigenetics and the Transgenerational Effects of White Racism," *Critical Philosophy of Race* 1, no. 2 (2013):190, 191, 210. Sullivan examines the "transgenerational biological impact of social forces" and offers evidence that "people of color can biologically inherit the deleterious effects of white racism." She suggests in fact that: "Epigenetics . . . gives striking new meaning to William Faulkner's . . . famous comment that 'the past isn't dead. It isn't even past.'" Alison Landsberg invokes Faulkner's *Absalom, Absalom!* as an illustration of both "transgenerational memory," in which one generation transmits memories to another, and intragenerational memory," in which memories are "constructed or reconstructed by peers." See *Prosthetic Memory*, 84. Ruffins finds that: "How contemporary African Americans may be experiencing psychic losses associated with this history has yet to be fully studied in the psychological literature," "Revisiting the Old Plantation," 419.

64. Emmanuel Lévinas, *Otherwise Than Being, or, Beyond Essence*, trans. Alphonso Lingis (Pittsburgh: Duquesne University Press, 1998), 81–82, 89, 116.

65. Ruffins argues that "the concept of the slave trade and slavery as genocide" is key "for most African Americans" and "is an article of faith, a key element of identity as true as any other clear historical fact." However, "For Americans not from those states where the 'Cause' was lost, and especially for that 70 percent of living white Americans who are descendants of turn-of-the-century immigrants from Europe, slavery is not a personal legacy." See "Culture Wars Won and Lost, Part II: The National African-American Museum Project," 85, 87.

66. Landsberg, *Prosthetic Memory*, 2, 83.

67. Elizabeth V. Spelman, *Fruits of Sorrow: Framing Our Attention to Suffering* (Boston: Beacon Press, 1997); see chapter 2, "Slavery and Tragedy," 43–47. Spelman uses Harriet Jacobs's *Incidents in the Life of a Slave Girl* to illustrate how hard that author needed to work to cultivate her audience's compassion. For example, Spelman observes that "Jacobs's reliance on a plea for the compassion of some [northern white] women occurs in the context of her fully expecting the cruel ministrations and daily humiliations of others."

68. Orlando Patterson, *Slavery and Social Death*, viii–ix, 5. As Patterson explains: "Not only was the slave denied all claims on, and obligations to, his parents and living blood relations but, by extension, all such claims and obligations on his more remote ancestors and . . . his descendants. He was . . . a genealogical isolate." He notes that slaves "were not allowed freely to integrate the experience of their ancestors into their lives . . . or to anchor the living present in any conscious community of memory." However: "That they reached back for the past, as they reached out for the related living, there can be no doubt . . . doing so meant struggling with and penetrating the iron curtain of the master, his community, his laws, his policemen or patrollers, and his heritage."

69. András Sajó, *Constitutional Sentiments* (New Haven: Yale University Press, 2011), 151, 156.

70. Joshua Reeves, "Suspended Identification: *Atopos* and the Work of Public Memory," *Philosophy and Rhetoric* 46, no. 3 (2013): 307.

71. Dominick LaCapra, *Writing History, Writing Trauma*, 46–48, 78–79.

72. Bonnell and Simon investigate dimensions of the "intimate encounter" in which "one inhabits a world but does not settle it." At such times "the museum visitor is confronted by the 'burdensome' gift of other people's histories of violence and suffering"; this may take them "beyond the idealized responses of empathy, identification, and solidarity." "Intimacy in the exhibit hall then references a moment when one becomes undone, absorbed in the singularity of another's existence. It is that moment in which words fail and meaning is unresolved, yet one still faces an unabated demand to acknowledge the life which one now encounters." Jennifer Bonnell and Roger Simon, "'Difficult' Exhibitions and Intimate Encounters," *Museum and Society* 5, no. 2 (July 2007): 67, 70, 77–78, 81.

73. Kristin L. Gallas and James DeWolf Perry, "Comprehensive Content and Contested Historical Narratives" in *Interpreting Slavery at Museums and Historic Sites*, eds. Gallas and Perry, 11–12.

74. This was found to be the case in the United Kingdom when, in 2007, many museums mounted exhibitions to commemorate the bicentennial of the Act of Parliament that ended British involvement in the transatlantic slave trade. As Geoffrey Cubitt, Laurajane Smith, and Ross Wilson explain, visitors revealed "anxious and ambiguous" attitudes "reflecting uncertainties . . . about the social role of museums in contemporary society" and the relationship between the work of museums and "established narratives about national identity." "Introduction: Anxiety and Ambiguity in the Representation of Dissonant History," in *Representing Enslavement and Abolition in Museums: Ambiguous Engagements*, Laurajane Smith, Geoff Cubitt, Kalliopi Fouseki, Ross Wilson, eds., (New York: Routledge, 2011), 1. In another essay in this volume Geoffrey Cubitt notes that each visitor is pre-disposed to perceive the exhibition content based on "reports or images or orally transmitted memories that have a temporal history of their own." He finds that: "In the case of transatlantic slavery, the relationship of the viewer is to violence and suffering in previous centuries, to which people today may feel an important connection, but to which they are cognitively linked by less immediate chains of communication." See Geoff Cubitt, "Atrocity Materials and the Representation of Transatlantic Slavery," in *Representing Enslavement and Abolition in Museums*, 230.

75. Huyssen, *Present Past*, 1.

76. Marianne Hirsch uses the term "postmemory" to identify "a structure of inter-and trans-generational transmission of traumatic knowledge and experience" that takes place "at a generational remove." See "The Generation of Postmemory," 106.

77. William James, "What Pragmatism Means," in *Pragmatism* (Cambridge, MA: Harvard University Press, 1975), 35–37.

Chapter Five

Publics

The new museum . . . does not build on an educational superstition. It examines its community's life first, and then straightaway bends its energies to supplying some of the material which that community needs, and to making that material's presence widely known, and to presenting it in such a way as to secure for it the maximum of use and the maximum of efficiency in that use.—John Cotton Dana. *The New Museum* (1917)[1]

. . . I want to explore what museums seeking to take up more activist positions on human rights issues might learn from culturally-specific museums that have very often been at the forefront of practice in this arena.—Dina A. Bailey. "The Activist Spectrum in United States Museums" (2019)[2]

The innovative museum maker John Cotton Dana insisted early in the twentieth century that a museum's mission and relevance should derive from the needs of the community it served. This understanding of the relationship between the institution and its publics has always been an important element of African American museums, and it has only become more pronounced in the first two decades of the twenty-first century.[3] The relationships are complex and varied, and the development of public programs depends on each museum's resources and the perceived needs of its constituents. Moreover, as Jennifer Barrett explains in *Museums and the Public Sphere*: "The term 'public' is slippery and evasive" and the "notion and associated practices" related to the concept clearly "change over time and space."[4] Each of the museums considered here fulfills the mission-related dimensions of public programming in a variety of ways, including lectures and symposia to supplement exhibitions. It may also undertake collection and preservation initiatives that aim to expand its holdings by attracting donors while also educating the public about conservation and preservation methods for the protection of personal collections. "Rapid Response" exhibitions and related collecting

145

initiatives may also be driven by contemporary events that demand immediate attention.[5]

Poetry readings, open mic performances, film series, book talks, holiday celebrations and commemorations, self-help and self-care workshops, local and regional heritage tours, and efforts to showcase and support local artists also comprise an important part of public programming. These programs can play a key role in extending a museum's borders and furthering its mission. They help to establish individual and communal relationships between the museum and its current constituencies; they attract new visitors; and they offer immediate and long-term practical benefits in the form of a multifaceted economic, political, and cultural education. Public programming may also include debates, community conversations, and other topic-driven events. The effort to document the building and/or rebuilding of culture and community through exhibitions is amplified through public programming, including symposia that supplement and amplify activist-oriented exhibitions. Activism has also begun to occupy the foreground of public programs and has arguably emerged as a defining, rather than an ancillary element. The study of how museums address civic life and human rights entails attention to town hall meetings and other museum-hosted conversations, as well as practical hands-on workshops that address education, family, self-care, inequality and socio-political injustices.

In this second decade of the twenty-first century, events have occurred, many of which involve violent and often fatal confrontations between police officers and black males, that highlight what has long been a chronic state of emergency stemming from systemic racism. These events have led to explicitly action-oriented rather than conventional educational or curatorial museum activities. I want to read the names of some of the victims into the record here and take up the details, including museum-based responses, later in this chapter. Looking back only as far as 2014, the deaths of Michael Brown in Ferguson, Missouri; Tamir Rice in Cleveland, Ohio; and Eric Garner in Staten Island, New York, enter the record. In 2015 the death of Freddie Gray in Baltimore, Maryland, must be added and in 2016, the deaths of Keith L. Scott in Charlotte, North Carolina, and Philando Castile in Falcon Heights, Minnesota. Incidents involving a wider spectrum of issues have included a "Unite the Right" rally in Charlottesville, Virginia in 2017 leading to the death of Heather Heyer, a white counterdemonstrator killed by a Neo-Nazi sympathizer as he drove his vehicle into the crowd. The practice of separating families at the US border with Mexico, which accelerated in 2018, announced another state of emergency that led to museum-based activism. These and other similar events—and museum-based responses—have shown that the role of the African American museum as an institution that reaches out to its publics has clearly expanded. Moreover, we see a reciprocal move on the part of the public as constituents take the lead and reach out to museums for support.

On May 25, 2020, George Floyd died on a street in Minneapolis, pinned to the ground by a white police officer who held his knee on Mr. Floyd's neck for what was initially reported to be eight minutes and forty-six seconds but was later found to be nine minutes and twenty-five seconds. A bystander's video offered incontrovertible evidence of the casual brutality with which four officers disregarded George Floyd's desperate cry: "I can't breathe."[6] The extended public outcry that followed led to protest marches and other non-violent actions across the United States and around the globe—united by the rallying cry that "Black Lives Matter" and by a gradual universal awakening to the scope of the problem of systemic racism. It would be a mistake to declare this eruption of conscience and action a culmination, since new evidence appears daily. However, this is a unique historical moment,[7] and these developments have exerted their influence on the work of museums and thus on the shape of this book.

COLLECTION, PRESERVATION, EXHIBITION, AND ACTION: A NEW MANDATE FOR MUSEUMS?

Whether the subject matter of an exhibition reaches back to the past for its specific content or draws upon contemporary events, the borders between the museum and the external world are proving more permeable. Moreover, the relationships between visitors and institutions are proving more dynamic and reciprocal. One recent influence on the museum/visitor relationship, and more specifically on public programming, stems from pressures felt *first* outside the museum. These pressures, exerted by events themselves and those most deeply affected by them, constitute states of emergency.

This condition is not new for African American museums. As we have seen, the corrective dimensions of the settlement, political, and cultural achievement themes are inherently activist in nature as they seek to move visitors to new ways of thinking (back) and being (now) in the world.[8] Similarly, stark confrontations with the slavery theme bring history to bear on the visitor's comprehension of the past. Beyond the exhibition platform itself, public engagement has always been present in the missions of African American museums, in their founding goals, and in their record of active involvement with communities.

Public programming has consistently included a focus on education and an awareness of civic and social responsibilities, which may entail activism beyond the museum's walls. Several of the exhibitions discussed in previous chapters—including *Women Hold Up Half the Sky* (National Underground

Railroad Freedom Center), *The Struggle Continues* (Birmingham Civil Rights Institute), *Kin Killin Kin [KKK]* (Reginald F. Lewis Museum), and *Welcome to Brookhill* (Harvey B. Gantt Center)—explicitly called for activism in the visitor's own time and place. *Philadelphia Conversations* (African American Museum in Philadelphia) and other permanent exhibitions that document the settlement theme and memorialize historically significant leaders and movements also explicitly or implicitly offer models for activism. Public programs that have been created in conjunction with activist-oriented exhibitions may engage directly with the exhibition's elements through docent-led and curator-led gallery talks, or they may amplify the exhibition's content through lectures and other events held outside the galleries. Additional historical background and contexts are frequently introduced in these formal presentations and thus add to the explanatory material provided by exhibition wall texts and object labels. Symposia, including day-long and longer gatherings of experts, may further extend an exhibition's reach, and town hall meetings may be organized and/or hosted by the museum to address exhibition-related subjects of often urgent importance to local communities.

Many activist-themed exhibitions look back at important historical events and rely on object-based material culture in their collections, but a significant number draw upon the visual arts. Although some visitors might not immediately associate fine art with activist goals, as I have noted in chapter 3, art exhibitions can make a strong case for that aspect of the work. As poet and philosopher Fred Moten reminds us, "to be interested in art is to be concerned with the constant and irruptive aspiration beyond the possible and the impossible."[9] Many exhibitions of African American art provide proof of that aspiration. The "irruptive" and "generative" instinct that Moten identifies in the arts in general (and jazz in particular)—the "capacity to break grammar," disrupt hierarchies, and combat exclusion—is often revealed in exhibitions and related symposia devoted to the visual arts.

For example, a *Black Radical Women Symposium* at the California African American Museum in 2017 marked the final day of *We Wanted a Revolution: Black Radical Women, 1965–1985*. The exhibition, organized by the Brooklyn Museum, focused on many of the women artists who had been virtually excluded from the (predominantly white male) art establishment and were also marginalized by the developing black (male-dominated) art movements of the period. *We Wanted a Revolution* began at the Brooklyn Museum (April–September 2017), then traveled to the California African American Museum (October 2017– January 2018), to the Albright-Knox Art Gallery in Buffalo, New York (February–May 2018), and finally to the Institute of Contemporary Art in Boston (June–September 2018).[10] The related symposium included conversations with several well-established artists represented in the exhibition as well as representatives of a new generation of local artists. It also included a performance piece titled "Women's Work" (originally performed in Paris in 2006 by Maren Hassinger, whose work was featured in the exhibition), and a "Radical Women Workshop" during which exhibiting artists participated in breakout sessions with emerging local artists.[11]

An annual series of daylong "ENGAGE" Symposia at the Museum of the African Diaspora in San Francisco is another key example. The symposium topic for 2022, *Transcending Boundaries in Contemporary African Art*, was inspired by temporary exhibitions featuring the work of Amoako Boafo and Billie Zangewa. One of the symposium panels addressed "Decolonizing Aesthetics in Contemporary African Art." The introductory statement (provided on the museum website and still available there) recalls issues I have noted in previous chapters that involve continuity, originality, and individual identity:

> One cannot discuss contemporary African aesthetics without addressing the impact of colonialism, de-colonialism and post-colonialism. Until very recently, the western world held tight expectations for artists from Africa and the African diaspora to produce work falling into narrow categories of aesthetics. Often artworks produced by Africans were expected to maintain close ties to traditional arts and cultural practices. As collectors, galleries, and scholars have embraced a wider range of aesthetic production from contemporary African artists, the variety of art work being shown is expanding exponentially. This panel will examine the changing aesthetics in contemporary African art and the promise of an African canon which is divorced from Eurocentric expectations.[12]

The *ENGAGE* series has also included *Picturing Blackness* (2020), inspired by the temporary exhibition *Black Is Beautiful: The Photography of Kwame Brathwaite* (December 2019–March 2020), and *Black Refractions* (2019), inspired by the exhibition *Black Refractions: Selections from the Studio Museum in Harlem* (January–April 2019). These events (held on site before the COVID-19 pandemic) were also live-streamed on the museum's YouTube channel.[13] The *Picturing Blackness* symposium included conversations with "scholars, artists, curators, and art writers" who addressed "the ways in which our contemporary understanding of Blackness has been informed by photographers since the dawn of photography in the 1890s through the present." The *Black Refractions* symposium included conversations between newly emerging/contemporary artists and well-established artists who were represented in the *Black Refractions* exhibition.

In a broader effort to integrate exhibitions and public programming, the Harvey B. Gantt Center announced that *Revealed: Where Art Meets Activism* would be their "season-long theme" for 2018–2019. In an email to the museum's LISTSERV, president and CEO David R. Taylor described a combined focus for exhibitions and programming and noted that these efforts "will inspire you to think more about how we live, how we learn, and how we relate to each other in our daily lives."[14] The Gantt's season began with a free community opening during which visitors were able to meet the "artist and image activist" Alvin C. Jacobs Jr. the creator of a new photo exhibition titled *Welcome to Brookhill*. The exhibit focused on the destructive effects of redlining in one Charlotte neighborhood and the issue was examined in several public programs, including lectures and book talks. The opening week of the new season also included "Reducing High-Poverty Schools & Creating Educational Opportunities for All Students in Charlotte: A Community Town Hall and Call to Action" which emphasized the related goals of "economic mobility, education, and equity." Subsequent events throughout 2018–2019 included a *Talk about It Tuesdays* series (a recurring feature of the Gantt's yearly programming) devoted to the practical and theoretical dimensions of economics and social mobility.

The Gantt's other 2018–2019 offerings included three exhibitions featuring the work of artist and activist Hank Willis Thomas: *Question Bridge: Black Males* (a permanent installation); *Hank Willis Thomas: What We Ask Is Simple* and *For Freedoms*. Each one approached twentieth-century history from a human rights perspective and brought that history to bear on twenty-first-century realities. *Question Bridge: Black Males*, created by Thomas, Chris Johnson, Bayeté Ross Smith, and Kamal Sinclair, used a video platform to interrogate black male identity. The viewpoints of more than 160 black males from around the United States were projected on the gallery wall and seemed to be engaged in conversation via the multichannel installation. *What We Ask Is Simple*, an exhibition of Thomas's still photography, focused on protests and direct action in a variety of contexts: women's suffrage, the civil rights movement, the American Indian movement, and the Stonewall riots. As the Gantt website explains, in these highly manipulated digital images, Thomas "challenges his audience to think differently about their role in society's evolution. He reminds us that the societal tumult witnessed in the news and on the streets is part of a hard-fought, perennial battle for equality and that we should not fail to acknowledge the overwhelming mass of people who use their creativity, courage and ambition to inspire change within their communities."[15] When COVID-19 closures disrupted public programming at the Gantt and other museums, a shift to virtual events became necessary. This will likely continue even as on-site exhibitions and related programs slowly return.

For Freedoms is a particularly vibrant example of multifaceted programming that may be situated in a museum but also extends beyond institutional walls. An ongoing fifty-state initiative founded by Hank Willis Thomas and

Eric Gottesman in 2016, *For Freedoms* is described on the Gantt website as "the largest creative collaboration in U.S. history" and "a platform for creative civic engagement, discourse, and direct action." The inspiration for the larger project came from Norman Rockwell's paintings of Franklin D. Roosevelt's *Four Freedoms* (1941): freedom of speech, freedom of worship, freedom from want, and freedom from fear. As the Four Freedoms website explains:

> exhibitions, installations, and public programs use art to deepen public discussions on civic issues and core values, and to advocate for equality, dialogue, and civic participation. As a nexus between art, politics, commerce, and education, *For Freedoms* aims to inject anti-partisan, critical thinking that fine art requires into the political landscape through programming, exhibitions, and public artworks.

Other "activations" (exhibitions, billboards, and other installations) under the banner of the *For Freedoms* initiative continue throughout the United States.[16] They include collaborations with organizations like Sankofa.org to bring social justice issues into the foreground through films, plays, art installations and discussion forums. In addition to the fifty-state billboard initiative that "literally advertises" local and regional issues, the *For Freedoms* "Super PAC" sponsors Town Hall meetings on issues of local, national, and global importance.[17]

TOWN HALL MEETINGS AND OTHER
MUSEUM CONVERSATIONS

When my research questions were still coming into focus, very early in my fieldwork for this book, I visited the August Wilson Center in Pittsburgh and learned that a town hall/community meeting was going to be held there the following evening.[18] At the time I was not aware of the extent to which large public gatherings devoted to the discussion of political issues had become a common occurrence at this and other African American museums. They would become even more frequent following the deaths in 2014 of Michael Brown and Tamir Rice.

The town hall at the August Wilson Center came at a moment when the case of Jordan Miles, an eighteen-year-old honors student, was slowly making its way through the courts. Miles had been beaten by white undercover police officers while he was visiting his grandmother in a Pittsburgh suburb in January 2010. The case, urgent in its own right, was evidence of an ongoing problem: the often excessively violent treatment of black males by police in Pittsburgh.[19] The Justice Department would later decide not to prosecute the three police officers involved.[20] Although the August Wilson Center itself did not organize "The Disappearing Black Community—The Endangered Black Man" (6/17/2011), it provided space for a discussion of Jordan Miles's case and the larger issues it brought to light. The Wilson's central downtown location and large theater provided a venue to address the unequal treatment of specific racial minorities by members of law enforcement. This was in fact the third in a series of four town hall meetings devoted to the "Disappearing Black Community."[21] It was an occasion for constituents to gather and voice their concerns, to protest the treatment of Jordan Miles in particular, to recognize the emblematic nature of that treatment as a far-reaching and long-standing problem, and to make demands for change.

The event at the August Wilson Center was consistent with the use of the (transformed) town hall meeting as an inherently democratic and potentially activist device. The town hall meeting structure, utilized at the August Wilson Center and adapted by the Gantt in 2018 to explore issues of "economic mobility, education, and equity," has been a staple of political life since the colonial period. As sociologist Andrew Perrin notes, town halls functioned as "deliberative places" where citizens could "come close to their ideals of direct democracy."[22] This model is increasingly employed in African American museums to address the pressing issues that bear upon communities and constituencies. However, in the colonial period and the early years of the Republic, the town hall meeting had upheld the "hierarchy of the community" and discouraged dissent. In an analysis of their history, sociologist and journalism specialist Michael Schudson explains that the town hall meetings were exclusive—"limited to property-owning adult males.'"[23] Their use in the public programming of African American museums can be seen as a corrective adaptation consistent with the formation, community oriented nature, and culturally specific missions of these institutions.[24]

For Freedoms partnered, for example, with the California African American Museum, IDEA (Institute for Diversity & Empowerment at Annenberg), and the University of Southern California's RAP (Race, Arts, & Placemaking) Initiative to host a Town Hall on March 2, 2020, part of a multiday *For Freedoms Congress*. The event, curated by Sankofa.org, aimed to unite "artists and activists to discuss freedom of speech in anticipation of the 2020 Presidential Election."[25] The town hall is also utilized at African American museums in conjunction with exhibitions that explicitly advance activist goals. These exhibitions exist as ends in themselves, but their subject matter also functions as a means to further ends. At the Gantt Center, for example, "Reducing High-Poverty Schools & Creating Educational Opportunities for All Students in Charlotte: A Community Town Hall and Call to Action" (2018) and "Responses—Economic Mobility, Education & Equity" (2019) spoke directly to the issues raised in the exhibition *Welcome to Brookhill*.

EDUCATION, FAMILY, SELF-CARE, AND CIVIC LIFE AT THE MUSEUM

Stand-alone events not directly related to exhibitions are an equally important aspect of public programming at African American museums, and this element of public outreach arguably distinguishes them from their mainstream counterparts. The representation of history and culture is inherently issue-oriented and politically charged, and thus the activist role of African American museums in current affairs is to be expected. The museum functions as a venue for community-initiated events, like the town hall meetings at the August Wilson Center, the Harvey B. Gantt Center, and the California African American Museum, and other exhibition-related events noted here, but the museum itself also becomes a source of (borrowing Fred Moten's terms) an "irruptive" and generative force of activist conversations.

This is consistent with a long tradition embodied first in The African Meeting House, now part of the Museum of African American History in Boston, which once functioned as a crucial planning ground for the abolitionist movement in the nineteenth century. That activist tradition has been carried on by the museum in "Peculiar Patriotism" (2018), a discussion of the prison industrial complex and patriotism as an example of "resisting structural oppression," in "The Power of Public Monuments and Why They Matter" (2019), and in an ongoing series on *Freedom, Justice and Race* in collaboration with PEN America. These gatherings address national "states of emergency" as well as equally urgent local conditions. Examples at the California African American Museum have included a Radical Self-Care workshop series as well as discussions of "Collective Action: Artists for Housing and Homeless Rights" and "Youth Now" (2018) which sought to "inspire activism in the next generation of leaders" through "art, critical thinking, and community organizing." At the Harvey B. Gantt Center, they have included "Black Male Identity," timed to coincide with their "Question Bridge" installation and "The Debate over Compensating Student Athletes" (2019). The Gantt has also added a "new dimension to its mission" with the launch of the "Initiative for Equity + Innovation" [IEI]. In partnership with Bank of America the initiative will address "unconscious bias, discrimination and social injustice" through exhibitions, community dialogues, and public programs.[26]

Public programs at the DuSable Black History Museum have addressed the "Economic Vestiges of Enslavement" (2014), "Unreasonable Doubt: Emmett Till, Trayvon Martin, Michael Brown and the Presumption of Black Guilt" (2015), and "Hope Is Vote: Educating Young Adults to the Power of Their Voting Rights" (2016). Under the title "Straight Talk: Black/Brown Unity in a Changing America" (2016) the museum offered "a daring discussion about the uniqueness and similarities of Black/Brown worlds" in terms of "low socioeconomic status, unparalleled rates of incarceration, police brutality, low wages and unsafe working conditions."[27] The regularity and the scope of museum-based responses to states of emergency continued to increase. In 2018, for example, the Reginald F. Lewis Museum hosted public discussions to address several current controversies, including "Is Kaepernick the Rosa Parks of the Next Generation?" and "The Long Arm of History: Monuments and Statues Really Do Matter."

Debates surrounding the removal of Confederate statues—and the broader question of the status of monuments to the Confederacy in public spaces—had already escalated in frequency and intensity when, on August 12, 2017, Heather Heyer was killed by James Alex Fields Jr. as she participated in a counterprotest against a "Unite the Right" white supremacist rally. The occasion for the rally was the proposed removal of a statue of Confederate General Robert E. Lee from Charlottesville's Emancipation Park. Fields drove his car into the crowd of counter-protesters, killing Heyer and injuring more than twenty others.[28] In the wake of the Charlottesville riot, the Reginald F. Lewis Museum in Baltimore took a firm stand, issuing an official statement on August 18, 2017, in support of the removal of "vestiges of history that serve to subjugate a group of citizens based on race."[29] The Lewis continued to host issue-oriented discussions in 2019, including "Baltimore After Freddie Gray," in partnership with the Maryland Commission on Human Rights, and "Blackface and Its Legacy."

The "Rapid Response" exhibition—which often involves rapid collection efforts—is another example of museum responses to states of emergency. These initiatives are added unexpectedly to a museum's pre-existing (generally long-term) schedule and speak directly to contemporary events. Such efforts have now become a vital, spontaneous aspect of the twenty-first-century activist turn as they seek to directly influence the conditions that give rise to these events. The concerted effort to document historical events through quotidian objects as well as stark fragments of destruction was undertaken immediately in the wake of the 2001 terrorist attacks on the World Trade Center in New York by the New-York Historical Society, the Museum of the City of New York, and the 9/11 Memorial Museum. These efforts have a clear, future-oriented dimension but are arguably less explicit in their immediate goals than a number of recent examples that focus on racism and explicit and implicit bias.

At the National Civil Rights Museum [NCRM] in Memphis, Tennessee, for example, the *I AM A CHILD* exhibition was mounted in 2018 in response to Immigration and Customs Enforcement actions and the separation of children at the Mexican border. Noelle Trent, director of interpretation, collections, and education at the NCRM, was inspired by a Twitter post containing an image by photographer Paola Mendoza of children carrying "I AM A CHILD" signs as they stood on the steps of Immigration and Customs Enforcement headquarters in New York City. Although the location and specifics of the protest differed, the group's pose hearkened back to an iconic 1968 photograph by Ernest Withers in which a group of striking Memphis sanitation workers carried signs that read "I AM A MAN." The assertion of humanity—and human rights—was clearly the same in both cases. In her Twitter post Mendoza had written: "'A child is a child no matter what country they were born in. A child is a child even when they cross the border. A child's desire to stay with their parents is a human right. In homage to the iconic I AM A MAN photo, I am proud to present *I AM A CHILD*.'"[30]

This sparked immediate interest from teachers who wanted to use Mendoza's image(s) in their classrooms. Trent and Mendoza subsequently met and collaborated on an exhibition at NCRM which, as Trent explains, remains "dedicated to telling the African American civil rights story." Trent reports on the project in *Museum* (a publication of the American Alliance of Museums) and includes a brief sidebar/guide entitled "Rapid-Response Exhibition 101" that draws upon lessons learned at NCRM. She concludes with this position statement: "Museums are not direct service agencies; however, they have a unique role in shining a light on social injustices and compelling audiences to re-examine a variety of issues. If museums are to be engaging public spaces, deploying exhibitions on contemporary issues is a critical piece of our work."[31]

It is also important to recognize the efforts of those museums that do not self-identify as culturally specific. Before the *I AM A CHILD* exhibition opened at the NCRM in Memphis, for example, the Minneapolis Institute of Art (Mia) had mounted a rapid response exhibition in collaboration with MASS Action (Museum as Site for Social Action). The focus was the death of Philando Castile, a thirty-two-year-old black male who was killed by police officer Jeronimo Yanez on July 6, 2016, during a traffic stop in Falcon Heights, Minnesota, eight miles from the museum. Castile's girlfriend, Diamond Reynolds, recorded his death and made the event available on social media. His mother, Valerie Castile, asked Mia if they would consider presenting an exhibition of artwork created to honor her son and to document the circumstances of his death. The result was *Art and Healing: In the Moment* (June–July 2017). As Matthew Welch, Mia's deputy director and chief curator, explained: "This was not something Mia had ever done before. And as an institution that receives public funding, the museum could not take a political stand, especially with the court case against Officer Jeronimo Yanez still pending. In the end, museum leadership decided to work with community members. . . . It was the right call." The Mia museum staff "recognized from the beginning that the exhibition was intended particularly for the African American community" yet the message about the "therapeutic ability of the creative process and art's role in helping people cope with trauma and loss" was a unifying theme for all visitors. In this case the focus was on the "empathic response of the artists" and the exhibition's "message of recovery and healing in the aftermath of this trauma."[32] The shooting of Philando Castile had understandably outraged his local community but perhaps, like so many similar tragedies, the outrage and reactions might have not extended beyond these boundaries. Because his girlfriend had documented and live-streamed his death, the outrage and reactions spread, resulting in protests in Minneapolis and St. Paul and leading to Mia's response.

The museum was well situated to respond. It had already launched the MASS Action (Museum as Site for Social Action) initiative in 2016 and went on to receive a grant from the Andrew W. Mellon Foundation to establish The Center for Empathy and the Visual Arts. Here, as Welch explains, "researchers, philosophers, content experts, artists, and thought leaders are grappling with how to make compassion and empathy a part of the museum's learning strategies with the ultimate goal of fostering social change." This initiative continues to function as a collective composed of museum staff from various institutions. Together they seek to prepare museums "to become 'sites for social action'" and to address the "inequity of exclusionary hiring practices."

MASS Action members have also collaborated to create an online tool for professionals in multiple "tracks" of museum work and, via Twitter, they have launched meetings to discuss the analyses, case studies, and practical instructions posted online. Structuring their efforts in the form of eight discrete "chapters" (as of July 2019), they have initiated a "Community of Practice Platform" to address the "Internal Transformation" of "attitudes and frames of mind," including legacies of colonialism, racism, and white privilege in the operations of traditional mainstream museums. MASS Action also takes up the need for diversity and inclusion by seeking ways of "Liberating the Narrative" and making exhibitions more "poly-vocal, multi-directional, and self-aware."[33] The goal is to achieve equality (in training, opportunity, and advancement) within the museum profession, and seems to mirror the broader movement to address inequality and injustice at every level of society beyond the museum's walls. Initiatives like MASS Action—that critique and seek to change the profession and make it more inclusive—involve consciousness-raising and outreach within existing institutional frameworks as well as reforms in museum studies programs to effectively attract, mentor, and prepare underrepresented groups.

INCLUSION, STATES OF EMERGENCY,
AND THE ACTIVIST TURN

The COVID-19 pandemic, which forced so many to take shelter, has shed light on social inequities that are by no means new. Here in the United States, it has had a disproportionate effect on communities of color, whose rates of infection and mortality far exceed those of other demographic groups. In the realm of museums, as a statement from the MASS Action Collective insisted, the pandemic has also shed light on inequalities within the museum profession:

> As we have seen over the past few weeks, this crisis is exposing already-deep inequities that exist in American society—impacting marginalized communities more immediately and severely than the rest of the population. . . . In light of all of the high-priority financial factors that must be considered in this time of crisis, the MASS Action collective urges museum leaders to center equity as the most critical value in the decisions that lay ahead. (*Equitable Institutional Sustainability in Times of Crisis* Disseminated April 17, 2020)

Layoffs and "parity" cuts (or equal percentage cuts at all salary levels) have had a greater effect on the lives of the lowest paid and least able to absorb that loss. The MASS Action statement targets all museums, calling them to devote greater attention to their publics:

> How strong is our commitment to our community if we abandon it when it counts? This is not a time to preserve ourselves at the expense of our communities. Keeping relationships active with community is crucial. It sends a message that the museum understands that we do not operate in isolation, that we are part of a larger community ecosystem. It also reminds people that museums can be important civic leaders, all the time, but especially during this time.[34]

That challenge entails a choice between passivity and engagement: museums can "weather this crisis in relative isolation, or step out as leaders in our field, shifting the paradigm to model a values-driven response, taking a human-centered, empathetic approach to the challenges ahead, and centering those most affected."

This call for responsibility and empathy has always been at the forefront of the work of African American museums. Caregiving has long been an integral part of their individualized yet shared sense of missions and goals and that aspect of their missions has become even more critical as museums have had to shut their doors and defer to the safety of virtual visits. While museums in general have responded to shelter-in-place orders by offering robust online platforms that make their exhibitions and collections available, many African

American museums have made a particular commitment to public programs that address the pandemic in its immediate medical, economic, and social contexts. Fulfillment of this primary, mission-related goal includes but also reaches beyond access to exhibitions and collections in order to provide practical knowledge and, where possible, reduce suffering. Public programs continue to include cultural events—curator-led tours, interviews with artists, poetry readings, film screenings, and book talks. The California African American Museum is an excellent example with its Artist/Curator Talks, Children's Reading Hour, Zoom-Self-Care Yoga, CAAM Reads Book Club, and a YouTube archive of exhibition-related events. The African American Museum in Philadelphia also offers poetry readings, screenings, and performances. However, what arguably sets African American museums apart from their mainstream counterparts is the emphasis on social justice.

An excellent example of this programmatic commitment is the Harvey B. Gantt Center's *Unmasked: Initiative for Equity and Innovation Series* which began in mid-April 2020. It has been live-streamed weekly and remains available on YouTube. These moderated conversations with medical experts, office holders, civic leaders, artists, and other stakeholders provide real time practical information on a variety of COVID-19 related subjects along with an analysis of relevant issues and identification of their deeper historical contexts. The *Unmasked* series began on April 14, 2020, with "How the Virus Impacts the Black Community" and continued weekly with: "Healthcare in the Black Community beyond the Virus"; "Will Black Businesses Survive the Virus? Part 1"; "The Digital Divide Leaves Students Offline"; "An Introspective Conversation with Creatives"; "Dehumanization of the Incarcerated during the Pandemic"; "Exposing Food Deserts in a Pandemic"; and a "retrospective analysis" of the impact of the George Floyd incident" titled "The Turning Point."

In the midst of our sheltered COVID-19 state, the killing of George Floyd—recorded and widely disseminated on videotape—brought racism and police brutality to the foreground alongside the COVID-19 pandemic.[35] Faced with the stark realities of systemic racism, Americans (of many races) responded with widespread protests and were soon joined by protesters around the world. While museums worldwide had already responded to the COVID-19 pandemic by finding ways to open their virtual doors to visitors, African American museums had found ways to provide space for analysis and debate—as well as to offer means and methods for self-care. When the devastating and ongoing effects of systemic racism became a subject that demanded equal attention, some museums launched focused comprehensive public programs in order to address the past, present, and future of race-based social and criminal justice-related inequities.

The Harvey B. Gantt Center's *Unmasked* series responded quickly with "We Can't Breathe" on June 3, 2020. President and CEO David R. Taylor provided the historical context:

> During the stress of a pandemic, the Gantt Center has highlighted the many ways Black Americans suffer its effects at a disproportionately higher rate. Although the reasons have social, economical, and historical contexts, they are all sourced from the same foundation: racism and white-supremacy. Recent events, as expounded on by various social and news media platforms, have shown that Black lives today are threatened by much more than a potentially deadly virus.[36]

"We Can't Breathe" opened with an arresting graphic instruction to viewers. In order to bear witness, we were told to "Say Their Names." A rollout of the names of victims then slowly appeared, materializing as an archive of losses emerging in measured time. The names appeared one by one, as if typed directly on the screen, and hovered there in list formation until the screen was full only to be replaced by a new blank screen and the appearance of more names.

It took approximately three minutes for the introduction to this pandemic, starting with the name Eric Garner and ending with the full-screen solitary appearance of George Floyd. An accompanying, now iconic soundtrack featured an acapella performance by twelve-year-old Keedron Bryant of "I Just Want To Live," a song composed by his mother Johnetta Bryant.[37] The discussion among the panelists who participated in "We Can't Breathe" covered a range of issues, including the training of law enforcement officers, the need for lawmakers to exert their legislative authority, and the role that artists can continue to play in the service of human rights activism.

While the Museum of the African Diaspora continued to offer non-COVID-19 specific programming, including an African Book Club, an African Diaspora Film Club, and Open Mic Nights, it also presented a regular program of webinars—under the main title "Community Resilience during COVID-19"—focused on wellness, maternal health, the democratic process, and safety and justice. A blog affirming that "Black Lives Matter. Black Art Matters. Black Museums Matter. Black Voices Matter" includes an extensive list of "Resources to Support Black Lives" with multiple practical uses: bail funds, freedom funds and mutual aid networks, and mental health resources. The museum also sponsored "Diaspora Unite! Support for Artists of African Descent Benefit Auction" which raised over $450,000.

The C. H. Wright Museum has launched *Wright Now* (described as a "long-term exhibition") which makes an extensive archive of previous public programs available. It stands on its own as more than a simple "rebroadcast" and includes exhibition walkthroughs, oral histories, poetry readings, music, and lectures. Under the themes "Be Entertained! Be Educated! Be Inspired! In Memoriam" the museum framed the "exhibition" in activist terms: "Witness emboldening performances and conversations that spark creativity and drive change."[38] In partnership with Detroit Public Television (DPTV) the Wright also embarked on a web-based series to address "COVID-19: African Americans and Racial Health Disparities," and The Museum of African American History in Boston hosted "Race in the Public Dialogue: The Economic Impact of COVID-19 in the African American Community."

In addition to an ongoing online collection portal, in 2020 the Reginald F. Lewis offered "Educate at Home with Resources from the Lewis Museum" and "Current Voices: Uprising + 5 Part 2" (in collaboration with the Jewish Museum of Maryland). This marked the fifth anniversary of the death of Freddie Gray and addressed a current exhibition of photos by Joseph Giordano. It also hosted "Freddie Gray: Five Years Later—Activists," a *Talks and Thoughts* series, "COVID-19 in Black and White," and "Objects Revealed: Jazz and the Blues" (featuring images from their collection). The museum also sponsored a three-part professional Virtual Education Webinar series in 2021 focused on "Slavery from a Different Point of View and Its Relevance in Education."

The pandemic resulted in the physical closure of museums worldwide but by late 2020 some had reopened and others had announced imminent reopening plans. As we can see from the examples mentioned here, however, African American museums continued to maintain a presence in the lives of their publics despite the temporary suspension of on-site events.

CONTEXTS AND THEORY:
BEST PRACTICES—GETTING IN HARM'S WAY

Agents of change—true, lasting change—require skills that most museum staff do not possess and weren't trained to practice. The debate over the purpose of museums is drawing attention to skills many of us need to acquire. But I feel we should exercise caution as we pursue this dramatic change in capacity building. . . . As museum professionals, we need to be fully aware of the need for new knowledge and skills. But, to assume that we be masters of those skills, to become social workers, urban planners, psychologists, developers is to put more expectations on us than most of us are able to meet.—Chet Orloff, "Should Museums Change Our Mission and Become Agencies of Social Justice?"[39]

. . . museums increasingly face situations in which competing moral visions of the good society must be negotiated. Where human rights claims revolve around these fundamentally clashing moral positions, it is no longer appropriate . . . for museums to operate as impartial observers or spaces for dialogue in which alternative viewpoints are respected, aired, and debated. Rather they must, as far as is practically possible, be prepared to take sides and speak out unequivocally against attempts to justify unequal treatment of people on the basis of gender or sexual differences.—Richard Sandell. *Museums, Moralities and Human Rights*[40]

The goals and accomplishments of African American museums in the realm of public programming activities need to be seen in the context of current debates within the museum profession and among museum studies scholars. In the twenty-first century these debates address more than what a museum collects and exhibits; they address what a museum supports, condones, tolerates, or opposes regarding conditions in the wider world. Museums like the Birmingham Civil Rights Center and the National Underground Railroad Freedom Center continue to be guided by founding principles and evolving missions that address human rights issues and the fight for social justice.[41] Their sense of purpose is clear and, for example, it is clearly reflected in this statement on the Freedom Center's website: "The National Underground Railroad Freedom Center is a museum of conscience, an education center, a convener of dialogue and a beacon of light for inclusive freedom around the globe."[42]

However, strong disagreements exist among mainstream museum professionals about the extent to which they can and should be actively involved in the public and civic lives of their visitors.[43] Museum leaders, staff, and academics do not agree about an institution's responsibility to its visitors and other constituencies, or to the broader sociopolitical contexts in which an institution operates. As Richard Sandell explains: "The past decade has seen a significant and sustained increase, among practitioners, policy makers and researchers, in the social role of museums and, more particularly, their potential to engender support for social justice and human rights . . . " However, he also observes that "there is still a tendency to view engagement with human rights work as optional . . . "[44] These complex conversations ultimately bear upon a museum's mission and can extend beyond local and regional matters to address national and global issues. The specific focal points are wide ranging. They address inclusion, the social role of the museum, and museum-based activism—the museum's responsibility to become actively involved in issues of social and criminal justice, human rights, and the modes and efficacy of exhibiting "difficult knowledge."

Under pressure to make the profession more inclusive, mainstream museums in the United States are becoming more aware of the need for racial and ethnic diversity in hiring at every level. This is but one aspect of the broader question of inclusion and an interrogation of what is/is not being collected and exhibited, and whose narratives are/are not being represented.[45] Critiques of mainstream museums focus on the exclusion of certain groups from collection and exhibition practices, the lack of diversity among museum professionals at all levels, and the failure to extend public outreach beyond a fairly limited audience base. However, there have been signs of progress, and even clearer signs of agitation for change.

One early example was the "Joint Statement from Museum Bloggers and Colleagues on Ferguson and Related Events" issued on 12/11/14 by a diverse group of museum professionals and scholars.[46] They recognized a "watershed moment" in the wake of "recent events from Ferguson to Cleveland to New York" and insisted that not only African American museums but all museums had a role to play in achieving justice and social change. The authors argued that museums, as "mediators of culture . . . should commit to identifying how they can connect to relevant contemporary issues irrespective of collection, focus, or mission."[47] One of the concrete developments that followed from this formal statement was a regular series of Twitter chats and other forms of consultation and collaboration. When they described the enthusiasm as well as the resistance they encountered in the process of composing the statement, participants Aleia Brown and Adrianne Russell offered some provocative "What ifs" for the museum community to ponder: *What if we developed restorative justice programs where both victims and perpetrators had to identify with something in collections and publicly share their reflections?*[48]

Questions like these continue to provoke wide-ranging debates about the museum's responsibility as a participant in the fight for human rights, civil rights and social justice. They also give rise to discussions within specific institutions about the degree and nature of their active involvement. As we might expect, these questions also reappear in—or are often generated by—academic literature. In the Introduction to *The Idea of a Human Rights Museum* the editors observe that "Over the past two decades, self-identified human rights museums have opened around the world; they even established their own organization." The missions of the institutions belonging to the Federation of International Human Rights Museums, for example, "range from social reconciliation, reparation, symbolic memorialization, calling to action, or providing the opportunity for what Piotr Cywinski . . . describes as 'a deep private individual experience.'" In "The Museology of Human Rights" Jennifer Carter explains that this new genre of museums makes "human rights concepts, stories, and practices the core of their institutional mission, curatorial praxis, and exhibition and programming initiatives."[49]

Richard Sandell, demonstrably one of the strongest advocates for the activist/social role of the museum, explains that "The concept of activism highlights the inherently political character of the processes through which moral standpoints—on a variety of issues—become embodied in museums." He finds that in recent years there has been "significant and sustained increase in interest, among practitioners, policy makers, and researchers, in the social role of museums and, more particularly, their potential to engender support for social justice and human rights." However, Sandell observes that "there is still a tendency to view engagement with human rights work as optional." He notes that in their "daily practice" most museums do not have "a specific human rights mandate."[50]

The presence of a human rights perspective does not, of course, guarantee that visitors will regard themselves as possible agents for change. In *The Social Work of Museums* Lois H. Silverman looks at "interactive social experiences of communication" and how "relationships are activated and people make meaning of objects." She finds that this "yields beneficial consequences" as "people may meet . . . needs like the need for self-esteem and self-actualization; achieve change in essential areas such as knowledge, skills, values, and behavior; build and strengthen social connections and relationships, including social capital; address social problems; and promote social justice and equality."[51] If visitors have these experiences then they may become activists.

In "Posterity Has Arrived: The Necessary Emergence of Museum Activism," Robert R. Janes and Richard Sandell define activism as "museum practice, shaped out of ethically-informed values, that is intended to bring about political, social and environmental change." They argue that "the civic arena is where important decisions are made about individual and community needs, and our sense is that mainstream museums remain largely disconnected from this interaction." Although they admit that there are "notable exceptions" they find that "the museum community is not responding to the world, be it climate change, species extinction, or social justice issues such as poverty and homelessness." For Janes and Sandell, activism "also means resistance—the critical questioning and re-imagining of the status quo." Thus, they remind us of a critical difference in commitment between awareness (the result of a successful exhibition) and activism (the behavior that seeks change).[52]

As mainstream museums reevaluate their relationships with the public and as they compete for public and private funding,[53] the social impact of the institution has become an important focal point for discussions regarding their missions and goals. In recent years many mainstream museums have expanded the traditional emphasis on collection, preservation, and exhibition and they have extended their reach through the creation of expansive websites. These digital zones of contact provide more than a standard overview of hours, location, fees, exhibitions, and amenities and now include virtual tours and online access to objects and archival materials. In addition, many museums bring public programs into the foreground.

Yet, with some important exceptions, gallery tours and lectures directly related to current exhibitions are still the primary point of contact. The head of the education staff may now hold the title of "curator," which suggests an elevation in standing for that aspect of the institution's mission; but the development of curriculum-specific materials and services for K–12 classes, without comparable higher education and community engagement programs, remains their primary focus. In a gradual expansion of exhibition and programming initiatives—if not in officially stated missions—some mainstream museums also go beyond exhibition-based and specialized scholarly programming to provide a venue for the discussion of local, community-based, national, and global issues.[54] Interactive exhibition elements also make new demands and create new contact zones.

These changes are not widespread, nor are they always welcome. Sandell's claim that the "social role" of museums must include "nurturing a more respectful, fair, and equitable society" has not received universal support.[55] The position statement by historian and museum director Chet Orloff, for example, quoted above stands in stark contrast to the stand taken by Sandell. Arguments for and against continue to be made and questions about purpose and process continue to be raised. Should a museum try to alter a visitor's beliefs and/or affect their actions, particularly if these alterations bear upon pressing political, social, and other issues and are thus *life*-changing? Who should be consulted on these matters? Who should decide what these institutions will support? "How should museums respond to situations in which moralities clash," Sandell asks, "where the rights of groups are contested and when there is little in the way of public consensus?"[56]

The goal of maintaining neutrality in the midst of controversy may now be a relic of past practice for some museums, but problems identified two decades ago by William Yeingst and Lonnie Bunch, based on trial and error at the Smithsonian, remain: "Clearly, exploring contemporary history is a reminder to us all that the past is political. As curators begin to delve into contemporary issues that are unresolved or still painful to the American psyche, they are made aware of the limits of their institutions, their collections, and their ability to educate in a museum setting." Yeingst and Bunch explained that visitors "often come seeking reaffirmation or answers," yet they advocated for space for the representation and potential eruption of controversy: "Our task is not to retreat from this opportunity but to continue to craft exhibitions that give meaning, hope, and understanding, rather than to produce presentations that attempt conflict resolution."[57] This task has been taken up more often in the last decade and, as Jennifer Carter observes," it suggests that a "profound rethinking of the traditional social and cultural functions of museums" is taking place.[58] Bunch, the founding director of the National Museum of African American History and Culture and now secretary of the Smithsonian Institution, has restated his commitment to taking on controversial issues: "I believe very strongly," he explains, that museums have a social justice role to play . . . to be at the center of their community, to help the community grapple with the challenges they face, to use history, to use science, to use education, to give the public tools to grapple with this."[59]

To place this position in a deeper historical context we can look back to John Cotton Dana and his insistence in *The New Museum* (1917) that traditional "conventions of purpose" should be reassessed. He explained that, when founding the Newark Museum on the principles of that "new museum idea," the focus had to be "the needs of the people of Newark." In doing so, the new museum project "examines its community's life first, and then straightaway bends its energies to supplying some of the material which that community needs."[60] More than fifty years later, at the Seminar on Neighborhood Museums in Brooklyn, New York (1969), participants were still insisting on the need for "new ways of thinking about museums and the public they serve," especially when that public is comprised of "militant minority groups."[61] When that seminar was convened in New York, the DuSable Museum in Chicago had been in existence for eight years and the Charles H. Wright Museum in Detroit for four years and they were already hard at work thinking about the publics they served.

Perhaps the most controversial and complex dimension of human rights-related museum work is the representation of difficult knowledge and the role of empathy in that implicitly (or explicitly) activist project. In "Adopting Empathy: Why Empathy Should Be a Required Core Value for All Museums—Period," authors Jon Carfagno and Adam Reed Rozan quote Roman Krznaric, founder of the first Empathy Museum in the UK, who defines empathy as "'the art of stepping imaginatively into the shoes of another person, understanding their feelings and perspectives, and using that understanding to guide your actions.'"[62] As Dina Bailey observes in her contribution to the volume *Museum Activism*, a number of subject-specific and culturally specific museums, including the Birmingham Civil Rights Institute and the National Underground Railroad Freedom Center, have taken up "the role of 'platform' or 'staging ground' for activism.[63] Julia Rose also outlines a method of "Comprehensive Museum Pedagogy" that "takes into account the learners' responses" and "allows for history workers to sensitively develop historical representations of the oppressed, victimized, and subjugated groups." As she explains, the goal is to "produce historical empathy in learners."[64] Emerging technologies can in some cases encourage "ethical attentiveness" and prove conducive to the emergence of more "empathic communities." Turning to game theory, for example, Adam Muller, Struan Sinclair, and Andrew Woolford point out that the use of interactive technology and social media in museums "'opens up new ways to be attentive to diverse audiences and draw them into a discussion as ethical actors themselves.'"[65]

Claims for the efficacy of museum encounters and the force of empathy, however, need to be accompanied by the admission that we should not take desired effects for granted. The belief that exhibitions and programs can influence a visitor's thoughts and/or actions has been challenged, for example, by Roger Simon and Angela Failler, who urge us to reflect on our expectations of empathy and its efficacy. They focus on the act of witnessing (through museum exhibitions) and caution that:

> though a spectatorial sensibility might allow me to "see" connections between systemic violence carried out against Indigenous peoples and my own relative security in a white settler society, I must also learn to translate this seeing into an ability to respond to the conditions out of which such inequality, violence, and oppression arise. Learning from, in other words, is about more than recognizing the other's difference. Learning from involves learning to take the experiences and memories of others into our own lives and to live and to act as though they mattered.[66]

In *A Pedagogy of Witnessing* Simon argued that while an exhibition may have the potential to exert influence beyond the spatial and temporal limitations of the discrete museum visit, and may thus become a "form of difficult learning," this outcome cannot be assumed. He explains that an exhibition "must foster more than affective attachments." Giving due time to the complexity of this transaction, Simon insists that "curating must ultimately be concerned with the question of how exhibitions might be presented so as to serve a *transitive* function that could open up an indeterminate reconsideration of the force of history in social life." If an exhibition is able to "foster grief and shame" on the viewer's part, to elicit a sense of failure rather than "triumphalist fantasies of righteousness," he suggests that the difficult lesson might be carried forward.[67]

Simon's grammatical analogy (the "transitive function" of curatorial efforts) helps us to see that the content of the exhibition must act on the visitor-as-object, who might take on the weight of that content and perhaps become the subject, the one who then takes action. With a focus on exhibitions and a focus on music and the visual arts respectively, both Roger Simon and Fred Moten alert us to the possibility that (once again) *rhetoric* (the art of persuasion), *grammar* (the mechanics, principles, and rules of meaning-making), and *content* (objects, texts, images, and sounds) might function together as activist tools. As I have tried to illustrate, African American museums provide the model and the space for that consequential work.

CODA

While doing the field work for this book I took some notes under the provisional title of "efficacy" that were generative at that time and remain emblematic now. Keeping that page of notes in view was one way to ensure that I would use them as a guide and acknowledge them in closing this frame. The notes came from a reading of Thomas W. Laqueur's "Bodies, Details, and the Humanitarian Narrative." Written narratives are Laqueur's primary subject here. He considers the "causal chains that might connect the actions of its readers with the suffering of its subjects," he notes the "reliance on detail [in the narrative] as the sign of truth," and he argues that the "humanitarian narrative describes particular suffering and offers a model for precise social action." The specificity of that "analytic of suffering," he argues, "exposes the means for its relief."[68] The forms Laqueur analyzes include novels, case histories, autopsies, and inquests that recognize suffering in its social context. I have tried here to make a case for the addition of other forms to that list: the museum experience in all its specificity—including architectural and other informative frames.

NOTES

1. John Cotton Dana, *The New Museum* (Woodstock, VT: The Elm Tree Press, 1917), 32.

2. Bailey provides brief overviews of the DuSable and C. H. Wright museums and cites the work of the Birmingham Civil Rights Institute and the National Underground Railroad Freedom Center. Dina A. Bailey, "The Activist Spectrum in United States Museums," in *Museum Activism*, eds. Robert R. Janes and Richard Sandell (London: Routledge, 2019), 295. © 2019. Used with permission of Taylor & Francis Group, LLC, a division of Informa plc, permission conveyed through Copyright Clearance Center, Inc.

3. Deborah L. Mack and John S. Welch note that the "Black museums movement" has in principle always been "engaged in the practice of 'participatory history' and culture." "The State of Black Museums." *The Public Historian* 40, no. 3 (August 2018), 10. Also see Mary Jo Fairchild, who argues that an "often overlooked method of 'resistance' is the African American Museum Movement." See "The African American Museum Movement: New Strategies in the Battle for Equality in the Twentieth Century," *Proceedings of the South Carolina Historical Association*, 2008: 5–14.

4. Jennifer Barrett, *Museums and the Public Sphere* (Malden, MA: Wiley-Blackwell, 2011), 7. Barrett examines the long history of "the public" as a concept and the "way museums themselves use the term."

5. Jeff Hayward and Christine Larouche offer a general summary of "service to their communities" in "The Emergence of the Field of African American Museums," *The Public Historian* 40, no. 3 (August 2018), 169–71.

6. A video by seventeen-year-old Darnella Frazier, body-cam footage, eye-witness accounts, and trial testimony have contributed to the emerging documentation of the event.

7. In an article in the *New York Times* on July 8, 2020, titled "Black Lives Matter May Be the Largest Movement in U.S. History," Larry Buchanan, Quoctrung Bui, and Jugal K. Patel reported that "Four recent polls—including one released this week by Civis Analytics, a data science firm that works with businesses and Democratic campaigns—suggest that about 15 million to 26 million people in the United States have participated in demonstrations over the death of George Floyd and others in recent weeks." They went on to suggest that "these figures would make the recent protests the largest movement in the country's history, according to interviews with scholars and crowd-counting experts."

8. For example, in an article in *Museum* (published by the American Alliance of Museums) the director of the Princeton University Art Museum described the institution's "activist" response to the debate about climate change. See James Christen Steward, "The Activist Exhibition," *Museum* 98, no. 2 (March/April 2019).

9. Inspired by the work of Noam Chomsky on the "6.2-word sentence," Moten probes the "ungrammatical" and the extra-grammatical"; he is particularly interested in the "extra-legal" in the arts and focuses on the language of jazz improvisation, specifically its capacity to "break" with and/or exceed the limits of set forms. Fred Moten, "Jurisgenerative Grammar (For Alto)" in *The Oxford Handbook of Critical Improvisation Studies*, Volume 1, eds. George E. Lewis and Benjamin Piekut (New York: Oxford University Press, 2016), 130–32.

10. The Brooklyn Museum exhibition began with a symposium on April 21, 2017. A broader effort to expand the reach of the exhibition included two edited volumes: *We Wanted a Revolution: Black Radical Women, 1965–1985/A Sourcebook* is a collection of primary documents published during the period covered by the exhibition; it includes statements from individual artists and major artists' collectives—including Africobra, Spiral, The Combahee River Collective, and Third World Women Artists of the United States—and related material by prominent literary figures—including Toni Morrison, Alice Walker, and Audre Lorde; it also offers brief contextualizing analyses by the curators/editors of the volume and other experts. *We Wanted a Revolution: Black Radical Women, 1965–1985/New Perspectives* includes installation photographs and contextualizing essays by contemporary theorists, two poems by Alice Walker, an expansive bibliography, and an exhibition checklist. See *We Wanted a Revolution: Black Radical Women, 1965–1985/A Sourcebook*, eds. Catherine Morris and Rujeko Hockley (Brooklyn, NY: Brooklyn Museum, 2018) and *We Wanted a Revolution: Black Radical Women, 1965–1985/New Perspectives*, ed. Catherine Morris and Rujeko Hockley (Brooklyn, NY: Brooklyn Museum, 2018).

11. The opening keynote speaker at the event was Naima Keith, deputy director and chief curator, California African American Museum. The closing keynote speaker was author Aruna D'Souza, whose work considers "how museums

shape our views of each other and the world." The panel topics were: "On Artists of African Descent" and "Artist as Social Change Agent." See caamuseum. org/exhibitions/2017/we-wanted-a-revolution; caamuseum.org/programs/current/ we-wanted-a-revolution-black-radical-women-196585-closing-symposium.

12. *Transcending Blackness in Contemporary African Art*. www.moadsf.org/what -we-do/engage-symposium-2022.

13. Participants in the *Picturing Blackness* symposium included keynote speaker Deborah Willis and other distinguished academics, curators, and artists. Participants in the *Black Refractions* symposium included artists, curators, collectors, gallery owners, and art writers who considered subjects addressed by the work in the exhibition, including "identity, politics, and the role of institutions on the works and careers of artists of African descent." See www.moadsf.org/event/engage -black-refractions-symposium and www.moadsf.org/event/engage-symposium-2020 -picturing-blackness.

14. Email LISTSERV letter from David R. Taylor, president and CEO, 9/4/2018.

15. www.ganttcenter.org/exhibitions/hank-willis-thomas-what-we-ask-is-simple/. Accessed 3/22/2019.

16. forfreedoms.org/partners/for-freedoms/. Accessed 2/17/2019.

17. For an interview with Gottesman and Thomas on the origins and intentions of For Freedoms see medium.com/kickstarter/ behind-the-billboards-for-freedoms-on-the-50-state-initiative-dbffd9a90a89.

18. I had come to see to see the permanent exhibition *Pittsburgh: Reclaim, Renew, Remix* (an example of the settlement theme) and a temporary exhibition, *In My Father's House*, a multiroom, object-rich setting of African American life in Pittsburgh.

19. For local coverage of the confrontation between Jordan Miles and the officers, and the ensuing criminal and civil court cases, see: Alex Zimmerman. "99 Problems . . . ": pghcitypaper.cpm/pittsburgh/99-problems-run-in-with-jordan-miles-wasnt-fir . . . ; and Rich Lord, "Different Attorney, Evidence in Jordan Miles Retrial." *Pittsburgh Post-Gazette* [Pittsburgh, PA], 10 Mar. 2014. Infotrac Newsstand, link. galegroup.com/apps/doc/A360961370/STND?u=nysl_me_cuny&sid=STND&xid=8 1c6b2d0. In 2014 a jury found that the police had lacked probable cause for their actions; however, it was not until 2016 (in a civil suit) that Miles was awarded a settlement of $125,000. Also see "Settle It: The Jordan Miles Case Was Painful All Around" by The Editorial Board of the *Pittsburgh Post-Gazette*, May 29, 2016.

20. The August Wilson Center for African American Culture closed in 2014 due to financial difficulties and reopened in 2017 as the August Wilson African American Cultural Center, a venue for cultural and other community events.

21. The moderator of this event was Albert Dotson, Chairman of *100 Black Men of America*.

22. Andrew J. Perrin, *American Democracy from Tocqueville to Town Halls to Twitter* (Cambridge, UK: Polity, 2014), 86–87.

23. Michael Schudson, *The Good Citizen: A History of American Civic Life* (Cambridge, MA: Harvard University Press, 1998), 4–5, 16–18, 98–99.

24. The town hall meeting is considered distinct from the "town meeting" (which was a form of direct democratic rule common in the New England colonies), but I am not making that distinction here. The museums typically refer to these events as town halls.

25. caamuseum.org/programs/talks-and-workshops/for-freedoms-town-hall-on -freedom-of-speech

26. See www.ganttcenter.org/public/assets/IEI-Fact-Sheet-Web.pdf

27. DuSable website.

28. Fields was eventually convicted of first-degree murder and federal hate-crime charges and sentenced to life in prison. The statue of Robert E. Lee was subsequently removed and will be melted down into metal ingots to be used to create new work.

29. The "Lewis Museum Official Statement on the Removal of Confederate Monuments and Markers" was posted on the museum's website. The subsequent removal of many Confederate statues from public spaces has created a problem of storage or relocation. Several museums have provided new homes for these statues, sparking a debate about whether museums should be expected to provide safe (storage) space and, in some cases, exhibition space for these objects.

30. Quoted by Noelle Trent, "I Am a Child," *Museum* 98, no. 2 (March/April 2019): 29–33.

31. The original signs, in which the word "AM" was underlined, were created by Joe C. Warren and Rev. Malcolm Blackburn. Trent quotes the text from Paola Mendoza's initial post. Trent's article also includes a sidebar entitled "Rapid-Response Exhibition 101" in which she enumerates the practical principles that must replace typical timelines for exhibition development. Noelle Trent, "I Am a Child," 30, 32, 33.

32. Matthew Welch, "For and by the Community," *Museum* 98, no. 2 (March/April 2019): 41–44, 46. Officer Yanez was tried for second-degree manslaughter and was acquitted, but he left the police force. He was awarded $48,500 in a separation agreement.

33. See www.museumaction.org. The need for diversity among exhibition teams—designers, developers, and fabricators—has emerged as a specific focus within the overall movement to address the issue of representation in museums. A recent article in *Museum* titled "Is That Hung White?" outlines the genesis of the growing movement to address these disparities and the obstacles that still prevent "truly transformative changes." The items and organizations listed in the Resource Guide include the MASS Action Toolkit, Incluseum, and the AAM Facing Challenge Initiative. Joanne Jones-Rizzi and Stacey Mann, "Is That Hung White?" *Museum* 99, no. 3 (Summer 2020).

34. The statement was written by Elisabeth Callihan and edited by others involved in the MASS Action (Museum as Site for Social Action) Collective. The Incluseum is part of the Collective. See https://incluseum.com/2020/04/17/equitable-institutional -sustainability-in-times-of-crisis/ Accessed 4/20/2020. The statement advocates for, among other remedial actions, policies that would address the disproportionate economic effects on museum workers of museum closings during the COVID-19 pandemic.

35. See the Postscript to *The Civic Mission of Museums* (Lanham, MD: Rowman and Littlefield, 2021) where author Anthony Pennay reflects on recent events, including the COVID-19 pandemic and the killing of George Floyd—and the impact they had on his own research project.

36. Email to the LISTSERV from Gantt Center president and CEO David R. Taylor dated 5/31/20. The event, moderated by Glenn Burkins, publisher and editor of the online newsletter Qcitymetro.com, included former South Carolina State Representative and current CNN political commentator Bakari Sellers, US Congresswoman Alma Adams, Mecklenburg County Sheriff Garry McFadden, and Image Activist Alvin C. Jacobs Jr. The "recent events" alluded to by Taylor—in addition to the killing of George Floyd—have included the fatal shooting of Breonna Taylor in Louisville, Kentucky, while police were executing a search warrant at her home on 3/13/20, and a racist-motivated attack on Ahmaud Arbery by three white men in Glynn County, Georgia, on 2/23/20. These acts of violence, which did not receive appropriate attention/investigation at the time they occurred, have now been placed at the forefront of the broader protest movement.

37. One contributor to the livestream chat noted that the song (which runs fifty seconds in one YouTube performance) had to be replayed four times before all the names were listed.

38. Charles H. Wright Museum website 6/1/20.

39. Chet Orloff, "Should Museums Change Our Mission and Become Agencies of Social Justice?" *Curator* 60, no.1 (January 2017): 36. © 2017 John Wiley and Sons.

40. Richard Sandell, *Museums, Moralities and Human Rights* (London: Routledge, 2017), 7. © 2017. Reproduced by permission of Taylor and Francis Group, LLC, a division of Informa plc, permission conveyed through Copyright Clearance Center, Inc.

41. In the mission-related statement by Jamie Glavic and Dion Brown of the National Underground Railroad Freedom Center, for example, they insist that "we as an institution most certainly are not neutral" and that "we are vocal and present in taking positions on issues and offering a constructive path forward." See Jamie Glavic with Dion Brown, "Twenty Perspectives From Museum Leaders" in Gail Anderson, *Mission Matters: Relevance and Museums in the 21st Century*, 85.

42. Freedomcenter.org/about/history. Accessed 8/9/2022.

43. I am using the term "mainstream" to differentiate between museums that do not nominally/explicitly identify with one or more specific cultural groups and/or issues.

44. Richard Sandell, *Museums, Moralities and Human Rights*, 160–61.

45. See Johnnetta Betsch Cole and Laura L. Lott, eds. *Diversity, Equity, Accessibility, and Inclusion in Museums* (Lanham, MD: Rowman & Littlefield, 2019) for an in-depth look at the problem and potential solutions. Also see Laura-Edythe Coleman, *Understanding and Implementing Inclusion in Museums* (Lanham. MD: Rowman & Littlefield, 2018); Coleman argues that "Social inclusion asserts the importance of including more than representations of marginalized communities, but also engaging marginalized communities in the co-creation of community heritage exhibits." She also insists that "American graduate museum studies programs should develop courses to better explain the social role of the museum and expand the abilities of

their graduates with the skills to become agents of social change." Coleman envisions a space where inclusion can be modeled through a "shared curatorial voice" that could "benefit community health" as it also combats exclusion. See pages 26, 90, 67, 17.

46. This group included: historian and museum analyst Aleia Brown; museum educator Adrianne Russell; professor of American studies, history, and history of art and architecture Steven Lubar; and Nina Simon, museum director and author of *The Participatory Museum*.

47. Gretchen Jennings. "Joint Statement from Museum Bloggers and Colleagues on Ferguson and Related Events." www.museumcommons.com/2014/12/joint-statement -museum-bloggers-colleagues . . .

48. These comments were part of an interview conducted by Kami Fletcher, associate professor of African American and US history, Albright College. See www .aaihs.org/museumsrespondtoferguson-an-interview-with-aleia-brown-and-adrianne -russell/.

49. Introduction, *The Idea of a Human Rights Museum*, eds. Karen Busby, Adam Muller, and Andrew Woolford (Winnipeg, Manitoba: University of Manitoba Press, 2015). Also in this volume see Jennifer Carter, "The Museology of Human Rights," 208.

50. Richard Sandell, *Museums, Moralities and Human Rights*, 9, 161, 11. Also see Lois H. Silverman, *The Social Work of Museums* (Oxon, UK: Routledge, 2010). For a compelling focus on the practical and theoretical dimensions of making the visitor an active agent in the creation of exhibitions see the contributions to *The Constituent Museum: Constellations of Knowledge, Politics and Mediation*, eds. John Byrne, Elinor Morgan, November Paynter, Aida Sánchez de Serdio, and Adela Železnik (Amsterdam: Valiz, 2018). For example, curator Elinor Morgan argues that: "If the museum is understood as a set of constituent relationships, it must also acknowledge the conversations and relations that have not been formed, along with those that will never be made, and those that have been broken. Rather than speaking on behalf of others, in an attempt to imagine positions different from its own, the museum must involve a breadth of people in dialogue, but without absorbing, assimilating or owning their voices." Elinor Morgan, "Distributing Ownership," in *The Constituent Museum*, 221.

51. Lois H. Silverman, *The Social Work of Museums*, 21.

52. Robert R. Janes and Richard Sandell, "Posterity Has Arrived: The Necessary Emergence of Museum Activism" in Janes and Sandell, eds., *Museum Activism* (London: Routledge, 2019), 1, 13, 18, and 7. For an analysis of how the National Museum of American History engaged with the American Indian protest movement see Kylie Message, *Museums and Social Activism: Engaged Protest* (London: Routledge, 2014).

53. A recent pilot study in Utah sought to analyze the social impact of museums on visitors, in part in order to provide funding agencies with evidence of their "relevance and impact." The projected short-term outcomes of museum visits included a positive contribution to the development of altruism and empathy; long-term outcomes included "intercultural competence." See Stephen Ashton et al., "Brace for Impact," *Museum* 98, no. 3 (May/June 2019): 26–31.

54. See Ruth B. Phillips on the complications and pitfalls of these collaborations. "APEC at the Museum of Anthropology: The Politics of Site and the Poetics of Sight Bite," in *Imagining Resistance: Visual Culture and Activism in Canada*, eds. J. Keri Cronin and Kirsty Robertson (Waterloo, ON: Wilfrid Laurier University Press, 2011).

55. Richard Sandell, *Museums, Moralities and Human Rights*, xvi.

56. Richard Sandell, *Museums, Moralities and Human Rights*, 136.

57. William Yeingst and Lonnie G. Bunch, "Curating the Recent Past: The Woolworth Lunch Counter, Greensboro, North Carolina," in *Exhibiting Dilemmas: Issues of Representation at the Smithsonian*, eds. Amy Henderson and Adrienne L. Kaeppler (Washington, DC: Smithsonian Institution Press, 1997) 153–54. The controversial issues they addressed included the *Enola Gay* exhibition—featuring the plane that dropped the atomic bomb on Hiroshima; the chairs that regularly appeared on the set of the racially charged TV sitcom *All in the Family*; and the Woolworth lunch counter where, in 1960, antisegregationists staged a sit-in.

58. Jennifer Carter, "The Museology of Human Rights," in *The Idea of a Human Rights Museum*, eds. Karen Busby, Adam Muller, and Andrew Woolford, 211, 208.

59. Bunch made the statement during an interview conducted by David Gelles and published in *The New York Times*. See "Smithsonian's Leader Says 'Museums Have a Social Justice Role to Play,'" www.nytimes.com/2020/07/02/business/smithsonian -lonnie-bunch-corner-office.html retrieved 7/5/20.

60. John Cotton Dana, *The New Museum* (Woodstock, VT: The Elm Tree Press, 1917), 11, 12, 32.

61. Emily Dennis Harvey, "Preface: Anatomy of Anger," in *A Museum for the People: A Report of Proceedings at the Seminar on Neighborhood Museums*, eds. Emily Dennis Harvey and Bernard Friedberg (Cambridge, MA: Acanthus Books, 1971), ix–x. The seminar was held at MUSE, the Bedford Lincoln Neighborhood Museum in Brooklyn, at the same time as the highly controversial exhibition *Harlem on My Mind* was on view at the Metropolitan Museum of Art in New York.

62. Jon Carfagno and Adam Reed Rozan, "Adopting Empathy: Why Empathy Should Be a Required Core Value for All Museums—Period," 204. The essay appears in *Fostering Empathy through Museums*, ed. Elif M. Gokcigdem (London: Rowman & Littlefield, 2016). This is an excellent collection of recent developments from theorists and workers in the field. Comprehensive practical applications of theory are discussed by Emily Zimmern, Janeen Bryant, Kamille Bostick, and Tom Hanchett in "A Decade of Community Engagement through the Lens of Empathy" (219–37) which draws on experiences at the Levine Museum of the New South (Charlotte, NC), and by Laura Caldwell Anderson in "Walk With Me: The Birmingham Civil Rights Institute" (265–76).

63. Dina A. Bailey, "The Activist Spectrum," 294, 301.

64. Julia Rose, *Interpreting Difficult History at Museums and Historic Sites* (Lanham, MD: Rowman & Littlefield, 2016), 5.

65. Adam Muller, Struan Sinclair, Andrew Woolford. "Engaging Machines: Experience, Empathy, and the Modern Museum," in *The Idea of a Human Rights Museum*, 145, 148. For a thorough exploration of these claims see Aylish Wood, "Recursive Space: Play and Creating Space," *Games and Culture* 7.1 (2012): 87–105.

66. Angela Failler and Roger I. Simon, "Curatorial Practice and Learning from Difficult Knowledge," in *The Idea of a Human Rights Museum*, edited by Busby et al.

67. Roger I. Simon, *A Pedagogy of Witnessing: Curatorial Practice and the Pursuit of Social Justice* (New York: SUNY Press, 2014), 204–205, 213, 219. Roger Simon's work spanned decades, during which he made a vital contribution to our understanding of the interrelationship of curation, reception, education, and social justice. Many of us have been inspired by his dedication to exploring the promise and the limits of approaching "difficult knowledge."

68. Thomas W. Laqueur, "Bodies, Details, and the Humanitarian Narrative," in *The New Cultural History*, ed. Lynn Hunt (University of California Press, 1989), 177–78, 181, 195.

Bibliography

Abercrombie, Stanley. *Architecture as Art: An Aesthetic Analysis*. New York: Van Nostrand Reinhold, 1984.

Adair, Bill, Benjamin Filene, and Laura Koloski. "Introduction: Letting Go?: Sharing Historical Authority in a User-Generated World?" In *Letting Go?: Sharing Historical Authority in a User-Generated World*, edited by Adair, Filene, Koloski, 10–15. Philadelphia: Pew Center for Arts and Heritage, 2011.

African American Military Portraits. Exhibition Wall Text. California African American Museum (Los Angeles, California).

Alpers, Svetlana. "The Museum as a Way of Seeing." In *Exhibiting Cultures: The Poetics and Politics of Museum Display*, edited by Ivan Karp and Steven D. Lavine, 25–32. Washington, DC: Smithsonian Institution Press, 1991.

Anderson, Gail. *Mission Matters: Relevance and Museums in the 21st Century*. Lanham, MD: Rowman & Littlefield, 2019.

Anderson, Laura Caldwell. "Walk with Me: The Birmingham Civil Rights Institute." In *Fostering Empathy Through Museums*, edited by Elif M. Gokcigdem, 265–276.

And Still We Rise. Exhibition. Charles H. Wright Museum of African American History (Detroit, Michigan).

Apel, Dora. "Images of Black History." *Dissent* 48, no. 3 (Summer 2001): 90–95.

Appiah, Kwame Anthony. *In My Father's House: Africa in the Philosophy of Culture*. New York: Oxford University Press, 1992.

Apsel, Joyce. "'Inspiration Lives Here': Struggle, Martyrdom, and Redemption in Atlanta's National Center for Civil and Human Rights." In *Museums and Sites of Persuasion: Politics, Memory and Human Rights*, edited by Joyce Apsel and Amy Sodaro, 91–115. London: Routledge, 2020.

———, and Amy Sodaro, eds. *Museums and Sites of Persuasion: Politics, Memory and Human Rights*. London: Routledge, 2020.

Araujo, Ana Lucia, ed., *Politics of Memory: Making Slavery Visible in the Public Sphere*. New York: Routledge, 2012.

Arnheim, Rudolf. *The Dynamics of Architectural Form*. Berkeley: University of California Press, 1977.

————. *The Power of the Center: A Study of Composition in the Visual Arts.* Berkeley: University of California Press, 1988.

Asgedom, Araya. "The Unsound Space." In Lokko, *White Papers, Black Marks,* 236–77; 372–75.

Ashton, Stephen et al. "Brace for Impact." *Museum* 98, no. 3 (May/June 2019): 26–31.

Autry, Robyn. "The Political Economy of Memory: The Challenge of Representing National Conflict at 'Identity-Driven' Museums." *Theory and Society* 42 (2013): 57–80.

————. "The Politics of Race, Space, and Memory at San Francisco's Museum of the African Diaspora." In *Remembering Africa and Its Diasporas,* edited by Diptee and Trotman, 177–95.

Bailey, Dina A. "The Activist Spectrum in United States Museums." In *Museum Activism,* edited by Robert R. Janes and Richard Sandell, 293–303. London: Routledge, 2019.

Bann, Stephen. "'Views of the Past'—Reflections on the Treatment of Historical Objects and Museums of History (1750–1850)." In *Picturing Power: Visual Depiction and Social Relations,* edited by Gordon Fyfe and John Law, 39–64. Sociological Review Monographs 35. London: Routledge, 1988.

Banner-Haley, Charles. "The Necessity of Remembrance: A Review of the Museum of African American History." *American Quarterly* 51, no. 2. (June 1999): 420–25.

Barber, Lucy G. *Marching on Washington: The Forging of an American Political Tradition.* Berkeley: University of California Press, 2002.

Barrett, Jennifer. *Museums and the Public Sphere.* Malden: MA: Wiley-Blackwell, 2011.

Bazin, Germain. *The Museum Age.* Translated by Jane van Nuis Cahill. New York: Universe Books, 1967.

Bearden, Romare et al. "The Black Artist in America: A Symposium." *Metropolitan Museum of Art Bulletin* New Series 27, no.5 (January 1969): 245–61.

————, and Harry Henderson. *A History of African American Artists from 1792 to the Present.* New York: Pantheon Books, 1993.

Bedford, Leslie. *The Art of Museum Exhibitions: How Story and Imagination Create Aesthetic Experiences.* Walnut Creek, California: Left Coast Press, 2014.

"Behind the Billboards: For Freedoms on the 50-State Initiative." *Kickstarter Magazine,* June 15, 2018. medium.com/kickstarter/behind-the-billboards-for-freedoms-on-the-50-state-initiative-dbffd9a90a89.

Bennett, Tony. "Pedagogic Objects, Clean Eyes, and Popular Instruction: On Sensory Regimes and Museum Didactics." *Configurations* 6, no. 3 (1998): 345–71.

Benson, Susan Porter, Stephen Brier, and Roy Rosenzweig, eds. *Presenting the Past: Essays on History and the Public.* Philadelphia: Temple University Press, 1986.

Berger, Maurice. "Are Art Museums Racist?" *Art in America* 78, no. 9 (September 1990): 69–77.

————. "Speaking Out: Some Distance to Go." *Art in America* 78, no. 9 (September 1990): 78–85.

Berger, Stefan, and Christoph Conrad. *The Past as History: National Identity and Historical Consciousness in Modern Europe*. Basingstoke, UK: Palgrave Macmillan, 2015.

Bernier, Celeste Marie. *African American Visual Arts: From Slavery to the Present*. Chapel Hill: University of North Carolina, 2008.

Bethel, Elizabeth Rauh. *The Roots of African-American Identity: Memory and History in Free Antebellum Communities*. New York: St. Martin's, 1997.

Bevir, Mark. "National Histories: Prospects for Critique and Narrative." *Journal of the Philosophy of History* 1, no. 3 (September 2007): 293–317.

Bickford, Louis, and Amy Sodaro. "Remembering Yesterday to Protect Tomorrow: The Internationalization of a New Commemorative Paradigm." In *Memory and the Future: Transnational Politics, Ethics and Society*, edited by Yifat Gutman, Adam D. Brown, Amy Sodaro, 66–86. London: Palgrave Macmillan, 2010.

Bindman, David, and Henry Louis Gates Jr. Preface. In *The Image of the Black in Western Art, Volume II, Part 2*. New Edition: Cambridge: Harvard University Press, 2012.

Bishir, Catherine W. "Landmarks of Power: Building a Southern Past in Raleigh and Wilmington, North Carolina." In *Where These Memories Grow: History, Memory, and Southern Identity*, edited by W. Fitzhugh Brundage, 107–32. Chapel Hill: University of North Carolina Press, 2000.

Black Art—Ancestral Legacy: The African Impulse in African-American Art. Dallas, Texas: Dallas Museum of Art, 1990.

Black Refractions. ENGAGE Symposium. Museum of the African Diaspora (San Francisco, California). www.moadsf.org/event/engage-black-refractions -symposium.

Blake, W. O. *The History of Slavery and the Slave Trade, Ancient and Modern . . . and the Political History of Slavery in the United States. Compiled from Authentic Materials*. 2 vols. New York: Haskell House Publishers Ltd., 1969. (Reprint of 1858 edition).

Blassingame, John. *Slave Testimony: Two Centuries of Letters, Speeches, Interviews, and Autobiographies*. Baton Rouge: Louisiana State University Press, 1977.

Boime, Albert. *The Art of Exclusion: Representing Blacks in the Nineteenth Century*. Washington, DC: Smithsonian Institution Press, 1990.

———. "Invisible in the Foreground." Review of Hugh Honour's *The Image of the Black in Western Art*. *New York Times Book Review*, April 2, 1989.

Bonnell, Jennifer, and Roger I. Simon. "'Difficult' Exhibitions and Intimate Encounters." *Museum and Society* 5, no. 2 (2007): 65–85.

Bourdier, Jean-Paul, and Trinh T. Minh-ha. *Vernacular Architecture of West Africa: A World in Dwelling*. New York: Routledge, 2011.

Brawley, Benjamin. *A Social History of the American Negro, Being a History of the Negro Problem in the United States, Including a History and Study of the Republic of Liberia*. New York: Macmillan, 1921. Reprint. Johnson Reprint Corp., 1968.

Brazuel, Jana Evans, and Anita Mannur, eds. *Theorizing Diaspora: A Reader.* Malden, MA: Blackwell, 2003.

Brenson, Michael. "Black Images, American History." *New York Times*, April 20, 1990.

Bronbeck, Bruce E. "The Rhetorics of the Past: History, Argument, and Collective Memory." In *Doing Rhetorical History: Concepts and Cases*, edited by Kathleen J. Turner, 47–60, 252–56. Tuscaloosa, AL: University of Alabama Press, 1998.

Brooks, James. F., ed. "State of Black Museums: Historiography Commemorating the Founding and Existence of Black Museums over Four Decades." *The Public Historian* 40, no. 3 (August 2018).

Broun, Elizabeth. Preface. In *Free within Ourselves: African-American Artists in the Collection of the National Museum of American Art*, by Regenia Perry, 8–13. Washington, DC: Smithsonian Institution and Pomegranate Artbooks, 1992.

Brown, DeNeen L. "Looking Forward and Back at Once." *Washington Post*, February 19, 2012.

Brown, William Wells. *The Black Man: His Antecedents, His Genius, and His Achievements*. Boston: James Redpath, 1863.

Brundage, W. Fitzhugh, ed. *Where These Memories Grow: History, Memory, and Southern Identity*. Chapel Hill: University of North Carolina Press, 2000.

Buchanan, Larry, Quoctrung Bui, and Jugal K. Patel. "Black Lives Matter May Be the Largest Movement in U.S. History." *New York Times*, July 8, 2020.

Bunch, Lonnie G. III. *Call the Lost Dream Back: Essays on History, Race and Museums*. Washington, DC: American Alliance of Museums Press, 2010.

———. "Embracing Ambiguity: The Challenge of Interpreting African American History in Museums." *Museums and Social Issues* 2.1 (Spring 2007): 45–55.

———. *A Fool's Errand: Creating the National Museum of American History and Culture in the Age of Bush, Obama, and Trump*. Washington, DC: Smithsonian Books, 2019.

Burns, Andrea A. *From Storefront to Monument: Tracing the Public History of the Black Museum Movement*. Amherst: University of Massachusetts, Press, 2013.

———. "When 'Civil Rights Are Not Enough': The Creation and Work of the International Afro American Museum of Detroit." In *Remembering Africa and Its Diasporas: Memory, Public History and Representations of the Past*, edited by Audra A. Diptee and David V. Trotman, 197–215. Trenton, New Jersey: Africa World Press, 2012.

Busby, Karen, Adam Muller, and Andrew Woolford. Introduction. In *The Idea of a Human Rights Museum*, edited by Busby, Muller and Woolford, 1–24. Winnipeg, Manitoba: University of Manitoba Press, 2015.

Byrne, John, Elinor Morgan, November Paynter, Aida Sánchez de Serdio, and Adela Železnik, eds. *The Constituent Museum: Constellations of Knowledge, Politics and Mediation*. Amsterdam: Valiz, 2018.

Carbonell, Bettina. "The Afterlife of Lynching: Exhibitions and the Re-Composition of Human Suffering." *Mississippi Quarterly* 61, no. 1–2 (Winter–Spring 2008): 197–215.

Carfagno, Jon, and Adam Reed Rozan. "Adopting Empathy: Why Empathy Should Be a Required Core Value for All Museums—Period." In *Fostering Empathy through Museums*, edited by Elif M. Gokcigdem, 201–16. London: Rowman & Littlefield, 2016.

Carter, Jennifer. "The Museology of Human Rights." In *The Idea of a Human Rights Museum*, edited by Busby, Muller and Woolford, 208–26.

Caruth, Cathy. *Trauma: Explorations in Memory*. Baltimore: Johns Hopkins University Press, 1995.

Clark, Gregory C. "Rhetorical Experience and the National Jazz Museum in Harlem." In *Places of Public Memory: The Rhetoric of Museums and Memorials*, edited by Greg Dickinson et al., 113–35. Tuscaloosa: University of Alabama Press, 2009.

Clarke, Lewis Garrard. *Narrative of the Sufferings of Lewis Clarke, during a Captivity of More Than Twenty-Five Years, among the Algerines of Kentucky, One of the So Called Christian States of North America. Dictated by Himself*. Boston: David H. Ela, Printer, 1845.

Clarke-Hazlett, Christopher. "Review: Of the People." *American Quarterly* 51, no. 2 (June 1999): 426–36.

Clemetson, Lynette. "Long Quest, Unlikely Allies: Black Museum Nears a Reality." *New York Times*, June 29, 2003.

———. "Smithsonian Picks Notable Spot for Museum of Black History." *New York Times*, January 31, 2006.

Cole, Johnnetta Betsch, and Laura L. Lott, eds. *Diversity, Equity, Accessibility, and Inclusion in Museums*. Lanham, MD: Rowman & Littlefield, 2019.

Coleman, Laura-Edythe. *Understanding and Implementing Inclusion in Museums*. Lanham. MD: Rowman & Littlefield, 2018.

Coloring America: Selections from the California African American Museum's California Permanent History Collection. Exhibition. California African American Museum (Los Angeles, California).

Conn, Steven. "Narrative Trauma and Civil War History Painting, or Why Are These Pictures So Terrible?" *History and Theory* 41, no. 4 (2002): 17–42.

Coombes, Annie. "Museums and the Formation of National and Cultural Identities." *Oxford Art Journal* 11.2 (1988): 57–68.

Cooper, Priscilla Hancock. "A City Embraces Its Past, Looks to the Future: A Perspective on the Evolution of the Birmingham Civil Rights Institute." *The Public Historian* 40, no.3 (August 2018): 211–31.

Cotter, Holland. "Black Artists: Three Shows." *Art in America* 78, no. 3 (March 1990): 165–71.

Cubitt, Geoff. "Atrocity Materials and the Representation of Transatlantic Slavery." In *Representing Enslavement and Abolition in Museums*, edited by Laurajane Smith et al., 229–59. New York: Routledge, 2011.

Cubitt, Geoff, Laurajane Smith, and Ross Wilson. "Introduction: Anxiety and Ambiguity in the Representation of Dissonant History." In *Representing Enslavement and Abolition in Museums: Ambiguous Engagements*, edited by Laurajane Smith, Geoff Cubitt, Kalliopi Fouseki, and Ross Wilson, 1–19. New York: Routledge, 2011.

Dagbovie, Peter Gaglo. *What Is African American History?* Cambridge, UK: Polity, 2015.

Dana, John Cotton. *The New Museum.* Woodstock, VT: The Elm Tree Press, 1917.

Davis, Felecia. "(Un)Covering/(Re) Covering." In Lokko, *White Papers, Black Marks,* 348–55, 375.

Davis, Nancy. "Communities of Refuge in Frontier Illinois." In *Many Voices, One Nation,* edited by Margaret Salazar-Porzio, et al., 101–109.

Davis, Thomas J. "'They, Too, Were Here': The Afro-American Experience and History Museums." *American Quarterly* 41, no. 2 (June 1989): 328–40.

Dempsey, Anna M. "150 Years Later: Remembering Africa in the Museum." In *Remembering Africa and Its Diasporas,* edited by Diptee and Trotman, 217–48.

Denyer, Susan. *African Traditional Architecture: An Historical and Geographical Perspective.* London: Heinemann, 1978.

"Detroit Architect Harold Varner Dies at Age 78." *Associated Press,* December 18, 2013.

Dickerson, Amina Jill. *The History and Institutional Development of African American Museums.* MA thesis, The American University, 1988.

Dietsch, Deborah, K. "Building New History; Black Museum Plan Picked." *Washington Times,* April 15, 2009.

———. "Storyteller of Black America: Director Shapes Mission of Smithsonian's Newest Museum." *Washington Times,* September 27, 2009.

Diptee, Audra A., and David V. Trotman, eds. *Remembering Africa and Its Diasporas: Memory, Public History and Representations of the Past.* Trenton, NJ: Africa World Press, 2012.

Duncan, Carol, and Alan Wallach. "The Universal Survey Museum," *Art History* 3, no. 4 (December 1980): 448–69.

Dvorak, Petula. "African American Museum Poses a Siting Dilemma." *Washington Post,* November 17, 2005.

Dwyer, Owen J. "Interpreting the Civil Rights Movement: Contradiction, Confirmation, and the Cultural Landscape." In *The Civil Rights Movement in American Memory,* edited by Renee C. Romano and Leigh Raiford, 5–27.

Eco, Umberto. "Function and Sign: The Semiotics of Architecture." In *Rethinking Architecture: A Reader in Cultural Theory,* edited by Neil Leach. London: Routledge, 1997.

Edelman, Murray. *From Art to Politics: How Artistic Creations Shape Political Conceptions.* Chicago: University of Chicago Press, 1995.

Edwards, Brent Hayes. *Epistrophies: Jazz and the Literary Imagination.* Cambridge: Harvard University Press, 2017.

Eldredge, Charles C. Foreword. In Hartigan, *Sharing Traditions: Five Black Artists in Nineteenth-Century America,* 7–10. Washington, DC: Smithsonian Institution Press, 1985.

Elleh, Nnamdi. *African Architecture: Evolution and Transformation.* New York: McGraw-Hill, 1997.

Emerging Artists Program. Museum of the African Diaspora (San Francisco, California). www.moadsf.org/what-we-do/moad-emerging-artists-program.

Equiano, Elaudah. *The Interesting Narrative of the Life of Olaudah Equiano, or Gustavas Vassa, the African, Written by Himself*, ed. Robert J. Allison. New York: Bedford/St. Martin's, 1995.

Eskew, Glenn. "The Birmingham Civil Rights Institute and the New Ideology of Tolerance." In *The Civil Rights Movement in American Memory*, edited by Renee C. Romano and Leigh Raiford, 48–60.

Failing, Patricia. "Black Artists Today: A Case of Exclusion." *Art News* (March 1989): 124–31.

Failler, Angela, and Roger I. Simon. "Curatorial Practice and Learning from Difficult Knowledge." In *The Idea of a Human Rights Museum*, edited by Karen Busby et al., 165–79.

Fairchild, Mary Jo. "The African American Museum Movement: New Strategies in the Battle for Equality in the Twentieth Century." *Proceedings of the South Carolina Historical Association*, 2008: 5–14.

Farrington, Lisa. *African American Art: A Visual and Cultural History*. New York: Oxford University Press, 2017.

Fax, Elton C. *Seventeen Black Artists*. New York: Dodd, Mead & Co., 1971.

Feldman, Eugene P. R. *The Birth and the Building of the DuSable Museum*. Chicago: DuSable Museum Press, 1981.

Feldman, Judy Scott. "Turning Point: The Problematics of Building on the Mall Today." In *The National Mall*, edited by Nathan Glazer and Cynthia R. Field, 135–58.

Ferguson, Leland. *Uncommon Ground: Archaeology and Early African America, 1650–1800*. Washington, DC: Smithsonian Books, 1992.

Fields, Darryl Wayne. *Architecture in Black*. London: The Athlone Press, 2000.

Fleming, John E. "African-American Museums, History, and the American Ideal." *The Journal of American History* 81, no. 3 (December 1994): 1020–26.

———. "The Impact of Social Movements on the Development of African American Museums." *The Public Historian* 40, no. 3 (August 2018): 44–73.

Fletcher, Kami. "Museums Respond to Ferguson." www.aaihs.org/museumsrespondtoferguson-an-interview-with-aleia-brown-and-adrianne-russell/.

Focillon, Henri. *The Life of Forms in Art*. Translated by Charles B. Hogan and George Kubler. New Haven: Yale University Press, 1942.

For Freedoms Town Hall on Freedom of Speech. California African American Museum (San Francisco, California). caamuseum.org/programs/talks-and-workshops/for-freedoms-town-hall-on-freedom-of-speech.

Fraser, Peter, and Rozina Visram. *Black Contribution to History. Report Commissioned by CUES Community Division and the Geffrye Museum*. London: Geffrye Museum, 1988.

Freelon Group. Museum of the African Diaspora. www.architectmagazine.com/projcct-gallery/museum-of-the-african-diaspora-2712.

Fried, Michael. *Realism, Writing, Disfiguration: On Thomas Eakins and Stephen Crane*. Chicago: University of Chicago Press, 1987.

FuturePresent: Acquisition Highlights from the Permanent Collection. Exhibition. Harvey B. Gantt Center for African-American Arts + Culture (Charlotte, North Carolina).

Gaither, Edmund. Introduction. In *Afro-American Artists, New York and Boston.* Boston: The Museum of the National Center of Afro-American Artists, The Museum of the Fine Arts and the School of the Museum of Fine Arts, 1970.

Gallas, Kristin L., and James DeWolf Perry, eds. *Interpreting Slavery at Museums and Historic Sites.* Lanham, MD: Rowman & Littlefield, 2015.

Harvey B. Gantt Center. *Fact Sheet.* www.ganttcenter.org/public/assets/IEI-Fact -Sheet-Web.pdf.

Gates, Henry Louis. *Life upon These Shores: Looking at African American History 1513–2008.* New York: Knopf, 2011.

———. "The Face and Voice of Blackness." In McElroy, *Facing History: The Black Image in American Art, 1710–1940.*

Gayle, Addison, ed. *The Black Aesthetic.* New York: Doubleday, 1971.

Gelles, David. "Smithsonian's Leader Says 'Museums Have a Social Justice Role to Play.'" *New York Times,* July 2, 2020.

Glavic, Jamie, with Dion Brown. "The National Underground Railroad and Freedom Center." In *Mission Matters: Relevance and Museums in the 21st Century*, edited by Gail Anderson, 85–87.

Glazer, Nathan. Introduction. *The National Mall: Rethinking Washington's Monumental Core*, edited by Nathan Glazer and Cynthia R. Field. Baltimore: Johns Hopkins University Press, 2008.

Gokcigdem, Elif M., ed. *Fostering Empathy through Museums.* London: Rowman & Littlefield, 2016.

Goldberger, Paul. *Why Architecture Matters.* New Haven: Yale University Press, 2009.

Goodman, Nelson. "How Buildings Mean." In *Reconceptions in Philosophy and Other Arts and Sciences*, edited by Nelson Goodman and Catherine Z. Elgin, 31–48. London: Routledge, 1988.

Grant, Bradford C. "Accommodation and Resistance: The Built Environment and the African American Experience." In *Reconstructing Architecture: Critical Discourses and Social Practices*, edited by Thomas A. Dutton and Lian Hurst Mann. *Pedagogy and Practice* vol. 5, 203–233. Minneapolis: University of Minnesota Press, 1996.

Greene, Carroll. *The Evolution of Afro-American Artists: 1800–1950.*

Hale, Zack. "Monuments Face a New Landscape." *Roll Call,* March 22, 2010.

Hall, Stuart. "Cultural Identity and Diaspora." In *Theorizing Diaspora: A Reader*, edited by Jana Evans Braziel and Anita Mannur, 233–46. Malden, MA: Blackwell, 2003.

Hammond, Leslie King, and Lowery Stokes Sims. *Art as a Verb: The Evolving Continuum: Installations, Performances, and Videos by 13 African-American Artists: November 21, 1988–January 8, 1989, Maryland Institute, College of Art.* Baltimore: The Maryland Institute College of Art, 1988.

Hank Willis Thomas: What We Ask Is Simple. Exhibition. Harvey B. Gantt Center for African-American Arts and Culture (Charlotte, North Carolina). www.ganttcenter .org/exhibitions/hank-willis-thomas-what-we-ask-is-simple/.

Harper, Phillip Brian. *Abstractionist Aesthetics: Artistic Form and Social Critique in African American Culture.* New York: New York University Press, 2015.

Hartigan, Linda Roscoe. *Sharing Traditions: Five Black Artists in Nineteenth-Century America.* Washington, DC: Smithsonian Institution Press, 1985.

Harvey, Eleanor Jones. "Abolition and Emancipation." In *The Civil War and American Art.* Washington, DC: Smithsonian American Art Museum, 2013.

Harvey, Emily Dennis. "Preface: Anatomy of Anger." In *A Museum for the People: A Report of Proceedings at the Seminar on Neighborhood Museums*, edited by Emily Dennis Harvey and Bernard Friedberg. Cambridge, MA: Acanthus Books, 1971.

Hayward, Jeff, and Christine Larouche. "The Emergence of the Field of African American Museums." *The Public Historian* 40, no. 3 (August 2018): 163–172.

Herskovits, Melville J. *The Myth of the Negro Past.* New York: Beacon Press, 1941.

Hill, Jonathan. Introduction. In *Occupying Architecture: Between the Architect and the User*, edited by Jonathan Hill. London: Routledge, 1998.

Hindle, Brooke. Introduction. In *A Nation of Nations: The People Who Came to America as Seen Through Objects and Documents Exhibited at the Smithsonian Institution*, edited by Peter Marzio, xv–xviii. New York: Harper & Row, 176.

Hirsch, Marianne. "The Generation of Postmemory." *Poetics Today* 29, no. 1 (Spring 2008): 103–28.

Honour, Hugh. *The Image of the Black in Western Art, vol. IV, from the American Revolution to World War I.* Cambridge: Menil Foundation, Harvard University Press, 1989.

Hooper-Greenhill, Eilean. "Changing Values in the Art Museum: Rethinking Communication and Learning." *International Journal of Heritage Studies* 6 no. 1 (March 2000): 9–31.

Horton, James Oliver, and Spencer R. Crew. "Afro-Americans and Museums: Towards a Policy of Inclusion." In *History Museums in the United States: A Critical Assessment*, edited by Warren Leon and Roy Rosenzweig, 215–36. Urbana: University of Illinois Press, 1989.

Huebner, Michael. "Birmingham Civil Rights Institute's Mission of Diplomacy, Education and Human Rights Having a Global Impact," AL.com blog.al.com/entertainment_impact/Print.html?entry=2013/01/brimingham_civil_right. . . .

Hughes, David. *Afrocentric Architecture: A Design Primer.* Columbus, Ohio: Greyden Press, 1994.

Hughes, Langston. "The Negro Artist and the Racial Mountain." In *The Black Aesthetic*, edited by Addison Gayle, 175–84.

Huyssen, Andreas. *Present Pasts: Urban Palimpsests and the Politics of Memory.* Stanford University Press, 2003.

Ihejirika, Edward. "Intensive Continuity." In *White Papers, Black Marks*, edited by Lesley Naa Norle Lokko, 182–193 and 368.

Incluseum. "Equitable Institutional Sustainability in Times of Crisis." Incluseum.com. incluseum.com/2020/04/17/equitable-institutional-sustainability-in-times-of-crisis/.

Jackson, Ronald L., and Elaine B. Richardson, eds. *Understanding African American Rhetoric*: *Classical Origins to Contemporary Innovations*. New York: Routledge, 2003.

Jacobs, Jane M., Kim Dovey, and Mathilde Lochert. "Authorizing Aboriginality in Architecture." In Lokko, *White Papers, Black Marks*, edited by Lesley Naa Norle Lokko, 218–35 and 371–72.

James, William. "What Pragmatism Means." in *Pragmatism*. Cambridge, MA: Harvard University Press, 1975.

Janes, Robert R., and Richard Sandell. Introduction: "Posterity Has Arrived: The Necessary Emergence of Museum Activism." In *Museum Activism*, edited by Janes and Sandell, 1–21. London: Routledge, 2019.

Jennings, Gretchen. "Joint Statement from Museum Bloggers and Colleagues on Ferguson and Recent Events." museumcommons.com/2014/12/joint-statement-museum-bloggers-colleagues-ferguson-related-events.html.

Johnson, Charles. "The End of the Black American Narrative." *American Scholar* 77, no. 3 (Summer 2008), 32–42.

Johnson, Edward A. *A School History of the Negro Race in America from 1619 to 1890 Combined with the History of Negro Soldiers in the Spanish-American War, Also Other Items of Interest*. Revised Edition, 1911, Reprint New York: AMS Press, 1969.

Johnson, Philip. "Whence and Whither: The Processional Element in Architecture." In *Philip Johnson. Writings*, 150–55. New York: Oxford University Press, 1979.

Johnson, Walter. *Soul by Soul: Life inside the Antebellum Slave Market*. Cambridge: Harvard University Press, 1999.

Jones-Rizzi, Joanne, and Stacey Mann. "Is That Hung White?" *Museum* 99, no. 3 (Summer 2020): 26–31.

Karenga, Ron (Maulenga). "Black Cultural Nationalism." In *The Black Aesthetic*, edited by Addison Gayle, 32–38.

Kargon, Jeremy. "Architecture: The Reginald F. Lewis Museum of Maryland African American History and Culture." *Curator* 49, no.1 (January 2006): 90–94.

Karp, Ivan, Corinne A. Kratz, Lynn Szwaja, Tomás Ybarra-Frausto, eds. *Museum Frictions: Public Cultures/Global Transformations*. Durham: Duke University Press, 2006.

Karp, Ivan, and Corinne A. Kratz. "Preface: Museum Frictions: A Project History." *In Museum Frictions*, edited by Karp et al., xv–xxii.

Kelley, Robin D. G. "How the West Was One: The African Diaspora and the Re-Mapping of U.S. History." In *Rethinking American History in a Global Age*, edited by Thomas Bender, 123–47. Berkeley: University of California Press, 2002.

Kennedy, Randy. "Architects Chosen for Black History Museum." *New York Times*, April 15, 2009.

Kennedy, Roger. "Some Thoughts about National Museums at the End of the Century." In *The Formation of National Collections of Art and Archaeology*, edited by Gwendolyn Wright, 159-163. Washington, DC: The National Gallery of Art, 1996.

Kirshenblatt-Gimblett, Barbara. "From Ethnology to Heritage: The Role of the Museum." *SIEF* Keynote, Marseilles, April 28, 4 (2004).

Kliment, Stephen A. "Discovering African Identity in African-American Architecture, Parts I and II." *AIA*rchitect (August 3, 2007) and (September 7, 2007).

Kristof, Nicholas D., and Sheryl WuDunn. *Half the Sky: Turning Oppression into Opportunity for Women Worldwide.* New York: Knopf, 2010.

Kurashige, Scott. "Epilogue: Our Polycultural Past and Future Century." In *Many Voices, One Nation*, edited by Margaret Salazar-Porzio et al., 269–75.

LaCapra, Dominick. *Writing History, Writing Trauma.* Baltimore: Johns Hopkins, University Press: 2001.

Landsberg, Allison. *Prosthetic Memory: The Transformation of American Remembrance in the Age of Mass Culture.* New York: Columbia University Press, 2004.

Laqueur, Thomas W. "Bodies, Details, and the Humanitarian Narrative." In *The New Cultural History*, edited by Lynn Hunt. 175–204. Berkeley: University of California Press, 1989.

LaRoche, Cheryl J. *Free Black Communities and the Underground Railroad: The Geography of Resistance.* Urbana-Champaign: University of Illinois Press, 2014.

Lavine, Steven D., and Ivan Karp. Introduction. In *Exhibiting Cultures: The Poetics and Politics of Museum Display*, edited by Lavine and Karp, 1–9. Washington, DC: Smithsonian Institution Press, 1991.

Levinas, Emmanuel. *Otherwise Than Being, or, Beyond Essence.* Translated by Alphonso Lingis. Pittsburgh: Duquesne University Press, 1998.

Lewis, John R., Sam Brownback, Max Cleland, and J. C. Watts, Jr. "400 Years of Turbulent History: An African American Space at the Smithsonian." Op-Ed. *Washington Times*, June 4, 2001.

Locke, Alain. *Negro Art: Past and Present.* Bronze Booklet No. 3. Washington, DC: The Associates in Negro Folk Education, 1936.

———. "The Negro as Artist." In *The Negro in Art: A Pictorial Record of the Negro Artist and of the Negro Theme in Art.* Edited by Alain Locke. New York: Hacker Books, 1968.

Lokko, Lesley Naa Norle. Introduction. In *White Papers, Black Marks: Architecture, Race, Culture*, edited by Lesley Naa Norle Lokko, 10–35, London: The Athlone Press, 2000.

Lord, Rich."Different Attorney, Evidence in Jordan Miles Retrial." *Pittsburgh Post-Gazette*, March 10, 2014.

Lusaka, Jane. "Finding a Voice." *Museum News*, July/August 1997.

Mack, Deborah L., and John S. Welch. "The State of Black Museums." *The Public Historian* 40, no. 3 (August 2018): 9–12.

MacLeod, Suzanne, "Rethinking Museum Architecture: Towards a Site-Specific History of Production and Use." In *Reshaping Museum Space: Architecture, Design, Exhibitions*, edited by Suzanne MacLeod, 9–25. London: Routledge, 2005.

Majekodunmi, Olufemi. "Afrocentric Architecture: Myth and Reality." *Architectural Record* (January 1994): 16.

Making African America: A Virtual Symposium on Immigration and the Changing Dynamics of *Blackness*. National Museum of African American History (Washington, DC). nmaahc.si.edu/making-african-america.

Marshall, Christopher R. "When Worlds Collide: The Contemporary Museum as Art Gallery." In *Reshaping Museum Space: Architecture, Design, Exhibitions*, edited by Suzanne MacLeod, 170–84. London: Routledge, 2005.

Marzio, Peter, ed. *A Nation of Nations: The People Who Came to America as Seen Through Objects and Documents Exhibited at the Smithsonian Institution*. New York: Harper & Row, 1976.

MASS Action: Museum as Site for Social Action. "Community of Practice Platform." www.museumaction.org.

Mathur, Saloni. "Social Thought and Commentary: Museums and Globalization." *Anthropological Quarterly* 78.3 (Summer 2005): 697–708.

McElroy, Guy. "Introduction: Race and Representation." In *Facing History: The Black Image in American Art, 1710–1940*. New York: Chronicle Books, 1991.

Mcelya, Micki. "Unknowns: Commemorating Black Women's Civil War Heroism." In Savage, *The Civil War in Art and Memory*, 212–26.

Meadows, John. From Confinement to Liberty: The National Underground Railroad Freedom Center by Blackburn Architects with BOORA Architects," *ArchNewsNow.com*, November 17, 2006.

Message, Kylie. *Museums and Social Activism: Engaged Protest*. London: Routledge, 2014.

———. *New Museums and the Making of Culture*. Oxford: Berg, 2006.

Meyer, Jeffrey F. *Myths in Stone: Religious Dimensions of Washington, DC* Berkeley: University of California Press, 2001.

Miller, Adam David. "Some Observations on a Black Aesthetic." In *The Black Aesthetic*, edited by Addison Gayle, 397–404.

Minardi, Margot. "Making Slavery Visible (Again): The Nineteenth-Century Roots of a Revisionist Recovery in New England." In *Politics of Memory: Making Slavery Visible in the Public Sphere*, edited by Ana Lucia Araujo, 92–105. New York: Routledge, 2012.

Mitchell, Melvin L. *The Crisis of the African-American Architect: Conflicting Cultures of Architecture and (Black) Power*. Revised 2nd edition. New York: Writers Advantage, 2003.

Mitchell, Michelle. Exhibition Review: "Of the People." *The Public Historian* 23, no. 2 (Spring 2001): 124–26.

Morgan, Elinor. "Distributing Ownership." In *The Constituent Museum*, edited by Byrne et al., 220–23.

Morris, Catherine, and Rujeko Hockley, eds. *We Wanted a Revolution: Black Radical Women, 1965–1985/New Perspectives*. Brooklyn, NY: Brooklyn Museum, 2018.

———. *We Wanted a Revolution: Black Radical Women, 1965–1985/A Sourcebook*. Brooklyn, NY: Brooklyn Museum, 2018.

Moselle, Aaron. "Philly's African American Museum Moving to the Ben Franklin Parkway." *WHYY.org*, August 11, 2022.

Moten, Fred. "Jurisgenerative Grammar (For Alto.)" In *The Oxford Handbook of Critical Improvisation Studies,* volume 1, edited by George E. Lewis and Benjamin Piekut, 128–42. New York: Oxford University Press, 2016.

Muller, Adam, Struan Sinclair, and Andrew Woolford. "Engaging Machines: Experience, Empathy, and the Modern Museum." In *The Idea of a Human Rights Museum,* edited by Busby et al.

Mullins, Paul R. "African American Heritage in a Multicultural Community: An Archaeology of Race, Culture, and Consumption." In *Places in Mind: Public Archaeology as Applied Anthropology,* edited by Paul A. Shackel and Erve J. Chambers, 57–70. New York: Routledge, 2004.

Murray, Freeman Henry Morris. *Emancipation and the Freed in American Sculpture: A Study in Interpretation.* Washington, DC: Press of Arthur Murray Brothers, Inc., 1916.

Museum of the African Diaspora. "Our Mission." www.moadsf.org/about

National Museum of African American History and Culture. "The Vision for the Future of the National Museum of African American History and Culture." nmaahc.si.edu/about.

National Underground Railroad Freedom Center. Press Release. freedomcenter.org/ voice/press_release/freedom-center-mourns-the-loss-of-renowned-historian-carl-westmoreland/.

———. "A Slave Pen Journey." artsandculture.google.com/story/wAVxA-E2xxAA8A.

Nell, William Cooper. *The Colored Patriots of the American Revolution, With Sketches of Several Distinguished Colored Persons: To Which Is Added a Brief Survey of the Conditions and Prospects of Colored Americans.* Boston: Robert F. Walcutt, 1855. digital-research-books-beta.nypl.org/read/14238779?source=cata log.

Newman, Richard S., and Roy E. Finkenbein. "Black Founders in the New Republic: Introduction." *William and Mary Quarterly* 3rd Series, LXIV, no. 1 (January 2007). 83–94.

Nora, Pierre. "Between Memory and History: *Les Lieux de Mémoire.*" *Representations* 26 (Spring 1989): 7–24.

Norberg-Schultz, Christian. *Meaning in Western Architecture.* New York: Praeger, 1975.

Oakes, James. "The Summer of 1863: Lincoln and Black Troops." In Savage, *The Civil War in Art and Memory,* 53–64.

Okpewho, Isidore. Introduction. *The New African Diaspora,* edited by Isidore Okpewho and Nkiru Nzegwu, 3–30. Bloomington: Indiana University Press, 2009.

O'Meally, Robert C. "On Burke and the Vernacular: Ralph Ellison's Boomerang of History." In *History and Memory in African-American Culture,* eds. Geneviève Fabre and Robert G. O'Meally, 244–60. New York: Oxford University Press, 1994.

Open Your Mind: Understanding Implicit Bias. Exhibition. National Underground Railroad Freedom Center (Cincinnati, Ohio). freedomcent er.org/visit/permanent-exhibits/open-your-mind-understanding-implicit-bias/#:~:text=The%20Open%20Your%20Mind%20learning,realm%20of%20impl icit%20bias%20research.

Orloff, Chet. "Should Museums Change Our Mission and Become Agencies of Social Justice?" *Curator* 60, no. 1 (January 2017): 33–36.

Panofsky, Erwin. *Perspective as Symbolic Form*. Translated by Christopher S. Wood. New York: Zone Books, 1997.

Parry, Ellwood. *The Image of the Indian and the Black Man in American Art, 1590–1900*. New York: George Braziller, 1974.

Patterson, Orlando. *Slavery and Social Death: A Comparative Study*. Cambridge: Harvard University Press, 1982.

Patterson, Ruby, and Robin D.G. Kelley. "Unfinished Migrations: Reflections on the African Diaspora and the Making of the Modern World." *African Studies Review* 43, no. 1 (April 2000): 11–45.

Patton, Sharon F. *African-American Art*. Oxford History of Art. New York: Oxford University Press, 1998.

Pecora, Vincent P. "Towers of Babel." In *Out of Site: A Social Criticism of Architecture*, edited by Diane Ghirardo, 46–76. Seattle: Bay Press, 1991.

Pennay, Anthony. *The Civic Mission of Museums*. Lanham, MD: Rowman & Littlefield, 2021.

Pennington, Rev. James W. C. *A Text-Book on the Origin and History, &c. &c. of the Colored People*. Hartford: L. Skinner, 1841.

Perrin, Andrew J. *American Democracy from Tocqueville to Town Halls to Twitter*. Cambridge, UK: Polity, 2014.

Perry, Regenia. *Free within Ourselves: African-American Artists in the Collection of the National Museum of American Art*. Washington, DC: Smithsonian Institution and Pomegranate Artbooks, 1992.

Phillips, Ruth B. "APEC at the Museum of Anthropology: The Politics of Site and the Poetics of Sight Bite." In *Imagining Resistance: Visual Culture and Activism in Canada*, edited by J. Keri Cronin and Kirsty Robertson, 171–91. Waterloo, Ontario: Wilfrid Laurier University Press, 2011.

———. "Where Is 'Africa'? Re-Viewing Art and Artifact in the Age of Globalization." *American Anthropologist* 104, no. 3 (September 2002): 944–52.

Picturing Blackness. ENGAGE Symposium. Museum of the African Diaspora (San Francisco, California). www.moadsf.org/event/engage-symposium2020-picturing-blackness.

Pittsburgh Post-Gazette Editorial Board. "Settle It: The Jordan Miles Case Was Painful All Around." *Pittsburgh Post-Gazette*, May 29, 2016.

Powell, Richard J. "Art History and Black Memory: Toward a 'Blues Aesthetic." In *History and Memory in African-American Culture*, edited by Geneviève Faber and Robert G. O'Meally, 228–43. New York: Oxford University Press, 1994.

———. *Black Art and Culture in the 20th Century*. London: Thames and Hudson, 1997.

———. "The Wounded Zouave and the Cyrenian Paradigm." In Savage, *The Civil War in Art and Memory*, 65–80.

Preston, George Nelson. "Traditions and Transformations . . . " in *Traditions and Transformations: Contemporary Afro-American Sculpture*. Bronx, NY: The Bronx Museum of the Arts, 1989.

Raiford, Leigh, and Renee C. Romero. "Introduction," in *The Civil Rights Movement in American Memory*, edited by Renee C. Romano and Leigh Raiford. Athens, GA: University of Georgia Press, 2006.

Raven, Arlene. "Mojotech." *Village Voice*, March 28, 1989.

Rediker, Marcus. *The Slave Ship: A Human History*. New York: Viking Press, 2007.

Reed, T.V. *The Art of Protest: Culture and Activism from the Civil Rights Movement to the Streets of Seattle*. Minneapolis: University of Minnesota Press, 2005.

Reeves, Joshua, "Suspended Identification: Atopos and the Work of Public Memory." *Philosophy and Rhetoric* 46, no. 3 (2013): 306–27.

Rice, Kym. "African American Expression in Antebellum America: The Story of Dave Drake." In *Many Voices, One Nation*, edited by Margaret Salazar-Porzio et al., 111–121.

Risen, Clay. "Plinth and Crown." *Architect* 98, no. 7 (July 2009).

Robins, Corinne. *The Pluralist Era: American Art, 1968–1981*. New York: Harper & Row, 1984.

Robinson-Hubbuch, Jocelyn. "African-American Museums and the National Conversation on American Pluralism and Identity." *The Public Historian* 19, no.1 (Winter 1977): 29–31.

Romano, Renee C., and Leigh Raiford, eds. *The Civil Rights Movement in American Memory*. Athens, Georgia: University of Georgia Press, 2006.

Rose, Julia. *Interpreting Difficult History at Museums and Historic Sites*. London: Rowman & Littlefield, 2016.

Roth, Leland M. *Understanding Architecture: Its Elements, History, and Meaning*. New York: Icon Editions, 1993.

Rothstein, Edward. "Anecdotal Evidence of Homesick Mankind." *New York Times*, July 20, 2006.

Ruffins, Fath Davis. "Building Homes for Black History: Museum Founders, Founding Directors, and Pioneers, 1915–1995. *The Public Historian* 40, no. 3 (August 2018): 13–43.

———. "A Community Revealed: The Reginald F. Lewis Museum of Maryland African American History and Culture." *Curator* 49, no. 1 (January 2006): 81–89.

———. "Contesting the Nation, 1900–1965." In *Many Voices, One Nation*, edited by Margaret Salazar-Porzio et al., 137–63.

———. "Culture Wars Won and Lost, Part II: The National African-American Museum Project." *Radical History Review* 70 (Winter 1998): 78–101.

———. "Revisiting the Old Plantation: Reparations, Reconciliation, and Museumizing American Slavery." In Ivan Karp et al., eds., *Museum Frictions: Public Cultures/ Global Transformations*, 394–434. Durham: Duke University Press, 2006.

Sajó, András. *Constitutional Sentiments*. New Haven: Yale University Press, 2011.

Salazar-Porzio, Margaret, Joan Troyano, and Lauren Safranek, eds. *Many Voices, One Nation: Material Culture Reflections on Race and Migration in the United States*. Washington, DC: Smithsonian Institution, 2017.

Salazar-Porzio, Margaret, and Joan Fragaszy Troyano. Introduction. In *Many Voices, One Nation*, 11–25. Washington, DC: Smithsonian Institution, 2017.

Sandell, Richard. "Constructing and Communicating Equality: The Social Agency of Museum Space." In *Reshaping Museum Space: Architecture, Design, Exhibitions*, edited by Suzanne MacLeod, 185–200. London: Routledge, 2005.

———. *Museums, Moralities and Human Rights*. London: Routledge, 2017.

———. *Museums, Prejudice and the Reframing of Difference*. London, Routledge, 2007.

Savage, Kirk, ed. *The Civil War in Art and Memory*. Washington, DC: National Gallery of Art, 2016.

———. *Monument Wars: Washington, DC, The National Mall, and the Transformation of the American Landscape*. Berkeley: University of California Press, 2009.

———. *Standing Soldiers, Kneeling Slaves: Race, War, and Monument in Nineteenth-Century America*. Princeton: Princeton University Press, 1997.

Schudson, Michael. *The Good Citizen: A History of American Civic Life*. Cambridge, MA: Harvard University Press, 1998.

Schultz, Douglas G. Foreword. *The Appropriate Object*. Buffalo, NY: Buffalo Fine Arts Academy, 1989.

Scott, James C. *Hidden Transcripts: Domination and the Arts of Resistance*. New Haven: Yale University Press, 1990.

Scully, Vincent. Introduction—Note to the Second Edition. In Robert Venturi. *Complexity and Contradiction in Architecture*. 2nd edition. New York: Museum of Modern Art, 1977.

Shaw, Gwendolyn Dubois. "The Freedom to Marry for All: Painting Interracial Families during the Era of the Civil War." In Savage, *The Civil War in Art and Memory*, 5–14.

Silverman, Lois H. *The Social Work of Museums*. Oxon, UK: Routledge, 2010.

Simon, Roger I. *A Pedagogy of Witnessing: Curatorial Practice and the Pursuit of Social Justice*. New York: SUNY Press, 2014.

Sims, Howard F. Letter to the Editor. *Ebony Magazine*, June 1998.

Slave Narratives. Online Exhibition. Museum of the African Diaspora (San Francisco, CA). archive.ideum.com/creative-services/moad-slave-narratives/.

Slevin, Peter. "Black History Museum Has Artifacts but No Building: Organizer Envisions Center on Anacostia Waterfront." *Washington Post*, January 9, 2000.

Smallwood, Stephanie E. *Saltwater Slavery: A Middle Passage from Africa to American Diaspora*. Cambridge: Harvard University Press, 2007.

Smith, Barbara Clark. "Unsettling the Continent, 1492–1776." In *Many Voices, One Nation*, edited by Margaret Salazar-Porzio et al., 27–43. Washington, DC: Smithsonian Institution, 2017.

Sokol, David. "Marrying Content to Container." *Architectural Record* 197, no. 5 (May 2009): 82–84 and 86.

Spelman, Elizabeth V. *Fruits of Sorrow: Framing our Attention to Suffering*. Boston: Beacon Press, 1997.

Stavisky, Leonard Price. "Negro Craftsmanship in Early America." *The American Historical Review* 54, no. 2 (January 1949): 315–25.

Stegall, Christian. "Annotated Bibliography." *The Public Historian—Theme Issue* 40, no. 3 (August 2018): 319–44.

Steward, James Christen. "The Activist Exhibition." *Museum* 98, no. 2 (March/April 2019): 24–27.

Still, William. *The Underground Rail Road. A Record of Facts, Authentic Narratives, Letters, &c. . . . As Narrated by Themselves and Others, or Witnessed by the Author . . .* Philadelphia: Porter and Coates, 1872. Reprint. New York: Arno Press, 1968.

Stuckey, Sterling. *Going through the Storm: The Influence of African American Art in History*. New York: Oxford University Press, 1994.

———. *Slave Culture: Nationalist Theory and the Foundations of Black America*. New York: Oxford University Press, 1987.

Sullivan, Shannon, "Racist Disparities in Health Epigenetics and the Transgenerational Effects of White Racism. *Critical Philosophy of Race* 1, no. 2 (2013): 190–218.

Szwaja, Lynn, and Tomás Ybarra-Frausto. Foreword. In *Museum Frictions*, edited by Karp et al., xi–xiv.

Taylor, Edward K. Foreword. In *New Black Artists*. New York: Printed by Clarke & Way, 1969.

Taylor, Eric Robert. *If We Must Die: Shipboard Insurrections in the Era of the Atlantic Slave Trade*. Baton Rouge: Louisiana State University Press, 2003.

Taylor, Kate. "The Thorny Path to a National Black Museum." *New York Times*, January 23, 2011.

Theoharis, Jeanne. *A More Beautiful and Terrible History: The Uses and Misuses of Civil Rights History*. Boston: Beacon Press, 2018.

Thompson, Robert Farris. "African Influence on the Art of the United States." In *Black Studies in the University: A Design Symposium*, edited by Armstead L. Robinson et al., 122–70. New Haven: Yale University Press, 1969.

———. *The Flash of the Spirit: African and Afro-American Art and Philosophy*. New York: Vintage Books, 1984.

Tillet, Salamishah. *Sites of Slavery: Citizenship and Racial Democracy in the Post-Civil Rights Imagination*. Durham, NC: Duke University Press, 2012.

Tomkins, Calvin. "A Sense of Place." *New Yorker*, September 23, 2013, 76–85.

Transcending Boundaries in Contemporary African Art. ENGAGE Symposium. Museum of the African Diaspora (San Francisco, California). www.moadsf.org/what-we-do/engage-symposium-2022.

Trent, Noelle. "I Am a Child." *Museum* 98, no. 2 (March/April 2019): 29–33.

Trescott, Jacqueline. "Black History's Future; Grand Plans Unveiled for African American Museum on the Mall." *Washington Post*, March 28, 2009.

———. "Designer Chosen for Black History Museum; Team Wins Bid with Crown-Shaped Plan." *Washington Post*, April 15, 2009.

———. "Grounds for Serious Reflection: As African American Museum Site is Weighed, The Mall Looms Large." *Washington Post*, January 30, 2006.

———. "Study Weighs Four Sites for Museum; African American History Location to be Chosen in January." *Washington Post*, December 6, 2005.

Tschumi, Bernard. *Architecture and Disjunction*. Cambridge: MIT Press, 1994.

Turner, Edith L.B. "The People's Home Ground." In *The National Mall*, edited by Nathan Glazer and Cynthia R. Field, 69–78. Washington, DC: Smithsonian Institution, 2017

Turner, Frederick. "Washington as a Pilgrimage Site." In *The National Mall*, edited by Nathan Glazer and Cynthia R. Field, 79–92. Washington, DC: Smithsonian Institution, 2017

Vale, Lawrence J. *Architecture, Power, and National Identity*. 2nd ed. London: Routledge, 2008.

Verre, Philip. Introduction and acknowledgments. In *Traditions and Transformations: Contemporary Afro-American Sculpture*. Bronx, NY: The Bronx Museum of the Arts, 1989.

Vlach, John Michael. *The Afro-American Tradition in Decorative Arts*. Cleveland: Cleveland Museum of Art, 1978.

———. "Phillip Simmons: Afro-American Blacksmith." In *Black People and Their Culture: Selected Writings from the African Diaspora*, edited by Linn Shapiro. Washington, DC: Smithsonian Institution, 1976.

———. "The Shotgun House: An African Architectural Legacy," In *Common Places: Readings in American Vernacular Architecture*, edited by Dell Upton and John Michael Vlach, 58–78. Athens, GA: University of Georgia Press, 1986.

Wallace, Michelle. "Defacing History." *Art in America* 78, no. 12 (December 1990): 121–28; 184–86.

Wallach, Alan. "Revisionism Has Transformed Art History but Not Museums." *In Exhibiting Contradiction: Essays on the Art Museum in the United States*. Amherst: University of Massachusetts Press, 1998.

Watkins, C. Malcolm. "A Plantation of Differences—People from Everywhere." In *A Nation of Nations*, edited by Peter Marzio, 54–82. Washington, DC: Smithsonian Institution, 2017

Weil, Stephen. "Speaking about Museums: A Meditation on Language." *Alberta Museums Review* 18 (Spring/Summer 1992): 590–98.

Welch, Matthew, "For and by the Community." *Museum* 98, no. 2 March/April 2019: 40–45.

We Wanted a Revolution. Exhibition. California African American Museum (San Francisco, California). caamuseum.org/exhibitions/2017/we-wanted-a-revolution.

We Wanted a Revolution. Closing Symposium. California African American Museum (San Francisco, California). caamuseum.org/programs/current /we-wanted-a-revolution-black-radical-women-196585-closing-symposium.

Wilkins, Craig C. *The Aesthetics of Equity: Notes on Race, Space, Architecture, and Music*. Minneapolis: University of Minnesota Press, 2007.

Wilkins, Robert L. *Long Road to a Hard Truth: The 100-Year Mission to Create the National Museum of African American History and Culture*. Washington, DC: Proud Legacy Publishing, 2016.

———. "A Museum Much Delayed." *Washington Post*, March 23, 2003.

Williams, George Washington. *History of the Negro Race in America From 1619 to 1880. Negroes as Slaves, as Soldiers, and as Citizens*. Two Volumes. New York:

G.P. Putnam's Sons, 1882. Project Gutenberg: www.gutenberg.org/files/21851/21851-h/21851-h.htm.

Wilson, Joseph T. *The Black Phalanx: A History of the Negro Soldiers of the United States, In the Wars of 1775–1812, 1861–1865*. Hartford, CT: American Publishing Company, 1888.

Wilson, Mabel O. *Negro Building: Black Americans in the World of Fairs and Museums*. Berkeley: University of California Press, 2012.

———. *Begin with the Past: Building the National Museum of African History and Culture*. Washington, DC: Smithsonian Institution Press, 2016.

Wittgenstein, Ludwig. *Philosophical Investigations*. Translated by G. E. M. Anscombe. Oxford: Oxford University Press, 1997.

Wood, Aylish. "Recursive Space: Play and Creating Space." *Games and Culture* 7, no. 1 (2012): 87–105.

Wood, Christopher H. Introduction. *Perspective as Symbolic Form*. Erwin Panofsky. Translated by Christopher S. Wood. 7–24. Washington, DC: Smithsonian Institution, 2017

Wood, Marcus. *Black Milk: Imagining Slavery in the Visual Culture of Brazil and America*. Oxford: Oxford University Press, 2013.

———. "Slavery, Memory, and Museum Display in Baltimore: The Great Blacks in Wax Museum and the Reginald F. Lewis." *Curator* 51, no.1 (January 2009):147–67.

Wright, Beryl. Introduction. *The Appropriate Object*. Buffalo, NY: Buffalo Fine Arts Academy, 1989.

Yeingst, William, and Lonnie Bunch. "Curating the Recent Past: The Woolworth Lunch Counter, Greensboro, North Carolina," In *Exhibiting Dilemmas: Issues of Representation at the Smithsonian*, edited by Amy Henderson and Adrienne L. Kaeppler, 143–55. Washington, DC: Smithsonian Institution Press, 1997.

Zeitlin, Steve. "Where Are the Best Stories? Where Is My Story?: Participation and Curation in a New Media Age." In *Letting Go?*, edited by Adair et al., 34–43.

Zimmerman, Alex. "99 Problems . . . " pghcitypaper.cpm/pittsburgh/99-problems-run-in-with-jordan-miles-wasnt-fir.

Zimmern, Emily, Janeen Bryant, Kamille Bostick, and Tom Hanchett. "A Decade of Community Engagement through the Lens of Empathy." In *Fostering Empathy through Museums*, edited by Elif M. Gokcigdem, 219–37.

Index

Page references for figures are italicized.

Abercrombie, Stanley, 33–34
Abiel Smith School, 59–60, 78n18
abjection, 83
abolition, 61, 153
absorption, 111–12, 133–34n3
activism, 86, 93; art exhibitions and,
    147–51; black art and, 99; collection,
    preservation, and, 147–51; human
    rights and, 124–25, 128–29, 146–67;
    immigration and, 155, 170n31; place
    and, 152–53; public programming
    and, 146, 147–48; publics, 147–60;
    slavery and, 120, 122; for social
    justice, 146–47, 150–67; town hall
    meetings and, 151–53. *See also* civil
    rights movement
Adams, Derrick, 89
Adjaye, David, 35, 51n29
The Aesthetics of Equity (Wilkins,
    C. L.), 25
Africa, 11–12, 33; African identity and,
    42–43, 45–46, 101, 123; ancestry
    and, 45–47, 123, 140n51; cultural
    identity and, 45–46, 55nn60–61;
    difficult history and, 123–28; Egypt
    and, 50n17, 54n58, 97, 124–25;
    heritage and, 45–47, 123, 125;

homogenization of, 45–46; human
    rights and, 124–25; as point of
    origin and point of return, 123–28;
    representation of, 123–28; traditions
    in, 100. *See also* diaspora
African American aesthetic. *See*
    black aesthetic
African American art, 15; activism
    and, 99; African American history
    and, 90–95; articulation, narrative,
    and, 84–88; "The Black Artist in
    America" symposium and, 44;
    craftsmanship and, 90–91; culture
    and, 99–101; debates about, 98–100;
    definitions of, 94–95; diaspora and,
    87–89, 93; Egypt and, 97; exclusion
    and, 96–98; exhibitions, catalogues,
    and, 89–95; exposure and, 101;
    Hughes on, 99; identity and, 44,
    101; Locke on, 90–91; Patton and,
    93–94; representation and, 96–101,
    103n9; slavery and, 91–92, 94, 96;
    types of, 94; white artists and, 95; by
    women, 86. *See also specific artists,
    specific topics*
African-American Art (Patton), 93–94

African American history, 12–13; "American ideal" and exclusion of, 2; black art and, 90–95; cultural awakenings to, 10–12; difficult history and, 111–33; living history and, 129–33; memory and, 72; military and, 63–68, 74–75, 90; narrative and, 58–65, 72–73; national history and, 10–11; politics and, 59–60, 65–68; regional history and, 57–76; as rhetorical, 71–72; settlement narratives and, 58–65. *See also* slavery

African American identity, 91; architecture and, 35–36, 41–48; black male identity, 96–97, 146–47, 150, 151–54; cultural identity and, 41–48; diaspora and, 23n52; representation and, 101

The African American Journey West (exhibit), 121

African American Military Portraits from the American Civil War (exhibit), 68

African American Museum in Philadelphia, 4; 19n17, 148, 158; *Audacious Freedom* exhibit in, *62,* 62–63, 122; *Philadelphia Conversations* exhibit in, *63,* 63–64, 74; place and, 61–62; regional history and settlement narratives in, 59, 61–64, *62, 63*; virtual exhibitions at, 89, 104n24

African American museums, 1–2. *See also specific museums; specific topics*

African American Visual Arts: From Slavery to the Present (Bernier), 93

African art, 94, 100

"African Influence on the Art of the United States" (Thompson), 47

African masks, 100

African Meeting House, 59–60, *60,* 78n18, 153

Africa Speaks (exhibit), 124–25

Afro-American Artists, New York and Boston (Gaither), 96

Afrocentric architecture, 42–48, 54n55

Albright-Knox Art Gallery, 99–100

Alpers, Svetlana, 102n2

"American ideal," exclusion and, 2

American Revolution, 57, 65–67, 72–73

American Women's History Museum, 18n10

Ames, Robert Witt, 85

ancestry, 45–47, 123, 140n51

Anderson, John W., 115, 117

Anderson, Laura, 40, 129

And Still We Rise (exhibit), 114–15, 125

Apel, Dora, 136n18, 136n20

Appiah, Kwame Anthony, 123

approach (to museum buildings), 29–31, 39, 65, 77nn4–5

The Appropriate Object (exhibit), 99–100

Arbery, Ahmaud, 171n36

architecture: African American identity and, 35–36, 41–48; Afrocentric, 42–48, 54n55; approaches to, 28–36; Birmingham Civil Rights Institute and, 30, *30,* 36, *39,* 39–40; canon and, 14; Charles H. Wright Museum of African American History and, 28, *29,* 33–36, *34,* 50n17, 51n27, 52n30; context and, 41–48; cultural identity and, 35–48; of domes, 33–35; Egyptian, 50n17, 54n58; experience and, 26–28, 31–32, 35, 40, 42–48; forms in, 26–28; frames in, 25–26, 33–48; heritage and, 45–47; identity and, 44–46; inclusion in, 41, 46–47; movement in, 36–41; National Museum of African American History and Culture and, 35, 44; National Underground Railroad Freedom Center and, 30–31, *31, 32,* 36, 40–41, *41*; National Organization of Minority Architects and, 46; in "New South," 49n8; perspective and, 25–26, 33; Reginald F. Lewis

Museum of Maryland African
American History and Culture and,
28–30, 36, 37–38, *38*; stairways and,
36–41, 52n34; substance and, 33;
symbolism in, 35–41, 52n30
Architecture as Art
(Abercrombie), 33–34
Architecture in Black (Fields), 45–46
Aristotle, 131
Arnheim, Rudolf, 10, 33
Art and Healing (exhibit), 155–56
Art as a Verb (exhibit), 99, 108n63
art exhibitions: activism and, 147–51;
articulation as argument and, 84–89;
catalogues and, 89–95; military
history and, 66–68; narrative
dimension of, 66–68, 83–84;
preservation and, 73; rapid response,
145–46, 154–55; as rhetorical space,
83–101; slavery as subject and,
87–88, 112–22; virtual, 88–89. *See
also specific exhibits and texts*
art history: education and, 93, 101, 129
articulation: art exhibitions and,
84–89; black aesthetic and, 89–95;
black art, narrative, and, 84–88; at
DuSable Black History Museum and
Education Center, 84–85; at Museum
of African American History, 86
artistic autonomy, 47–48
The Art of Exclusion (Boime), 97
*The Art of Protest: Culture and Activism
from the Civil Rights Movement to
the Streets of Seattle* (Reed), 83
Asgedom, Araya, 42
aspect blindness, 11–12
Attucks, Crispus, 73
Audacious Freedom (exhibit), *62*,
62–63, 122
August Wilson African American
Cultural Center, 4, 14,
151–53, 169n20
Autry, Robyn, 126

Bailey, Dina A., 145, 165

Bailey, Radcliffe, 87
Barber, Lucy G., 4
Barrett, Jennifer, 145
Bazin, Germain, 11, 20n31, 22n38
Bearden, Romare, 88, 92–93, 94–95
Bedford, Leslie, 137n24
Bell, Nancy, 137n22
Berger, Stefan, 71
Bernier, Celeste-Marie, 93
Bethel, Elizabeth Raul, 72, 123, 127
Bethune, Mary McLeod, 6, 85
Bevir, Mark, 69, 71, 81n31
bias, recognition of, 120, 153–55
Bickford, Louis, 13
Bindman, David, 107n52
Birmingham Civil Rights Institute, 4,
59, 120–21, 161, 165; architecture
of, 26, 30, *30*, 32, 36, *39*, 39–40,
50n19, 52n39; on human rights, 128–
29, 148; stairways in, *39*, 39–40
Bishir, Catherine W., 49n8
black aesthetic, 15; African
American aesthetic and, 96–101;
articulation of, 89–95
The Black Aesthetic (anthology), 99, 100
"Black Americans in Illinois"
(portraits), 85
Black Art—Ancestral Legacy
(exhibit), 109n66
*Black Art and Culture in the 20th
Century* (Powell), 98–99
"The Black Artist in America: A
Symposium," 44
"Black Artists: Three Shows"
(Cotter), 99–100
Black Arts Movement, 94
black body, as subject, 87
Black Emergency Cultural Coalition, 94
"Black Heritage Trail," 60
Black Lives Matter, 147, 159–60, 168n7
black male identity, 96–97, 146–47,
150, 151–54
*The Black Man: His Antecedents, His
Genius, and His Achievements*
(Brown, W. W.), 73–74

Black Panther Party, 93
The Black Phalanx (Wilson, J.
    T.), 107n53
black proletariat, 98–99
Black Radical Women Symposium
    (exhibit), 148–49
Black Refractions (exhibit), 149, 169n13
black subjectivity, 98–99
black veterans, 5–6
"Bodies, Details, and the Humanitarian
    Narrative" (Laqueur), 167
Bodies of Information (exhibit), 121
Boime, Albert, 97, 107nn53–55
Bond, Max, 45
Bonnell, Jennifer, 111, 132, 142n72
Brawley, Benjamin, 75–76
Bronbeck, Bruce, 71–72
The Bronx Museum of the Arts, 100
Brooklyn Museum, 94, 101,
    103n15, 168n10
Broun, Elizabeth, 96, 100–101
Brown, Aleia, 162
Brown, Dion, 120, 171n41
Brown, Michael, 151
Brown, William Wells, 73–74
Brownback, Sam, 6
Bryant, Johnetta and Keedron, 159
Building Maryland, Building America
    (exhibit), 64–65
Bunch, Lonnie G., III, 6, 13,
    18–19nn15–16, 19n19, 113, 164–65
burdensome gift, 132–33, 142n72
"A Burial Party, Cold Harbor"
    (Reekie), 90
Burns, Andrea, 4, 79n20, 125
Burroughs, Margaret, 17n5, 85

California African American Museum,
    4, 14, 59, 84–86; on African
    American military service, 68;
    Coloring America exhibit at, 125–26;
    public programs at, 152–53, 158,
    168n11; slavery exhibits at, 121–22,
    125–26; *We Wanted a Revolution:*

Black Radical Women, 1965–1985
    exhibit at, 86, 148–49, 168n10
Carter, Jennifer, 162, 164
Castile, Philando, 155–56
catalogues: art exhibitions and, 89–95;
    The Civil War and American Art, 90;
    Facing History, 101, 109n70
Catlett, Elizabeth, 88
Charles H. Wright Museum of African
    American History, 4, 6, 13, 165;
    architecture of, 28, *29,* 33–36,
    34, 50n17, 51n27, 52n30; slavery
    exhibits at, 113, 114–15, 125,
    130–31; *And Still We Rise* exhibit
    at, 114–15, 125; *Wright Now* exhibit
    at, 159–60
children: immigration and, 155, 170n31;
    and slave traders, 119, 135n16
citizenship, 64, 73–75;
    insurgent, 3, 18n11
civic life, 153–57. *See also* publics
civil religion, 10
civil rights movement, 6, 21n37, 40,
    81n31, 85; human rights and, 58,
    128–29; Jim Crow and, 46, 58
Civil War, 5–6, 63–64, 104n25, 105n26;
    African American military service
    during, 68, 90; Brown, W. W., on,
    73–74; slavery and, 73–74
The Civil War and American Art
    (exhibit and catalogue), 90
The Civil War in Art and Memory
    (anthology), 90
Clarke, Lewis Garrard, 119
Clarke-Hazlett, Christopher, 136n20
Cleland, Max, 6
Clovese, Joseph "Uncle Jo," 68
Collins, Hubert, 86
colonialism, 62, 96, 122–23, 149
*The Colored Patriots of the American
    Revolution* (Nell), 57, 67
Coloring America (exhibit), 125–26
commemorative system, 3
Confederate statues, 154, 170nn28–29
Conover, Lewis I., 68

consequential / pragmatic spaces, 12–14, 16
Constitutional Sentiments (Sajó), 131
contaminated space, 42
contemporary slavery, 120, 128–29
"Contesting the Nation, 1900–1965" (Ruffins), 80n27
Coombes, Annie, 20n31
Corcoran Gallery, 101
corrective anthropology, 102n3
corrective history, 2
Cotter, Holland, 99–100, 108n63
Cotton, William, 119
counternarratives, 12
COVID-19 pandemic, 17n4; public programming and, 150, 157–60; race and, 157–60; virtual exhibitions and, 88
craftsmanship, 90–91
Crew, Spencer, 2
Cubitt, Geoffrey, 143–44n74
cultural awakenings, 10–12, 58
cultural centers, 9–10
cultural continuity, 133–34n3; African traditions and, 54n53, 65, 91, 94, 98, 100, 109n66, 124, 126–27, 129, 149; architecture and, 33, 40–48, 53n49; go-between and, 133; loss of, 53n46, 134n5
cultural identity: Africa and, 45–46, 55nn60–61; architecture and, 35–48; heritage and, 45–47; personal identity and, 44
culture: African American art and, 99–101; deculturation and, 69–70; diaspora and, 87; diversity, inclusion, and, 12, 162–67; power and, 11–12; wars, 11
Cywinski, Piotr, 162

Dallas Museum of Art, 109n66
Dana, John Cotton, 145, 165
Davis, Nancy, 80n27
Davis, Thomas J., 58, 77n5
deculturation, 69–70

"Defining Black Art" (Patton), 93–94
Dempsey, Anna M., 140n50
Denyer, Susan, 50n16
dialectical image, 3. *See also* aspect blindness
diaspora, 85–86, 159–60; African American identity and, 23n52; ancestry and, 45–47, 123, 140n51; black art and, 87–89, 93; black body and, 87; culture and, 87; identity and, 12, 123, 127–28; Museum of the African Diaspora and, 4, 87–89, 126–27, 140n51, 149; representation and, 123–28
Dickerson, Amina, 138n34
"Difficult Exhibitions and Intimate Encounters" (Bonnell and Simon), 111
difficult history: Africa and, 123–28; African American history and, 111–33; identity and, 133; museum as living history and, 129–33; race relations and, 113; slavery as, 112–28
"Discovering African Identity in African-American Architecture" (Kliment), 45
diversity: inclusion and, 12, 162–67; rhetorical historiography and "diversity deficit," 69–76
domes, 33–35
Douglass, Frederick, 76, 121, 122
Dovey, Kim, 43
Du Bois, W. E. B., 80n27, 85, 124
DuSable, Jean Baptiste Pointe, 65
DuSable Black History Museum and Education Center, 4, 6, 59, 66, 84–85, 113, 165; Africa exhibits at, 121, 124–25; on African American military service, 67–68; public programming at, 154; regional history in, 65
DuSable Bust (exhibit), 65
The Dynamics of Architectural Form (Arnheim), 33

economic mobility, 150, 152–53
Edelman, Murray, 27–28
education, 59–60, 65, 79n20, 145–47,
    150–57, 161, 164–65. *See also*
    art history
efficacy, 5, 162, 166–67
Egypt, 50n17, 55n59, 97, 124–25
Eldredge, Charles C., 95
Elleh, Nnamdi, 39, 47, 55n59
Emancipation and the Freed in
    American Sculpture: A Study in
    Interpretation (Murray), 91–92
Emancipation Proclamation, 67, 74
Emerging Artists Program, 87–89
empathy, 128–33, 156–57, 158,
    165–66, 173n62
empire, 8–10, 20n31
employment, 157
endslaverynow.org, 120
ENGAGE Symposia, 149
epigenetic trauma, 141n63
Equiano, Olaudah, (*The Interesting*
    Narrative), 112
The Evolution of Afro-American Artists
    (exhibit), 94–95, 106n43
exclusion, 2, 96–98
Exhibiting Cultures: The Poetics and
    Politics of Museum Display (Karp
    and Lavine), 11
experience, 130–33; architecture and,
    26–28, 31–32, 35, 40, 42–48

"Face of the African Diaspora"
    (Silvers), 126–27
Facing History (exhibition catalogue),
    101, 109n70
Failler, Angela, 166
family, 153–57
Festival of American Folk Life
    (exhibit), 79n23
Fields, Darell Wayne, 45–46, 54n54
Fleming, John E., 2
Floyd, George, 147, 158–59
Focillon, Henri, 28, 50n15
For Freedoms (exhibit), 150–51, 152

For Freedoms Congress (event), 152
forms: in Afro-centric architecture,
    42–48; approaches to, 28–36; context
    of, 41–48; frames and, 26–48;
    narrative elements of, 26–27; power
    of, 26–28; space and, 26–28, 42–48,
    49n12. *See also* architecture
Forten, James, *63*, 63–64
Four Freedoms, 151
frames: approaches to, 28–36; in
    architecture, 25–26, 33–48; context
    and, 41–48; forms and, 26–48;
    narrative and, 62–63; space and,
    25–26, 35–36
Franklin, Jack T., 89
freedom fighters, 66–67
"Freedom Now" mural (Ames), 85
Freedom Rising (exhibit), 67, 73
Freelon Group, 36–37
Free within Ourselves: African-
    American Artists in the Collection of
    the National Museum of American
    Art (Braun), 96
Free within Ourselves
    (exhibit), 100–101
From Storefront to Monument: Tracing
    the Public History of the Black
    Museum Movement (Burns), 4
Fuller, Meta Vaux Warrick, 91
FuturePresent: Acquisition Highlights
    from the Permanent Collection
    (exhibit), 86–87

Gaither, Edmund Barry, 93–94, 96, 101
Gallas, Kristin, 120, 132
Garner, Eric, 159
Gates, Henry Louis, 82n37, 82n40,
    101, 107n52
Geffrye Museum, London, 79n24
geography, 120, 123–24. *See also* place
Gerstle, Gary, 70
Giordano, Joseph, 160
Glavic, Jamie, 120, 171n41
Glazer, Nathan, 20n29
go-between function, 129, 133

Goldberger, Paul, 32, 35
Goodman, Nelson, 27
Grant, Bradford C., 39–40,
    45, 46, 52n39
grassroots museums, 4
gravediggers, images of blacks as, 90
Gray, Freddie, 160
Great Depression, 6
Great Kings and Queens
    (exhibit), 124–25
The Greek Slave (Powers), 91–92
griot, 2

Hall, Stuart, 123
Harlem Cultural Council, 94–95
Harper, Phillip Brian, 103n9
Hartigan, Linda Roscoe, 95
Harvey, Eleanor Jones, 90, 105n26
Harvey B. Gantt Center for African-
    American Arts + Culture, 4, 26,
    36–37, *37*, 84–85, 148; Hewitt
    collection at, 86–88; public
    programming at, 152–53, 171n36;
    Revealed: Where Art Meets Activism
    exhibit at, 149–51; stairways
    in, 36–37, *37*; *Unmasked* series
    at, 158–59
Hassinger, Maren, 149
Henderson, Harry, 92–93
heritage, 45–47, 123, 125
Herskovits, Melville J., 102n3
Hewitt, John and Vivian, 86–88
hierarchies, 96–98, 101
Higgins, Chester, Jr., 126–27
Hindle, Brooke, 69–70
Hirsch, Marianne, 129, 133
historical consciousness, 2,
    19n18, 71, 118
historiographic work, 5, 57
history, museum representations of,
    4–5, 10–11. *See also* Africa; African
    American history; architecture; art
    history; corrective history; cultural
    continuity; difficult history; historical
    consciousness; identity; living

history; memory; military service;
    narrative; national history; New
    Social history; politics; regional
    history; rhetorical historiography;
    settlement narratives; slavery;
    *specific exhibitions, museums, and
    texts*; unclaimed history
*A History of African American Artists
    from 1792 to the Present* (Bearden
    and Henderson), 92–93
*History of the Negro Race in
    America from 1619 to 1880*
    (Williams), 57, 74–75
Holocaust, trauma and, 132
Holocaust Memorial Museum,
    Washington, DC, 84
Honour, Hugh, 97
Horton, James, 2
Huffman, David, 88
Hughes, David, 39, 47, 54n58
Hughes, Langston, 99
humanitarian narrative, 167
human rights, 58; activism and, 124–25,
    128–29, 146–67; Africa and, 124–25;
    immigration and, 155, 170n31;
    museums and, 145–47, 160–67;
    social justice and, 146–47, 150–67;
    trauma and, 128–33; universal,
    128–29; women and, 128–29,
    148–49, 168n10. *See also* civil
    rights movement
Huyssen, Andreas, 129

IAM. *See* International Afro-
    American Museum
iconographic program, 26, 52n34
The Idea of a Human Rights Museum
    (anthology), 162–63
identity: African, 42–43, 45–46, 101,
    123; architecture and, 44–46;
    black art and, 44, 101; black male,
    96–97, 146–47, 150, 151–53;
    colonialism and, 149; cultural,
    35–48, 55nn60–61; diaspora and,
    123, 127–28; difficult history and,

133; national, 9, 20n31, 111; racial
    other and, 98, 109n70; slavery and,
    111; stereotypes and, 101. *See also*
    African American identity
Ihejirika, Edward, 43, 53n49
*The Image of the Black in African and
    Asian Art* (series), 97–98
The Image of the Black in Western Art
    (exhibit), 96–97, 107n52
*The Image of the Indian and the Black
    Man in American Art, 1590–1900*
    (Parry), 96
immigration, 155, 170n31
Impasse of Desires (exhibit), 88–89
inclusion: in architecture, 41, 46–47;
    counter-movements dedicated to, 92;
    in cultural identity, 41–48; diversity
    and, 12, 162–67; publics and,
    157–60, 171n45
individuality, creative expression
    and, 41–48
insurgent citizenship, 3, 18n11
intensive continuity, 43, 53n49
*The Interesting Narrative of the Life of
    Olaudah Equiano* (Equiano), 112
intergenerational trauma, 2
International Afro-American Museum
    (IAM), 79n20

Jacobs, Alvin C., Jr., 150
Jacobs, Jane M., 43
"Jacob's Ladder School," 36–37
James, William, 133
Janes, Robert R., 163
Jim Crow, 46, 58
John and Vivian Hewitt
    collection, 86–88
John Brown movement, 74
Johnson, Edward A., 75
Johnson, Joshua, 95
Johnson, Philip, 31, 36
Johnson, Walter, 119
Jones, Anna Russell, 89

Karenga, Ron, 99

Kargon, Jeremy, 38
Karp, Ivan, 11
Kelley, Robin D. G., 123, 127
Kennedy, Roger, 10
King, Martin Luther, Jr., 21n37
Kirshenblatt-Gimblett,
    Barbara, 20–21n31
Kliment, Stephen A., 45, 54n53
Kratz, Corinne, 12
Ku Klux Klan, 80n27
Kurashige, Scott, 70–71

LaCapra, Dominick, 129, 131
Landsberg, Alison, 51n26, 131, 135n9
Laqueur, Thomas, 167
Lavine, Steven D., 11
Lawrence, Jacob, 88
Lawrence, Robert Henry, Jr., 68
Lévinas, Emmanuel, 130
Lewis, Edmonia, 91
Lewis, John, 6
lieux de mémoire, 72, 81n33
living history, 129–33
Lochert, Mathilde, 43
Locke, Alain, 90–91
Lokko, Lesley Naa Norle, 42
Lusaka, Jane, 35

MacLeod, Suzanne, 41–42
Majekodunmi, Olufemi, 46, 54n55
Making a Way for Democracy
    (exhibit), 67–68
Manned Orbital Laboratory Program, 68
Many Voices, One Nation (exhibit), 59,
    69–71, 80n27
Marshall, Christopher, 84, 102n5
Maryland Collects Jacob Lawrence
    (exhibit), 88
MASS Action initiative,
    156–57, 170n34
Massey, Hubert, 35–36
McElroy, Guy, 101
McKim, Charles F., 67
McWorter, Solomon, 80n27
Meadows, John, 115–16

memory, 57; African American history and, 72; *lieux de mémoire* and, 72, 81n33; space and, 31–32, 50n19, 60; trauma and, 131–33, 141n63
Mendoza, Paola, 155, 170n31
Menil, Dominique and Jean de, 98
Message, Kylie, 9, 18n14
Metropolitan Museum of Art, 44
Meyer, Jeffrey, 10
Middle Passage, 85, 112, 116, 121, 134n5, 135n13, 136n20
migration, 121–22
Miles, Jordan, 151–52, 169n19
military service, 5–6; African American history and, 65–68, 74–75, 90; African American veterans and, 5–6; art exhibitions on, 66–68; citizenship and, 74–75; freedom fighters and, 66–67; national history and, 65–68; patriots and, 66–67, 74; politics and, 65–68
Miller, Adam David, 99
Miller, Thomas, 65
Minardi, Margot, 79n19, 139n37
Minneapolis Institute of Art, 155–56
misrepresentation, 96–98, 101
Mitchell, Melvin, 35
Moore, Juanita, 19n19
Morgan, Elinor, 172n50
Moten, Fred, 148, 166–67, 168n9
Moutusseme, John, 47
"Ms. Precious, Tamale" (Higgins), 126–27
Muller, Adam, 165
Murray, Freeman Henry Morris, 91–92
The Museum Age (Bazin), 20n31
"museum effect," 73, 83, 102n2
Museum Frictions (Karp and Kratz), 11–12
Museum of African American History, Boston, 4, 14, *60*, 67, 73, 84, 86, 122, 153, 160; settlement theme and, 59–61
Museum of Modern Art, 92

Museum of the African Diaspora, 4, 84–85, 87–89, 93, 122, 126–28, 139–140n48, 140nn51–52, 149, 159–60
museums: as agents of change, 11, 160–67; as forum, 13–14, 27; human rights and, 145–47, 160–67; as living history, 129–33; mandates for, 12–14, 33, 147–51, 163–64; mission statements of, 12–14, 16; publics and, 145–67; technology and, 166; town hall meetings and conversations about, 151–53. *See also specific topics*
Museums, Moralities and Human Rights (Sandell), 161
Museums and the Public Sphere (Barrett), 145
museum-visitor relationship, 147–48, 172n53
Myers, Bill, 119
The Myth of the Negro Past (Herskovits), 102n3

narrative: African American history and, 58–65, 72–73; art exhibition as, 66–68, 83–84; articulation and, 84–88; counternarratives and, 12; DuSable Black History Museum and Education Center and, 85; forms in, 26–27; frames and, 62–63; humanitarian, 167; at Museum of African American History, 86; power and, 11–12; rhetorical historiography and "diversity deficit" in, 69–76; rhetorical space and, 83–88; settlement, 58–65, 80n27, 86; slavery, 58, 115–22
Narrative of His Sufferings (Clarke), 119
National Civil Rights Museum (NCRM), 154–55
National Council of Negro Women, 6
"National Histories" (Bevir), 69
national history: African American history and, 10–11; contexts and

theory, 69–76; defining, 71; military and, 65–68; regional history and, 5, 57–58; rhetorical historiography and, 71–73

national identity, 9, 20n31, 111

National Mall: National Museum of African American History and Culture and, 3–4, 6–7, 9–10; place and, 3–4; religion and, 10; sites, 9–10, 18n9, 18n11, 20n29

National Museum of African American History and Culture, 1–2; architecture of, 35, 45; background on, 5–7; construction of, 9, *9*; as custodian of future, 12–14; "four pillars" of, 12–13; groundbreaking ceremony for, 7; mission of, 12–14; National Mall and, 3–4, 6–7, 9–10; opening of, 4; photos of, *7*, *9*; Plan for, 6; regional history at, 35, 45, 76–77n4; site selection for, 6–7, *8*

National Museum of American History, 10, 69–70

National Museum of the American Latino, 18n10

National Organization of Minority Architects (NOMA), 46

National Park Service, 61

National Underground Railroad Freedom Center, 4, 13, 161, 171n41; architecture of, 30–31, *31*, *32*, 36, 40–41, *41*; on human rights, 128–29; "Slave Pen" exhibit at, 87–88, 115–20; slavery and, 87–88, 113, 115–20; stairways of, 40–41, *41*; Welcome Hall of, 40

nation-building, 8–10, 20n31

A Nation of Nations (exhibit), 59, 69–70, 77n6

Native Americans, museum exhibitions and, 70

Negro Art: Past and Present (Locke), 90

Negro Building (Wilson, M.), 4

The Negro in Art: A Pictorial Record of the Negro Artist and of the Negro Theme in Art (Locke), 91

Nell, William C., 57, 67, 71–72, 73, 74, 79n19, 82n37

Nelson, Richard-Jonathan, 87

"Neo-Africanism," 94

New Black Artists (exhibit), 94

"new black show," 96

The New Museum (Dana), 145, 165

New Museums and the Making of Culture (Message), 9

New Social History, 11

Nora, Pierre, 72, 81n33

Norberg-Schulz, Christian, 50n17

O'Meally, Robert G., 84

Orloff, Chet, 160

Oxford History of Art (series), 93

Painter's Refuge: A Way of Life—A Solo Exhibition of Recent Work by Reginald Sylvester II (exhibit), 88

Panofsky, Erwin, 8–9, 21n32

Parry, Ellwood, 96

The Past as History: National Identity and Historical Consciousness in Modern Europe (Berger), 71

patriots, 57–58, 66–68, 73–74, 76, 78n17, 107n53, 153

Patterson, Orlando, 131, 142n68

Patton, Sharon, 92, 93–94, 106n39

Pecora, Vincent, 49n4

A Pedagogy of Witnessing (Simon), 166

Pennington, James W. C., 73, 76, 81–82n36

Perrin, Andrew, 152

Perry, James DeWolf, 120, 132

perspective, 8–10, 21n32, 25–26, 33

Perspective as Symbolic Form (Panofsky), 8–9

Philadelphia Conversations (exhibit), *63*, 63–64, 74

Phillips, Ruth B., 123, 139n40

Philosophical Investigations
(Wittgenstein), 3
Picturing Blackness symposium,
149, 169n13
place: activism and, 152–53; African
American Museum in Philadelphia
and, 61–62; African Meeting House
and, *60*, 60–61, 153; consequential
spaces and, 12–14, 16; geography
and, 120, 123–24; National Mall
and, 3–4; power of, 3–5; site
placement and, 31–32; symbolic
spaces and, 8–10
Plato, 131
The Pluralist Era (Robins), 105n31
police brutality, 146, 155–56,
158–59, 171n36
politics, 84; activism and, 86, 93;
African American history and,
59–60, 65–68; military and, 65–68
postmemory, 129, 133, 143n76
Powell, Richard, 98
power: culture and, 11–12; force and,
10–12; of forms, 26–28; narrative
and, 11–12; of place, 3–5
The Power of the Center (Arnheim), 10
Powers, Hiram, 91–92
pragmatic spaces, 4–5, 12–14, 72, 131
Preston, George Nelson, 100
proximity, 129–32
public programming: activism and, 146,
147–48; African American museums
and, 16; COVID-19 pandemic
and, 150, 157–60; inclusion and,
157–60. *See also specific museums,
specific topics*
publics: activism and, 147–60;
education and, 145, 153–57; family,
self-care, and, 153–57; inclusion and,
157–60, 171n45; museum mandates
and, 12–14, 33, 147–51, 163–64;
museums as agents of change in,
11, 160–67; town hall meetings and,
151–53. *See also specific museums,
specific topics*

queer subjecthood, 89, 127
Question Bridge (exhibit), 150

race. *See* architecture; art history;
corrective history; COVID-19
pandemic; cultural continuity;
cultural identity; difficult
history; epigenetic trauma;
historical consciousness; identity;
intergenerational trauma; police
brutality; public programs; *specific
exhibitions, museums, and texts*
racism, 141n63; African American
aesthetic and, 98–99; bias and,
154–55; recent deaths related to,
146–47, 151–54, 158–60, 168n7,
171n36; segregation and, 80n27, 98;
stereotypes and, 88, 96–97; systemic,
146–47, 153–60; white supremacy
and, 80n27, 97, 154
rapid response exhibitions,
145–46, 154–55
*Reconceptions in Philosophy and Other
Arts and Sciences* (Goodman), 27
*Red White Blue and Black: A History
of Blacks in the Armed Forces*
(exhibit), 67–68
Reed, T. V., 83, 102n1
Reekie, John, 90
Reeves, Joshua, 131
reflective space, 84, 87–88
Reginald F. Lewis Museum of Maryland
African American History and
Culture, 4, 55n60, 113, 148, 154,
160; architecture of, 26, 28–30, 32,
36, 37–38, *38*; *Bodies of Information*
exhibit at, 121; *Building Maryland,
Building America* exhibit at, 64–65;
regional history and settlement
narratives in, 59, 64–65; stairways
in, 36, 37–38, *38*
regional history: African American
history and, 57–76; at African
American Museum in Philadelphia,
61–64, *62, 63*; at DuSable Black

History Museum and Education
Center, 65; at Museum of African
American History, 59–61; national
history and, 5, 57–58; at National
Museum of African American
History and Culture, 35, 45,
76–77n4; at Reginald F. Lewis
Museum of Maryland African
American History and Culture,
64–65; settlement narratives
and, 58–65
regional museums, pragmatic spaces
and, 4–6, 12–14, 57–58, 76–77n4
religion, 10, 73
Rendering Justice (exhibit), 89
representation: acts of, 101; of Africa,
123–28; African American identity
and, 101; black art and, 96–101,
103n9; diaspora and, 123–28;
misrepresentation and, 96–98, 101
Revealed: Where Art Meets Activism
(exhibit), 149–51
Reynolds, Diamond, 155–56
rhetorical historiography: African
American aesthetic and, 96–101;
"diversity deficit" and, 69–76;
national history and, 71–73
rhetorical space: art exhibitions as,
83–101; narrative and, 83–88;
reflective space and, 84, 87–88
Rice, Kym, 80n27
Rice, Tamir, 151
Ring of Genealogy mural (Massey), *34,*
35–36, 125
Risen, Clay, 45
*Robert Gould Shaw and Massachusetts
54th Regiment Memorial*
(Saint-Gaudens), 90
Robins, Corinne, 105n31
Rockefeller Foundation, 11, 12
Rockwell, Norman, 151
Roosevelt, Franklin D., 151
Rose, Julia, 165–66
Roth, Leland, 33
Rothstein, Edward, 140n50

Ruffins, Fath Davis, 3, 17n2, 17n5,
78nn13–14, 80n27, 113, 137n23,
141n63, 141–42n65
Russell, Adrianne, 162

Saint-Gaudens, Augustus, 67, 90
Sajó, András, 131
Salazar-Porzio, Margaret, 70
Sandell, Richard, 49n13, 103n8,
161, 162–63
Savage, Kirk, 3, 18n9, 18n11, 90
*A School History of the Negro Race in
the United States, from 1619–1890*
(Johnson, E. A.), 75
Schudson, Michael, 152
Schultz, Douglas G., 99–100
Scott, James C., 83
Scully, Vincent, 25–26
segregation, 80n27, 98
self-care, 153–57
self-reflection, 61
settlement narratives: at African
American Museum in Philadelphia,
61–64, *62, 63*; at Museum of African
American History, 59–61, 86; *A
Nation of Nations* exhibit on, 59,
69–70, 77n6; at Reginald F. Lewis
Museum of Maryland African
American History and Culture,
64–65; regional history and, 58–65;
slavery and, 58, 80n27
Seventeen Black Artists (exhibit), 92
*Sharing Traditions: Five Black Artists
in Nineteenth-Century America*
(exhibit), 95
Shaw, Robert Gould (Colonel), 67, 90
Shaw Memorial, 67, 78–79n18
Silverman, Lois H., 163
Silvers, Robert, 126–27
Simon, Roger, 111, 132, 142n72,
166–67, 174n67
Sims, Howard F., 51n27
Sinclair, Struan, 165
single-point perspective, 8–10

SITES. *See* Smithsonian Institution Traveling Exhibition Service

"Slave Pen" (exhibit): overview of, 115–20; pictures of, *116, 117, 118*; as reflective space, 87–88

slavery, 11–12, 35–36, 52n30; abolition and, 61, 153; activism and, 120, 122; African American military service and, 74–75; art exhibitions of, 87–88, 112–22; *Audacious Freedom* exhibit on, *62,* 62–63, 122; black art and, 91–92, 94, 96; *Bodies of Information* exhibit on, 121; in *Building Maryland, Building America* exhibit, 64–65; California African American Museum exhibits and, 121–22, 125–26; Charles H. Wright Museum of African American History and, 113, 114–15, 125, 130–31; children, slave trade and, 119, 135n16; citizenship and, 74–75; Civil War and, 73–74; contemporary, 120, 128–29; as difficult history, 112–28; Emancipation Proclamation and, 67, 74; European, 85, 98; identity and, 111; installations, 114–20; integration and incorporation within museums, 120–23; Middle Passage and, 85, 112, 116, 121, 134n5, 135n13, 136n20; migration and, 121–22; Museum of the African Diaspora exhibits on, 126–27; narratives, 58, 115–22; National Underground Railroad Freedom Center and, 87–88, 113, 115–20; Pennington on, 81–82n36; reflective space and, 87–88; religion and, 73; settlement narratives and, 58, 80n27; sites of, 111; slave ship exhibit and, 114–15, 134n5, 135n13, 135–36nn16–17

Slave Trade: From Africa to the Americas, 1650–1870 (exhibit), 121–22

"slow space effect," 84, 87–88

Smallwood, Stephanie, 112, 134n5, 135n13, 136n17

Smith, Barbara Clark, 80n27

Smith, Hamilton Sutton, 86

Smithsonian Institution, 11–12, 18n10; *The Civil War and American Art* and, 90; *Many Voices, One Nation* exhibit at, 59, 69–71, 80n27; *A Nation of Nations* exhibit at, 69–70, 77n6

Smithsonian Institution Traveling Exhibition Service (SITES), 96–97

Smithsonian Orientation Plaque, *8*

Smithsonian's National Museum of History and Technology, 69

social death, 119, 53n46, 142n68

A Social History of the American Negro, Being a History of the Negro Problem in the United States (Brawley), 75–76

social justice: activism for, 146–47, 150–67; agents of change and, 160–67; inclusion and, 157–60, 162–67. *See also* civil rights movement

The Social Work of Museums (Silverman), 163

socioeconomic class, 86

Sodaro, Amy, 13

Sokol, David, 44

space, 49n14; as consequential, 12–14, 16; forms and, 26–28, 42–48, 49n12; frames and, 25–26, 35–36; memory and, 31–32, 50n19, 60; reflective, 84, 87–88; rhetorical, 83–101; in "slow space effect," 84, 87–88; symbolic, 8–10

Spanish American War, 75

Spelman, Elizabeth, 131, 142n67

Spicer, S. E., 137n22

stairways: architecture of, 36–41, 52n34; in Birmingham Civil Rights Institute, *39,* 39–40; in Harvey B. Gantt Center for African-American Arts + Culture, 36–37, *37*; in National Underground Railroad Freedom Center, 40–41, *41*; in

Reginald F. Lewis Museum of
Maryland African American History
and Culture, 36, 37–38, *38*
stereotypes, 86; identity and,
101; racism and, 88, 96–97;
segregation and, 98
Still, William, 119, 138n28
The Strength of the Mind
(exhibit), 64–65
structural trauma, 132
Stuckey, Sterling, 43, 136n17
Sullivan, Shannon, 130, 141n63
Sylvester, Reginald, II, 88
symbolism, 8–10, 35–41, 52n30
systemic exclusion, 2
systemic racism, 146–47, 153–60
Szwaja, Lynn, 12

Tanner, Henry Ossawa, 95
Taylor, Breonna, 171n36
Taylor, David R., 159, 171n36
Taylor, Edward K., 95, 106n44
technology, 166
Terrell, Mary Church, 6
terrorism, 154–55
Terry, David, 138n33
A Text-Book on the Origin and History,
&c. &c. of the Colored People
(Pennington), 73, 76
Theoharis, Jeanne, 21n37
Things Hold, Lines Connect
(exhibit), 64–65
Thomas, Hank Willis, 150–51
Thomas, Phillip, 87
Thompson, Robert Farris, 47, 55n60
Through His Eyes: Youth Activism in
the Civil Rights Era in Philadelphia
(exhibit), 89
Tillet, Salamishah, 111, 133
town hall meetings, 151–53
Traditions and Transformations:
Contemporary Afro-American
Sculpture (exhibit), 100
trauma, 129–33, 141n63. *See also*
slavery; unclaimed history

"Traumanauts," 88
Treasures from the Collections
(exhibit), 67
Trent, Noelle, 154–55
Troyano, Joan Fragaszy, 70
Tschumi, Bernard, 27, 49n12
Tubman, Harriet, 121
Turner, Edith L. B., 10
Turner, Frederick, 10
Turner, Nat, 121
Tuskegee Airmen, 68

unclaimed history, 112
United Kingdom, museums,
representations of slave trade in, 85,
98, 143n74
universal human rights, 128–29
Unmasked series, 158–59
"The Unsound Space" (Asgedom), 42

Vale, Lawrence J., 49n14
Varner, Harold, 35, 51n27
vernacular art and architecture, 48,
55–56nn61–62, 84
Vernon, Sam, 88–89, 127
Verre, Philip, 100
virtual exhibitions, 88–89
Vlach, John, 48, 55n61, 84, 105n32

Waddell, Stacy Lynn, 87
Wadsworth Atheneum, 100–101
Walker, Kara, 103n9
Wallace, Michelle, 109n70
Washington, George, 122
Watkins, C. Malcolm, 69–70
Watts, J. C., 6
"We Can't Breathe" series, 159
Welch, Matthew, 156
Welcome to Brookhill (exhibit), 150
Westmoreland, Carl B., 117–18
We Wanted a Revolution: Black Radical
Women, 1965–1985 (exhibit), 86,
148–49, 168n10
white supremacy, 80n27, 97, 154
Whitman, Walt, 77n6

Wilkins, Craig L., 25
Wilkins, Robert L., 5–6
Williams, George
  Washington, 57, 74–75
Wilson, Joseph T., 107n53
Wilson, Mabel, 4, 19n18
Withers, Ernest, 155
witnessing, 166, 174n67
Wittgenstein, Ludwig, 3
women: American Women's History
  Museum and, 18n10; in *Art as a Verb*
  exhibit, 108n63; art by, 86; *Black
  Radical Women Symposium* and,
  148–49; human rights and, 128–29,
  148–49, 168n10; in National Council
  of Negro Women, 6

Women Hold Up Half the Sky
  (exhibit), 128–29
Wood, Christopher, 21n32
Wood, Marcus, 121, 135n16, 138n33
Wood, Thomas Waterman, 90
Woodson, Carter, 80n27
Woolford, Andrew, 165
Wright, Beryl, 108–9n64
Wright, Charles H., 79n20
Wright Now (exhibit), 160

Yanez, Jeronimo, 155–56
Ybarra-Frausto, Tómas, 12
Yeingst, William, 164–65

Zangewa, Billie, 88

About the Author

Bettina Messias Carbonell is an associate professor of English at John Jay College of Criminal Justice, City University of New York, where she designs and teaches topics-based courses on literature, ethics, and human rights; she also teaches in the College's Humanities and Justice Major where students approach justice-related issues from the perspectives of three disciplines: history, literature, and philosophy. Her publications include *Museum Studies: An Anthology of Contexts* (1st edition; Blackwell Publishing, 2004; 2nd edition; Wiley-Blackwell, 2012), review essays on the exhibition of African American history and culture in museums, and a critical analysis of ethical inquiry in the work of Charles Chesnutt.

www.ingramcontent.com/pod-product-compliance
Lightning Source LLC
Chambersburg PA
CBHW062024270326
41929CB00014B/2311